BI 0783457 8

L9203343
£10.95
LABA

The Arts in the
Primary School

KU-545-502

AM

29.

17.

13.

2

15

27

The Falmer Press Library on Aesthetic Education

Series Editor: Dr Peter Abbs, University of Sussex, UK

Setting the Frame

LIVING POWERS:
The Arts in Education
Edited by Peter Abbs (1987)

A IS FOR AESTHETIC:
Essays on Creative and
Aesthetic Education
Peter Abbs (1988)

THE SYMBOLIC ORDER:
A Contemporary Reader on the
Arts Debate
Edited by Peter Abbs (1989)

THE RATIONALITY OF
FEELING:
Understanding the Arts in Education
David Best

The Individual Studies

FILM AND TELEVISION IN
EDUCATION:
An Aesthetic Approach to the
Moving Image
Robert Watson

LITERATURE IN
EDUCATION:
Encounter and Experience
Edwin Webb

DANCE AS EDUCATION:
Towards a National Dance Culture
Peter Brinson

THE VISUAL ARTS IN
EDUCATION
Rod Taylor

MUSIC EDUCATION IN
THEORY AND PRACTICE
Charles Plummeridge

THE ARTS IN THE PRIMARY
SCHOOL
Glennis Andrews and Rod Taylor

EDUCATION IN DRAMA:
Casting the Dramatic Curriculum
David Hornbrook

Work of Reference

KEY CONCEPTS:
A Guide to Aesthetics, Criticism and the Arts in Education
Trevor Pateman

THE FALMER PRESS LIBRARY OF AESTHETIC EDUCATION

The Arts in the Primary School

Rod Taylor and Glennis Andrews

The Falmer Press

(A member of the Taylor & Francis Group)

London • Washington, DC

UNIVERSITY OF
INFORMATION
SERVICES
CENTRAL ENGLAND

UK The Falmer Press, 4 John St, London WC1N 2ET
USA The Falmer Press, Taylor & Francis Inc., 1900 Frost Road, Suite 101, Bristol, PA 19007

© Taylor and Andrews 1993

All rights reserved. No part of this publication may be reproduced, stored in a retrieval system, or transmitted in any form or by any means, electronic, mechanical, photocopying, recording or otherwise, without permission in writing from the Publisher.

First published in 1993

A catalogue record for this book is available from the British Library

ISBN 0 1 85000 7713 cased
ISBN 0 1 85000 7721 paper

Library of Congress Cataloging-in-Publication Data are available on request

Typeset in 10/12 Bembo by
Graphicraft Typesetters Ltd., Hong Kong.

UNIVERSITY OF
CENTRAL ENGLAND

Book no. 07634578

Subject no. 372.5/Tay

INFORMATION SERVICES

Contents

Contents of Plates

Acknowledgments

Many people have contributed in a variety of ways to the writing of *The Arts in the Primary School*. Thanks are especially due to Gill David, the headteacher of Tyldesley County Primary School, for her support; she was the first person to read and comment upon Chapters 5 to 8 utilizing school-based material. The help of her staff has likewise proved invaluable, with Viv Burrows, Liz Surman and Jean Nicholson, in particular, providing invaluable information through recorded interviews made specifically to assist in the writing. Much of the detailed pupil case-study material used was only available because of the school's unusual commitment to record and to document systematically aspects of primary school practice which often prove elusive. Some of this information arose directly out of an unusual commitment to Wigan's involvement in the Arts in Schools project, leading to the written formulation of a philosophy evolved over many years. The resulting material has been freely incorporated into our text.

Thanks are also due to Wigan Education, in particular Kevin Hampson, the Director of Education, and his predecessor Charles Hopkinson. Their vision and unflinching support was crucial to Wigan establishing the rich and diverse arts resources and services which have been influential in numerous schools developing whole-school policies in which the arts occupy a central role. Both authors acknowledge the benefits of having worked in such an enlightened authority; the range and scope of the book would have been less generous but for Wigan's support of, and pioneering work in, the arts in relation to a vigorously pursued entitlement policy.

Our philosophy and approach further reflects the close involvement we both share with the Drumcroon Education Art Centre and its dedicated team of art educators. For over a decade it has enjoyed close working relationships with Tyldesley County Primary School, based upon the partnership principles which have been central to its policy for many years. The close ties are evidenced in the richness of the TCP environment, with its abundance of original art works and children's practice reflecting Drumcroon visits and the work of its artists out in schools. Of the numerous artists who have influenced developments in the school's practice, particular thanks are due to Anne-Marie Quinn and Ian Murphy for their contributions to the content of this book.

We are also indebted to Carolyn Yates, Technology Coordinator, and Chris Hull, a primary music advisory teacher at the time of writing. Both offered invaluable evaluations of and insights into specific projects used in the text. Important Pitprop Theatre, Ludus Dance and Horse and Bamboo projects and initiatives also feature, and we offer our thanks to all those who contributed to the rich body of arts material published by Wigan, in particular the *Wigan Arts Policy* document and the accompanying publications arising out of the Arts in Schools involvement and Sue O'Brien and Christine Merton's writing about the Passing Through sculpture and its placement in the school's grounds.

Thanks are also due to Keith Walker, Fiona Norton and Robert Aitchison. All read the manuscript at key draft stages and their perceptive comments and observations greatly benefited the subsequent writing. We had the privilege of writing the last volume in the Library on Aesthetic Education, meaning that we were able to take account of other books in the series, aided by David Best making a couple of key sections of his manuscript available to us prior to publication, and we wish to acknowledge how helpful this was to us.

Finally, the tireless commitment and support of Dr Peter Abbs has been invaluable throughout. As Series Editor of the Falmer Library on Aesthetic Education, he invited us to contribute *The Arts in the Primary School* as the final volume in the series, and his perceptive help and sympathetic promptings constantly sustained us in the arduous task of writing it, for he consistently helped us to maintain a clear view of the ultimate goal. We hope that in its final form *The Arts in the Primary School* proves a worthy addition to the Library on Aesthetic Education; in the fight to redress the educational imbalance which reflects the impoverished and antipathetic climate of today, such a series in its completed form is sorely needed!

Series Editor's Preface

The Arts in the Primary School is the final volume in the Falmer Press Library on Aesthetic Education and, in one crucial sense, it is the most important as it concerns the first collective initiation of children into the arts. One can be fairly sure that if this does not take place or takes place in a drab and haphazard manner the consequences will be as severe as they will be long-term — for the arts are closely related to the senses and these are at their most acute and impressionable during childhood. To neglect the arts in the primary school is to impoverish the human personality, to leave children in exile from their own culture and to leave the future open to the chill forces of mass insensibility and mass standardization. Yet an initiation into all the arts for all our children has never, as yet, taken place in our culture. Nor, at the moment, does the National Curriculum secure what has long been missing. The great value of this volume is that, perhaps for the first time, it provides both the principles and practices of a democratic aesthetic education for all primary school children. It provides a necessary fusion of theory and teaching with a conviction born of hard experience. Both authors have had sustained experience of exactly what they are advocating, a characteristic which can hardly be said to be the mark of those who have formulated many of the recent policies for our schools. Glennis Andrews was for fifteen years Deputy Headmistress of Tyldesley County Primary School (a school whose extraordinary work is documented in this book), while Rod Taylor was for eighteen years Art Adviser for Wigan and, for almost as many years, Director of the Drumcroon Arts Centre (whose inspiring example is also documented here). It is their intimate knowledge of teaching the arts which, I believe, gives a quiet authority to every page of this book.

At the heart of the volume lies a single insight into the true nature of active learning. It is an insight which in the various ideological struggles over the nature and content of education has been betrayed again and again. What is this insight? It can best be formulated negatively: *Learning cannot be transferred, cannot be prescribed, cannot, to use the current jargon, be delivered.* No one can do our learning for us. This negative principle is as old as Socrates and Plato. It lies at the root of western culture. It was the merit of the progressive school of thinking that it recognized this truth; it grasped that learning can only be *released* in another, that logically, only the individual child can be agent of his or her own learning. This means that in the daily practice of good teaching the child must be given space to select, to judge, to innovate, to initiate, to ask questions, to explore. Now, it is transparently clear that the present National Curriculum has singularly failed to recognize the need for this open-ended action in the child-learner. In this it could well bring about a numbing return to rote-learning, to mere drill, to unvaried constant pre-scriptive teaching and, in doing so, unwittingly assassinate the deep educational impulses of the human mind. On the other hand, where the progressivists went so wrong was in their all but exclusive emphasis on 'self-expression' and 'self-discovery', without the constant challenge of the wider encompassing historic culture, without the achieved works of arts, the inherited theories, artefacts, categories of a rich and variegated culture. In brief, both the pro-gressivists and the Conservative government missed the point: learning is an ever evolving encounter between the innate creative energies of the student and the inherited energies of the general culture — and the teacher's primary task is to engender and deepen that encounter. What this means in practice for aesthetic education is fully demonstrated in *The Arts in the Primary School*, particularly in its last four expansive chapters.

I have already said enough to indicate that the authors of the book seek to delineate a comprehensive view of learning and aesthetic education, not just a partial view which fits the present and prevailing pragmatic requirements. Their book does, of course, address the dictates of the National Curriculum and many primary school teachers will be inspired by the examples and deeply heartened by what can be done inside the current curricular constraints and structures. At the same time, however, each book in the Library has been written to answer the question, 'What is the full and fitting form of arts education?' not 'How can we meet the current demands of the National Curriculum?' This has meant that, at many points in the argument, a critical rather than pragmatic view has been offered. How could it have been other-wise when in the National Curriculum, dance (a great arts discipline) has been amalgamated with physical education, when drama (as an arts subject) has not been recognized, when film (as an artistic medium) has been wholly absent, when only two of the six arts disciplines have been granted status as founda-tion subjects and then only to the age of 14? All these changes were driven through with little argument, little evidence and no real consultation. It is as if the educational argument for aesthetic coherence had not even entered the closed offices where the curricular decisions were made. Looking at the sad plight of current education in Britain, ever breaking down into smaller rival 'consumer' units, ever driven by an alien ideology, one cannot but recall Goethe's remark: *Nothing is so terrible as to witness ignorance in action.* In the present volume the authors extend the Library's critique of the *status quo* by insisting that the preoccupation with prescriptive teaching and the mechanical testing of inert knowledge could well murder all artistic creativity at birth, if not before. It is an observation that relates well to the Library's commitment to the dynamic and creative nature of all art-making and of the aesthetic field in which it works.

As the authors point out, it is a curious historical coincidence that during the identical period — 1987–1993 — that the National Curriculum has been conceived and executed, the Library on Aesthetic Education has been systematically coming out. It seems appropriate at the culmination of the project to reflect on what we have tried to achieve.

Our aim has been to propose a common framework for the arts so as to secure their comprehensive teaching in our schools, colleges and universities, together with a richer practice, both more energetically expressive and discerningly critical. It has been our intention to reclaim the whole cultural continuum for the teaching of the arts but always in relationship to the expressive and imaginative impulses of the actual pupils. Our arguments taken as a whole amount to something like a paradigm shift. What we advocate has not existed in the past and does not exist at present. To clarify the position we have had to attack both modernism and progressivism. We have also had to alter, at times, the current use of language and, at other times, to elaborate new phrases, concepts, models. In his *Life of Galileo* Brecht has his eponymous hero say to the senators: 'I'm telling you astronomy has stagnated for the last thousand years because they had no telescope'.[1] We feel that the teaching of the arts has been likewise impoverished by a lack of vivifying categories to determine and enhance their action. Some of our key formulations are as follows:

Aesthetic intelligence[2] (a concept to denote a form of intelligence, which works not primarily through propositions but predominantly through the senses, the feelings and the imagination);
The illuminating experience[3] (the autobiographical testimony of aesthetic experience);
Artistic knowing[4] (the revelatory understanding disclosed in illuminating experiences);
The vertical and horizontal axes of creativity[5] (the play between unconscious and biological elements and conscious and culturally inherited elements in the making of art);
The generic community of the arts[6] (the six major art forms: art, dance, drama, film, literature, music);
The four phases of the creative process[7] (namely, making, presenting, responding and evaluating);
The aesthetic field[8] (the whole interactive context of the symbol-system in which individual work is created and understood);

The significance of genre[9] (one way of formally demarcating the elements of the aesthetic field);

Contextualization[10] (the classroom practice of placing individual work inside the aesthetic field sometimes through genre);

Content, form, process, mood[11] (a series of related categories for the understanding and evaluation of works of art);

For the full elucidation of these concepts and their implication for the teaching of the arts the reader is urged to turn to the various volumes of the Library. However, the reader will also observe that they are all in play in the present volume, illuminating aesthetic education and the teaching of the arts in the primary school. Indeed some of the above formulations are the creation of Rod Taylor himself. How far we have achieved our aims, how far the Library represents a valuable paradigm-shift, only half-understood at the moment, remains for time (and each individual reader) to judge.

I would like now to draw attention to the general structure of the present book. The first four chapters are, essentially, theoretical in nature; they examine, in turn, the general principles used (Chapter 1), the recent histories of all six arts disciplines (Chapter 2), the case for a psychological approach towards arts education (Chapter 3) and a consideration of the demands on the training of teachers (Chapter 4). The remainder of the book is more practical in orientation. (Some teachers, no doubt, will want to turn to these chapters first and engage with the matrix of supporting principles later). Here the following themes are taken consecutively: the crucial importance of the whole environment and overall policy in the teaching of the arts (Chapter 5), the relationship of language to art and the art of language (Chapter 6), the place of the arts in the teaching of the sciences, the humanities and technology (Chapter 7), and the major significance of communal events and cultural festivals in the life of the primary school (Chapter 8). Finally, the book closes with a postscript on the Aesthetic Library and the National Curriculum. In this, it returns the reader to some of the earlier reflections of this preface and, indeed, brings the educational argument for the arts full circle and the Library to a fitting close.

One of the great purposes of art is to enhance our awareness of life by making vivid the essential lineaments of consciousness. In clarifying his own intentions as an art-maker, Edvard Munch once claimed: 'In my art I have tried to explain to myself life and its meaning. I have also tried to help others to clarify their lives'.[12] This is one of the reasons why the arts matter so much and why they are so vital to the curriculum. It is also the spirit of open enquiry and existential engagement in which the Library has been conceived and written. In this spirit we place our trust if not entirely, for the reasons given, in the present moment, then in the future, which is still ours to shape until the spirit of exploration is more fully housed both in our society (which, of course, *does* exist) and in our individual lives (without which there can be no true development). There can be no higher educational aim than animated enquiry and open reflection. We rest our case there; and look to the future.

Peter Abbs
Centre for Language, Literature and the Arts in Education
University of Sussex
January 1993

Notes and References

1 Brecht, B. (1980) *Life of Galileo* (translated by John Willett) London, Eyre Methuen, p. 21.
2 See, in particular, the entry on 'Aesthetic intelligence' in Pateman, T. (1991) *Key Concepts: A Guide to Aesthetics, Criticism and the Arts in Education*, London, Falmer Press, pp. 7–8.
3 For more on the illuminating experience see Taylor, R. (1983) *The Illuminating Experience*, Wigan, Critical Studies in Art Education Project, Drumcroon Art Centre; and Hargreaves, D. (1983) 'Dr Brunel and Mr Denning; Reflections on Aesthetic Knowing' in Ross, M. (Ed.) *The Arts: A Way of Knowing*, Oxford, Pergamon Press, pp. 127–160 and Abbs, P. (1992) 'Making the Art Beat Faster', *Times Higher Education Supplement*, 18 September, p. 18.
4 For a full discussion of the cognitive functions of art see Chapter 2 of Plummeridge, C. (1991) *Music Education in Theory and Practice*, London, Falmer Press; and Chapter 1 of Best, D. (1993) *Rationality of Feeling*, London, Falmer Press.
5 For a full account of the vertical and horizontal axes of creativity see Abbs, P. (1989) 'Creativity, the Arts and the Renewal of Culture', *A is for Aesthetic*, London, Falmer Press, pp. 1–25.
6 For further descriptions of the generic community of the arts see Abbs, P. (1987) *Living Powers: The Arts in Education*, London, Falmer Press, especially the individual essays on each arts discipline by Edwin Webb, Marian Metcalfe, Robert Watson, Anna Haynes, Christopher Havell and Robin Morris. See also the entry 'Arts in Education: The Idea of a Generic Arts Community' in Pateman (1991) pp. 12–17 (*ibid.*).
7 For an exposition of the nature and distinct phases of the creative process see Part VII, 'Art and the Creative Process' in Abbs, P. (1989) *The Symbolic Order; A Contemporary Reader on the Arts Debate*, London, Falmer Press, pp. 188–210.
8 Further accounts of the aesthetic field can be found in 'Towards a Coherent Arts Aesthetic' *Living Powers*, pp. 52–62 (*ibid.*). See also the entry 'Aesthetic field' in Pateman's *Key Concepts*, pp. 4–6 (*ibid.*).
9 For the significance of genre see, for example, Webb, E. (1992) 'Working within the Genres of Literary Form' in *Literature in Education: Encounter and Experience*, London, Falmer Press, pp. 43–45. See also 'Language, Genres and Television' in Watson, R. (1990) *Film and Television in Education*, London, Falmer Press, pp. 95–131.
10 For an account of contextualization see Chapter 1 of this book pp. 9–29.

11 For a full description of 'content, form, process, mood' see Taylor, R. (1992) 'Four Necessary Categories for the Teaching of Art' in *Visual Arts in Education*, London, Falmer Press, pp. 67–88. See also the present volume.

12 Munch, E., quoted in *Edvard Munch: The Frieze of Life* (1992) (edited by Mara-Helen Wood) London, National Gallery Publications, p. 52.

Introduction

> We want to see not only a programme for the arts, but also a body
> of arts teachers who actively feel they form a unified community with
> a common purpose and a common aesthetic . . . we believe that the
> individual arts — literature, drama, dance, music, film and art —
> must be conceived as forming a single community in the curriculum.
> This does not necessarily mean that they should be integrated in their
> teaching, but that they should be understood as serving similar aes-
> thetic processes and purposes. They all belong together under the
> category of the aesthetic.
>
> Peter Abbs[1]

The arts constitute one of the major areas of human endeavour and achievement, and have done so throughout time. They are firmly rooted in the
aesthetic, representing a form of knowing which is pre-eminently to do with
sensory awareness. A worthwhile arts education is therefore rigorous and
demanding as well as creatively satisfying and enjoyable. Throughout time,
the arts have represented one of humankind's most potent means of giving
expression to, and communicating ideas and concepts about profound issues
to do with the human condition — issues of birth, life and death made manifest
through the sensory exploration of the world we inhabit. Individuals are able
to understand themselves more fully by coming to terms with their identity
and uniqueness through arts experiences. Profound ideas concerning the
spiritual, political and social are made manifest through the arts in ways which
cannot be expressed and made apparent by other means.

Nevertheless, our current materialistic society does not afford the arts the
attention they warrant — a neglect also inevitably reflected in education. In
September 1992 the National Curriculum assumed a complete form, with
physical education, art and music the last foundation subjects to be introduced. Within physical education is to be found dance, optional beyond the

primary school years. Art and music are the only arts disciplines which appear in their own right — and they need only be studied to 14 years of age, as opposed to 16 in every other core and foundation subject. Equally significantly, the National Curriculum provides no coherent view of the place of the arts in education — and yet aesthetic experience allied to the imaginative and creative modes of thinking and practice epitomized by the arts are arguably more essential in society today than ever before. Peter Abbs' plea for the arts to form a 'unified community with a common purpose and a common aesthetic' remains unheeded at government levels in an increasingly centrally controlled educational system.

Parallel with the introduction of the National Curriculum, all the various volumes of the Falmer Press Library on Aesthetic Education have been written and introduced — both unfolded simultaneously from the publication of the *National Curriculum Consulation Report* and *Living Powers*, the first volume in the Library, in 1987. Might the latter provide the coherent framework so lacking in the former? Is the Library relevant to the hard-pressed primary practitioner fighting to preserve more imaginative approaches to teaching? *The Arts in the Primary School* is the last volume in the Library; it complements other works in the series, being consistent with them in its arguments. However, the series would remain incomplete without a volume specifically addressing issues peculiar to the primary sector.

This book utilizes detailed case-study material drawn from the practice of one primary school, Tyldesley County Primary. Examples could easily have been drawn from here and there, but specific use has been made of one school because no primary school possesses specialist expertise in *all* the arts. How might that school therefore build upon and develop whatever skills, interests and expertise it does enjoy — or rectify their omission? This process is best illustrated by focusing upon one school with a commitment to the central place of the arts within a whole-school policy, exploring how it has extended its arts practice and approaches over a period of time. The risk of bias towards the most fully established and developed art forms in that one school seemed preferable than the selection of random examples of good practice plucked from different places. The practice of the school is utilized in detail from Chapter 5 onwards.

In addition to National Curriculum developments, this book has been written against the backdrop of other wide-ranging changes. Those with most direct bearing on the issues addressed in *The Arts in the Primary School* are local management of schools (LMS) and the parallel reduction in the scope afforded to local education authorities. One author is the former deputy headteacher of the Wigan primary school used, the other is the former Wigan LEA Art Adviser. Both have advocated the principles of partnership over many years, and the case-study material used demonstrates close working partnerships between school and authority. The central principle of partnership is that of collectively providing something of greater benefit to pupils than can be offered when individuals or groups work in isolation.

However, the school in question is not an indiscriminate consumer of resources. It uses them as they directly relate to its overall philosophy and curricular needs. It is an irony of the National Curriculum that its introduction has provided the rationale for the widespread use of these resources, illustrating their paramount importance, just as another wing of central policy is committed to dismantling them. In the future, access to, even provision of, some of the resources referred to will have become the direct responsibility of schools themselves. Procedures designed to make schools compete with each other at ever more intense levels are also being implemented, yet an immediate need is that of close partnership between schools on a local or consortia basis to enable them to acquire resources collectively which will otherwise remain beyond their individual reach. In addition, though, further case-study examples illustrate the wide range of possibilities that lie within the reach of any school capable of identifying its arts needs and determining the necessary priorities, resources and strategies. Access to the kinds of rich stimuli highlighted here should be part of all children's entitlement — denial of such access means an inevitable impoverishment of experience.

The school was actively involved in the Schools Curriculum Development Council (SCDC) 1985 to 1990 Arts in Schools project. Glennis Andrews was a Wigan coordinator and member of the primary working group. The concept behind the group's publication, *Some of the Arts All of the Time*, influenced the school's practice in significant ways.[2] No school can possibly practice all of the arts all of the time, but the recognition that it *can* practice some of them all of the time commits it, on the one hand, to making constant use of the arts strengths it already possesses. On the other, staff can *then* easily identify which art forms it is most insecure about and are therefore most neglected. Are there any personal enthusiasms among the staff relevant to these forms? What opportunities are available for staff development in them? What provision is there locally for pupils to experience them and increase their understanding of them and their significance? In turn, the concept 'some of the arts all of the time' leads naturally to an equally important counterpart: 'all of the arts some of the time', the major theme of this volume's final chapter.

A special issue which the arts in the primary sector raises, as distinct from the vast majority of secondary practice, is that of learning *in* and *through* the arts. Learning through only takes place satisfactorily if the arts are sufficiently prized and valued in their own right to exist in their full aesthetic complexity. In other words, learning in the arts has to be satisfactorily developed *before* learning through can become a real possibility, otherwise the arts are reduced to servicing agencies and the degree to which they successfully enhance wider learning is correspondingly diminished. However, once learning in them is properly valued, the power of the arts to inform what takes place in other curricular areas is extraordinary. Given the importance they have assumed in the National Curriculum, a priority has been placed on examples involving English, the sciences and technology. Space precluded a chapter on the equally enriching power of the arts to inform the humanities curriculum, environmental studies and other specific curriculum areas, but evidence of how they can illuminate humanities practice permeates the book as a whole.

The Arts in the Primary School provides a clear rationale for determining the place of the arts in the primary curriculum. However, the current obsession with accountability is leading to an ever-increasing emphasis on a factually based curriculum, the return to so-called 'basics', and to formal class teaching methods appropriate to testing by simple — meaning standardized — means. The arts empower children to interpret, understand and respond to the world from personal perspectives in personally involving ways which can never be fully anticipated, requiring flexibility and adaptability on the part of the teacher. Standardized class teaching of the type currently being advocated does not readily accommodate the arts. To this end, *The Arts in the Primary School* takes account of individuality and personality in learning, and the implications this raises for classroom practice.

We are constantly being enticed to use an alien language which unsuspectingly draws us into its web, imperceptibly changing our attitudes and outlook in the process; 'delivery of the curriculum' is systematically replacing 'teaching' as a term. Implicit in its use is the insidious assumption that an externally conceived curriculum can be 'delivered' to one and all without any consideration for the individual or for negotiated learning. Local management of schools has led to the introduction of managerial approaches and attitudes derived from the business and commercial worlds, most succinctly encapsulated by what are being referred to as the 'Three Es' of Economy, Efficiency and Effectiveness. These priorities devalue the arts and force them to the periphery of the curriculum — the arts will always fit uncomfortably into an education determined by purely mechanistic priorities.

Any school that sits back, assuming a National Curriculum can solve all its problems of what to teach and how, is doomed. The results will be arid and lifeless. A National Curriculum, however precisely defined, still demands the creative and interpretative skills of the teacher, born of firmly held beliefs and convictions. All children are entitled to a broad and balanced education which is also vital, stimulating and life-enhancing in its own right. Our aspirations must also be to develop powers of adaptability in a generation of children who, because of ever-accelerating rates of change, will live their adult lives in a world likely to be distinctly different to that we know now. Their education must therefore surely take account of the sensory and aesthetic dimensions of life and encourage creative and imaginative thought, action and response. What is urgently required is a quite different form of education than that governed by the overriding concerns of economy, efficiency and effectiveness alone. It should equally be shaped by three Es of a dramatically different nature — the 'Healthy Addititive Es' of *Enhancement, Enrichment* and *Enlightenment*. The arts will then assume their rightful place at the very heart of the curriculum.

References

1 Abbs, R. (1987) *Living Powers*, London, Falmer Press, pp. 2–3.
2 *The Arts in the Primary School: Some of the Arts All of the Time* (1990) Metropolitan Wigan Arts in School publication.

Part I:

Theory

Chapter 1

The Arts in the Primary School: Addressing the Aesthetic

It will be found that the varieties of children's play are capable of being coordinated and developed in four directions, corresponding to the four basic mental functions, and that when so developed, the play activity naturally incorporates all the subjects appropriate to the primary phase of education.

From the aspect of *feeling* play may be developed by personification and objectivation towards DRAMA.
From the aspect of *sensation* play may be developed by modes of self-expression towards visual or plastic DESIGN.
From the aspect of *intuition* play may be developed by rhythmic exercises towards DANCE and MUSIC.
From the aspect of *thought* play may be developed by constructive activities towards CRAFT.

These four aspects of development, DRAMA, DESIGN, DANCE (including MUSIC) and CRAFT, are the four divisions into which a primary system of education naturally falls, but together they form a unity which is the unity of the harmoniously developing personality.
Herbert Read[1]

The Library on Aesthetic Education

The Arts in the Primary School is the final volume in a series of twelve which, in total, comprise a unique Library on Aesthetic Education — a manifesto for the arts. The series contains books of a general nature, dealing with the arts in education from the theoretical and philosophical standpoints, plus individual studies dealing with each of the major art forms in turn — Film and Television, Literature, Dance, Music, the Visual Arts and Drama. How might these art forms best be approached in the primary school in the age of the

National Curriculum? How might they most effectively inform learning *across* the primary curriculum? The role of the arts is crucial in the primary curriculum, enabling teachers to harness constructively and to build upon children's play through approaches to learning which involve the senses, imagination and personal experience. These sensory approaches allied to the life-issues and concerns which mature artists can make comprehensible to children are crucial to worthwhile arts experiences, but also have profound implications for learning in many other curriculum areas.

Individual primary teachers and, indeed, whole schools have successfully demonstrated during the last half-century that when the arts are afforded their rightful place in the curriculum, the creative dimensions they bring to learning *in general* are beneficial to children's development in countless ways. However, the arts sometimes become the handmaidens of other subjects without their own essential needs being realized; they must never become just servicing agencies for the rest of the curriculum. There are also schools where the hold of the arts has always been tenuous, reinforced by attitudes within society which undervalue them, with them perceived as distractions to — or relief from — the 'real' business of teaching children 'the basics'. There was, therefore, a clear need for the Library on Aesthetic Learning to contain a volume specifically devoted to the place, nature and function of the arts in the primary school.

The Gulbenkian Report *The Arts in Schools* (1982) highlighted the need to look specifically at the ways in which the arts manifest themselves in the primary sector, 'because the kinds of provision they need and the problems involved are different. Where the curriculum of the primary school is teacher-based, that of the secondary school is teachers-based. This involves more complicated patterns of organisation'.[2] The arts, the report emphasizes, 'are *natural* forms of expression and communication. Part of the job of education is to develop these natural capacities into practical capabilities.' This process should begin in the primary school 'and be extended through the secondary school, *as a continuous process.*' A major benefit of a National Curriculum should be that, by identifying the essential principles underlying each discipline through the key stages, the resulting continuity should give added coherence and meaning to children's learning. Having initially failed to take account of curriculum developments regarding the areas of experience — a fundamental one being the *aesthetic and creative* — a problem created by the National Curriculum is that its subject-specific structure has tempted some primary schools to move to more rigid secondary-type systems, with core and some foundation subjects inflexibly timetabled. It is even now being extended to subject-specific teachers being timetabled at the upper primary level. Ironically, in the period immediately prior to the introduction of the National Curriculum, there was a growing concern that secondary methods of organization and timetable structures had become ends in themselves — straitjackets, inhibiting rather than facilitating learning of benefit to the whole child.

In *Education through Art*, Read argued that each arts discipline grew naturally out of play to form the unity which is that of the 'harmoniously developing personality'. The National Curriculum poses special challenges — and problems — to the primary teacher who believes in the arts as fundamental to human growth and development. Read consciously entitled his book *Education through Art*, and many primary teachers readily identify with a philosophy which emphasizes how learning might become more holistic and cohesive as well as subject-based when and as appropriate. Unfortunately, Read's emphasis on the child as natural creator contributed to a divorce between the study and practice of the arts, the consequences of which are still with us. However, strategies to bridge the resulting divide are now being addressed in positive ways, sanctioned particularly by specific attainment targets for art and music.

Some primary schools forcibly demonstrate the extent to which the arts can be valued and enjoyed in their own right, while also informing learning in subject areas like the sciences, mathematics and environmental studies, likewise contributing to language development in a variety of invaluable ways. It would be a tragedy if these developments, so essential to real learning, were curtailed by the National Curriculum leading to rigid timetable structures compartmentalizing subjects at the expense of the education of the whole child.

Such concerns highlighted the need for a book focusing on the arts in the primary sector to conclude a series born of a concern that many of the major developments currently taking place in education are marginalizing the arts, and the time devoted to them, to the detriment of all children and, ultimately, of society as a whole. Peter Abbs in *Living Powers* sets the scene for the whole series.[3] The arts comprise an essential and substantial area of the curriculum to do with the aesthetic; the aesthetic is the common bond which gives them their common purposes. *Living Powers* defines the philosophical framework upon which the Library is founded — a kind of microcosm for the series as a whole in terms of both content and structure, with the second section of the book examining how each art form entered the curriculum and now manifests itself in relation to these aesthetic considerations.

It is fitting that the series concludes with *The Arts in the Primary School*. All the art forms, having been examined separately in subject-specific volumes, are once again considered together in relation to the primary curriculum as a whole, but with attention paid to the essential distinguishing characteristics of each. The chosen approach illustrates theory through practice, in-depth case-study material illustrating the centrality of the arts to learning in one Wigan primary school. The school is a typical one in many respects; the staff are generalist primary practitioners with no arts specialists. It is perhaps untypical, though, in that it demonstrates the richness and diversity which the arts can bring to all children's learning on an ongoing basis. This book complements other volumes in the series but should be of especial use to all primary teachers with a concern as to how they can make maximum use of essential artistic experiences within the framework, context and demands of an inevitably National Curriculum-focused curriculum.

The Library on Aesthetic Education is certainly timely. *Living Powers* was published during 1987 in close proximity to the National Curriculum *Consultation Document* which led to such a huge response from all sectors of education, albeit one that was largely ignored. *The Arts in the Primary School* is published with a National Curriculum firmly in place, the first modifications to the core subjects in the light of practice already made, programmes of study and attainment targets in the ten designated core and foundation subjects known, testing by law of 7-year olds a reality, the initial tests already modified to fit more narrow paper and pencil criteria, thus testing schools rather than diagnosing individual pupil needs. The series has therefore been written and published against the constantly shifting backdrop of sweeping educational changes through imposed legislation. *Living Powers* highlighted the inadequacy of arts practice and provision in the majority of schools at the outset of this process. The most ardent advocate of the National Curriculum will readily concede that, whatever its virtues, the accompanying debate has paid little attention to any coherent view of the arts, or of how aesthetic education might or should comprise an essential part of all children's entitlement.

Living Powers argues for a shift of emphasis in how the arts are taught and for more allocation of arts time, the arts representing, as they do, a fundamental area of profound human achievement, expression and understanding. Secondary school time available for their study has, if anything, diminished since 1987. In the primary sector, there is a very real danger of the arts being marginalized and only taught in isolated pockets. There is a long tradition of some schools successfully harnessing the arts to facilitate learning across the curriculum, permeating everything while they also flourished in their own right. The pressures to teach only that which is to be tested risk fragmenting the primary curriculum with 'subjects' taught in isolation and the in-depth experiences necessary for engagements of an aesthetic nature in danger of disappearing. The need for the Library on Aesthetic Education is therefore more pronounced now than when *Living Powers* was published such a relatively short time ago.

The Nature of Aesthetic Experience

A central argument in *Living Powers* is that it is the aesthetic which the six major art forms share. Each discipline has a different and distinct history in education, though, having come into the curriculum at different times and for different reasons. As creative subjects, their history is a relatively short one in primary education, as Sir Alec Clegg emphasizes:[4]

By the 1930s, the *infant* schools — schools for children 5 to 7 years of age — had already embarked on the course that has followed ever since. Teachers in training for these schools learned the value of clay, sand, water, and all manner of sense-training apparatus. The physical education of infants already included dramatic games, even though they erred on the side of sentiment. Music teaching had elicited the support of percussion instruments. And whatever the training of infant teachers in those days did *not* do, it most certainly insisted on the importance of learning how to manage the many and varied teaching materials already available at that time. . . .

But these improvements in the infant school were not immediately accomplished by improvements in the primary schools. The schemes of work in use in the primary or junior schools of the late 1930s still showed little evidence of the transformation that was to begin some ten years later.

As illustration, Clegg sets out a scheme of work in use in one school in the early 1940s. It comprised English, speech training, arithmetic, history, nature study and art and craft. Art has played a particularly notable part in primary education, but there it comprised:

— The relationship between primary and secondary colours (provide each classroom with a simple colour wheel);
— Complementary colours;
— Simple exercises in the laying on of colour;
— Design in circle and lozenge;
— Paper and card wash, leading to bookbinding;
— Jotters, notebooks, mounting Christmas cards, blotters, bookmarkers, purses, table mats, comb cases, friezes, and repeat patterns.

English comprised comprehension exercises and dictations, punctuating sentences, rearranging words, blanks to be filled in and spelling lists to be learnt. English composition was on an assigned topic with suitable words listed on the blackboard to be woven in. Handwriting was practised daily. Art and craft and English were the two art forms that specifically appeared on the timetable, but the main thing they shared in common was that neither addressed the aesthetic other than, at best, marginally.

Particularly in the primary sector, where the arts have subsequently fulfilled two functions — being taught for their own sake and as an aid to wider learning — it is hardly surprising that teachers have not always recognized what they share in common, invariably to the detriment of aesthetic education. For Abbs, 'Aesthetic denotes a mode of sensuous knowing essential for the life and development of consciousness; aesthetic response is inevitably, through its sensory and physical operations, cognitive in nature.' In order to focus more fully upon the significance of the aesthetic, he draws attention to its opposite, anaesthesia. Interestingly, this word was in use in 1721, decades before 'aesthetic' came into the language. Anaesthesia, of course, denotes 'loss of feeling or sensation: insensibility', as when one is being treated on an operating table. An education which ignores or excludes the aesthetic is therefore an impoverished one because of its failure to cultivate and develop fundamental feelings, sensations and sensibilities:

> The aesthetic, then, must be considered with all that works through and on feeling, sensation and sensibility. . . . *T o u c h, t a s t e, f e e l, t a c t*: these are the words, suggesting in their uses the intimate relationship between sensation and feeling, which best bring out the nature of the aesthetic mode.[5]

In addition to lack of continuity in arts teaching and inadequate time allocations, the problem is further compounded; much of what is actually done in arts lessons is not 'deeply aesthetic in nature'. Many of the activities undertaken lie virtually outside what Abbs defines as the aesthetic field. He focuses on a comprehensive school timetable in support of his case, but the issues are just as pertinent to the primary sector where time allocations in relation to what is actually undertaken often similarly lead to aesthetic concerns being addressed, at best, only fleetingly.

Immediately prior to the introduction of the National Curriculum it was *still* possible to see art and English taught in ways not dissimilar to those highlighted by Clegg in that 1940s scheme of work. Abbs suggests that a major cause behind the neglect of aesthetic activity emanates from the intertwining of modernism in the arts with progressivism in education, the most articulate advocate of both being, of course, Herbert Read. It is now possible to see that just as the arts, in the latter phases of modernism, often failed to replenish themselves adequately by drawing upon the wider cultural tradition, so arts teaching too tended to turn in on itself, the resulting pupil work becoming predictable, failing to develop because of a narrowness of scope and focus. In proposing an alternative to what was *then* the norm, though, Herbert Read became an influential visionary. Prior to the publication of *Education through Art* in 1943 there was little scope for *feeling, sensation, intuition* and *thought* in primary education, as Clegg illustrates, but the concepts and learning requirements implied by those words are under constant threat — never more so than at the present time.

Progressivism undoubtedly broadened the scope of arts teaching, but the debit side was that children often became locked in a world of their own art activity totally divorced from that of all others. The aesthetic field enables the arts as practised by children to be reconnected to the wider world of the arts as practised by others, both now and through time. As opposed to a view of art as constituting a series of artefacts or art objects, Abbs uses 'field' metaphorically to suggest 'a highly complex web of energy linking the artist to the audience, and both artist and audience to all inherited culture as now an active, now a latent shaping force'. Within this web of energy, 'the parts are seen in relationship, in a state of reciprocal flow between tradition and innovation, between form and impulse, between the society and the individual', and, in order to chart this aesthetic field, he proposes the four phase model of *making, presenting, responding* and *evaluating.*

The dynamic nature of this web of energy, and its relevance to the creative act, is vividly illustrated in a recent review of the 'Mingei: The Living Tradition of Japanese Arts' exhibition, Charles Hall noting that:

> The exhibition takes off when contemporary artists begin to look to their predecessors to enrich their vocabulary in works which engage equally with contemporary influences.One artist inflects bawdy Ukiyo-e images with expressionist mark-making, and perhaps with the self-parodying taste for the grotesque of contemporary cartoons.
>
> Anonymous craft forms emerged from a remarkably rich and stable tradition; the sureness of their execution is testimony to that. Work which simply replicates its forms simply condescends to its apparent simplicity. Work which turns its legacy into collision with contemporary issues implies a respect for the tradition's continued vitality, even though it implies the artist's distance from the admired original.[6]

Within this dynamic aesthetic field the child, too, can move freely between being art-maker and art critic and receiver through responding to the art of others — but the teacher must facilitate the necessary access.

The Aesthetic Field of Making, Presenting, Responding and Evaluating

The concept of a dynamic aesthetic field 'in which all art moves and has its being' is summarized diagramatically in *Living Powers* (p. 56), the central significance of making, presenting, responding and evaluating becoming immediately apparent (see Figure p. 16). The teacher of the arts can break into the aesthetic field at any point and be led by an invisible pattern of relationships into the whole circuit — for the parts are not self-contained but gain their meaning through connection with all the other parts. All points, therefore, can be starting points and there can be no one way of sequencing the teaching of the arts. What is important is that the teacher discerns the whole complex interaction of the field and makes full use of that knowledge in the organization, planning and implementation of work.

The art medium is the tangible material which makes the act of making possible. Its particular character invites certain movements, resists others. It is through technique that definite shape is given to 'an unknown entity already possessed but not yet intelligible'. Every artistic material has its own history, with which the artist also engages — at both the conscious and unconscious levels — during the creative process, the artist might actively study other artists' work as an essential part of that process: 'Each work of art in its making manifests the whole field'. An artist can identify so passionately with the material that he or she can be 'lost' in it. However, there comes a stage in the making process, most obviously towards resolution, when the work begins to assume its own independent existence.

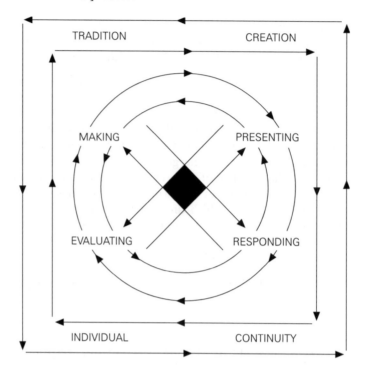

Abbs cites John Dewey, who observed that 'the completed artefact is not in itself an aesthetic object but an object that invites aesthetic response from others'; the aesthetic meaning resides in the dynamic interaction between the work and those who engage with it: *'No audience — no aesthetic'*. The presenting dimension of the aesthetic field is therefore an essential act of communication without which the work remains incomplete. It is the viewer, reader or listener who completes the work, though in aesthetic education the child will 'move constantly from one position to another, now making, now responding, now performing, now evaluating'.

This notion is in marked contrast to certain views of art history which assume that art works have 'fixed' messages to be learned from expert art historians — the only possessors of the real truth. This has often led to the study of facts and data about art works, with their true essence neither envisaged nor addressed. Equally significant, it has inhibited teachers in *every* sector of education, the message being that these areas are the exclusive preserves of a few experts; only via their knowledge is any engagement possible. John Berger was one critic who raised fundamental questions about whether this *status quo* should be maintained:

> No artist's work is reducible to *the* independent truth; like the artist's life — or yours or mine — the life's work constitutes its own valid or worthless truth. Explanations, analyses, interpretation, are no more

than frames or lenses to help the spectator focus his [*sic*] attention more sharply on the work. The only justification for criticism is that it allows us to see the work more clearly.[7]

Response can be to the work as a whole but might be to some compelling part which, in turn, draws us deeper into the work as a whole. There may be the wish to submit oneself further to a work so that it might release more fully what was sensed to a degree but somehow withheld in the initial engagement; it is not uncommon for a person to return to favourite works over and over again throughout a whole lifetime, constantly making new discoveries. In the initial stages, though, expressions of response are often along the lines of 'Terrific!', 'Fantastic!', 'Dreadful!' or 'Deeply moving!', for all these responses 'are not logical but intuitive apprehensions working through our senses and our feelings, through our sensibility'. The non-specialist primary teacher can feel vulnerable at this stage — should knowledge now be being imparted? However, in keeping with Berger's viewpoint, Abbs emphasizes that the educational temptation should be resisted to overlay this stage with too much theory, explanation and knowledge. In isolation from aesthetic experience, this can block the sensuous, physical, dramatic and imaginative 'indwelling' aspects so crucial to artistic response at this essentially pre-verbal stage; 'the point and purpose of the art lies in the field of its action'.

Nevertheless, we *do* wish to make judgments and to understand the nature of the transformation of media brought about by the artist — equally, at many crucial moments in responding we also require information to help us make sense of what we see or hear: 'Evaluating is, then, in large part, an attempt to organize the complex elements of our aesthetic response — to state intellectually our relationship to the work of art, to formulate the aesthetic response . . . conceptually.'[8] Great pleasure can be derived from this process of seeing how something works and how it has been made to add up to a unified whole. 'Evaluation makes intelligible (and communicable) the aesthetic response'; 'It is post-event'. It is here that knowledge of traditions, awareness of history and culture, understanding of craft — and possession of an appropriate critical vocabulary — can develop and deepen aesthetic judgments and responses. These key areas all require careful examination in the primary context, and will constantly be returned to throughout this text.

The Library on Aesthetic Education demonstrates that all the major art forms in the curriculum, irrespective of their different origins and developments to date, fit into this dynamic aesthetic field. However, their previous histories can obscure that this is so — drama and art have tended to be dominated by an almost exclusive emphasis on making alone, so much so that both the secondary specialist teacher and the primary general practitioner have felt guilty when their pupils have not been 'doing'. Opportunities for discussion, analysis and response were reduced to a minimum. The music lesson, by comparison, would just as likely focus on appreciation aspects to the exclusion of the pupils' practical engagement. At both these extremes, the circle of the aesthetic field was damagingly broken. By accepting the significance of the aesthetic field, therefore, the teacher is also accepting the relevance of the four phases of making, presenting, responding and evaluating. Having accepted their relevance, it is then a matter of thoughtful planning and careful provision of appropriate resources to ensure that they are held in equilibrium throughout the whole course. On many occasions, one aspect will inevitably come sharply into focus, but over a period of time all pupils should have the necessary opportunities to engage fully and interactively in the whole field, so that each can be seen and understood in relation to the others.

Recent Developments in Critical Studies

Just as the aesthetic field of Making, Presenting, Responding and Evaluating is essential to the arts being approached in a fully rounded manner, the *Content, Form, Process* and *Mood* model facilitates direct engagement with art works of all kinds. It is empowering to childen for it enables them to interpret works by using their own senses and judgments as opposed to passively receiving others' opinions. It is therefore a crucial aid to Dewey's notion of the audience completing the art work. Before looking at this model in more detail, though, it will be helpful to trace its evolution, originating in the visual arts through the critical studies developments of the 1980s, with subsequent developments across the arts, largely through the practical participation of teachers in the Schools Curriculum Development Council 'Arts in Schools' Project which began in 1985. It culminated in 1990 with the publication of *The Arts 5–16 Project Pack*, which emphasized that the 'best practice in primary as well as secondary schools gives equal weight to developing young people's critical understanding of other people's work and their knowledge of different cultural practices and traditions. This calls for a shift in the balance of work in many classrooms.'[9] Much still needs to be done in this respect!

The Arts in Schools Project was the first National Curriculum development initiative of the SCDC, formed on the demise of the Schools Council. Its emphasis on critical studies approaches across the arts shows a debt, at least in part, to one of the last Schools Council projects. In 1981, the two year national Critical Studies in Art Education (CSAE) Project was set up by the Arts and Schools Councils, Crafts Council involvement extending it to a third year. A major concern was that the vast majority of children were leaving school having had ample opportunities to make art, but with virtually no chances to aid their understanding and enjoyment of the works of others across time and place. Host centre to the project was the Drumcroon Education Art Centre, recently opened in Wigan. Children of all ages use this Centre, it being a local education authority initiative with the building serving the needs of all Wigan's young people in all its schools, as well as being open to the general public. The Centre's Policy Statement is always clearly displayed; it aims:

> To give all Wigan's young people — irrespective of age — their teachers and the local community access to the range, breadth and variety of the Visual Arts through the focus of contemporary makers, taking into account such issues as those of race, gender and special needs. To give further insight and understanding, the Centre provides its visitors with opportunities to engage in related practical activities, and it also attempts to place each exhibition into a contextual framework by demonstrating process through resident artists and craftspeople and through the use of secondary source material which has the potential to range across time, place and cultures.

This policy provides the bedrock for Drumcroon activities, being formulated from existing practice as well as being a statement of intent. Drumcroon proved an ideal CSAE host centre, for children of all ages can be observed daily working within a practical environment in which they constantly engage with the art of others. It ensured that CSAE research was action-based and practical as well as theoretical. Enjoying, as it does, particularly close ties with teachers while functioning as an art gallery within a locality, Drumcroon breaks down many of the traditional barriers which frustrate working partnerships between the two.

Drumcroon receives and accommodates children of all ages, but in keeping with Schools Council policy the CSAE Project had a designated age range in mind — 11 to 16. The initial project outline indicated that much of the material produced would also be of value to the primary practitioner. Rod Taylor, as Project Director, pointed out the inherent dangers in running a secondary-based project and passing specialist packages down, as if from on high, to the primary practitioner. Teachers would feel patronized — equally important, primary approaches raise specific problems and issues of a different nature to those encountered in the secondary sector. From an early stage, the scope of the CSAE project was consequently broadened to embrace the 7 to 18 age range and *Educating for Art*, (1986) the book of the project, addressed and illustrated specific primary issues and practice.

'Free expression' were words in common usage in 1981 when CSAE began, indicating the considerable influence 'Child Art' still exerted. They had a profound influence on primary classroom approaches and, though many secondary specialists also embraced the concept, in practice they tended to begin Year 7 courses with exercises designed to develop a basic art 'vocabulary' (frequently on the assumption that nothing of worth had been done at the primary level!). In consequence, widely different upper primary and lower secondary approaches made continuity across the phases a virtual impossibility, so marked was the change in emphasis and approach at 11-plus transfer. It was commonplace to find natural and manufactured forms attractively arranged throughout primary schools and for young children to be taken into the local environment and on museum outings as part of humanities-based environmental studies projects, but there was still a widespread acceptance that art galleries were boring places. The resulting divide between the aesthetic in nature and in the arts will be considered in Chapter 7.

The CSAE Project demonstrated that children of all ages can study and enjoy a wide variety of the arts, past and present, and engage in related studio practice to the benefit and enrichment of both aspects, making continuity and coherence practically realizable and not just abstract notions inviting theoretical discussion but no positive action. Instead of their engagement with adult art stultifying children's imaginations and creativity, as many still maintained, the evidence was to the contrary — such contacts opened up a wider range of practical possibilities, actually feeding and nurturing the imagination.

Another highly desirable outcome of properly structured art gallery visits is that they often have a dramatic — sometimes immediate — impact on children's use of an extended vocabulary. During the Ted Roocroft exhibition, including many pig sculptures, a family visited Drumcroon early one evening. The mother was holding the 10-year old daughter's hand and the father was carrying her 7-year old sister. The elder child had constantly mithered to be taken to this exhibition, but only because her younger sister had already been! At the meal table for a whole week she had talked about nothing but wallowing and farrowing sows and saddleback pigs. 'We've never heard her use words like that before!' Her sister was fascinated. What had generated this interest, enabling a 7-year old to use confidently words with which she herself were unacquainted? David Hargreaves[10] argues that teachers should consciously transmit their enthusiasm for the arts to pupils (teachers being society's greatest consumers of the arts) as an effective means of generating wider interest in them; in this case a young child transmits her enthusiasm, arousing within her elder sister the desire likewise to experience what had affected her so potently.

Illuminating Experiences

Rather than art galleries being boring, as was still widely assumed, they could therefore be exciting places, opening children's eyes to new, unexpected stimuli, values and attitudes with potential to inform their own work and meet a wide variety of aesthetic needs. The younger sister had enjoyed what Rod Taylor called an 'illuminating experience'. This constitutes:

> . . . a relatively sudden and frequently unexpected form of initiation into an art form, and in its clearest form is dramatic, intensive and therefore memorable. There are four main elements in this experience or set of experiences. The first is a powerful concentration of attention. The individual becomes totally caught up and absorbed in the art object. 'In a strong form of the trauma, one's sense of time and space is suspended and one loses consciousness of all extraneous matters. One is lost in the art object. . . .' The second is a sense of revelation.

'One has a sense of new and important reality opening up or of entering a new place of existence which is somehow intensely real'. The third is inarticulateness. 'Only after the trauma has done its work does one have something to talk about and . . . the motivation to find a language in which to communicate one's feelings. . . .' The fourth is arousal of appetite. 'One simply wants the experience to continue or be repeated, and this can be felt with considerable urgency'.[11]

The term was coined during the CSAE project to convey the nature and kind of impact which particular art works can have on young people, sometimes against their expectations and in circumstances when they anticipate boredom. In the relevant section in *Educating for Art*, examples are also drawn from music and literature to illustrate that such aesthetic responses can occur in *all* art forms.[12] The impact can be profound enough to reshape lives — Ben Kingsley recounted on *Desert Island Discs* how his future as a doctor was more or less decided until he went on a school trip to Stratford to see Richard III: 'It was that afternoon with Ian Holm that rocketed all the molecules that were there dormant to the surface'. He left the theatre determined to become an actor.

The resulting *arousal of appetite* is of singular importance in educational terms, and Hargreaves contrasts such sudden and unexpected moments with the incremental learning approaches which predominate in schools — colour-coded reading books indicate an incremental approach in use in many primary schools. Learning builds upon what has gone before, knowledge and skills developing slowly but systematically. Whatever the virtues of incremental learning, however, high levels of motivation do not normally feature among them. Hargreaves does not suggest that incremental learning is mistaken, but indicates it is only part of the account. The missing element, epitomized by the illuminating experience, is essential to aesthetic learning, having to do with appreciation as well as mere skill acquisition. Once this is understood, the teacher can periodically consciously plan surprise.

The illuminating experience possesses further important characteristics, experienced in varying degrees, and these can lead to equally important outcomes. Hargreaves identifies a number of them through the testimonies of adults who, as consumers of the arts, could reflect over considerable time spans, identifying how and when their arts interests were initially aroused, often because of illuminating experiences. These invariably occurred *outside of the classroom*, leading Hargreaves to suggest that the art gallery, concert hall, theatre and opera house are the natural arenas for the illuminating experience (or conversive trauma, as he termed it).

Hargreaves' findings were further substantiated by the testimonies of young people interviewed as part of the CSAE Project research. These provided vivid accounts of *concentration of attention*: 'It just flew past . . . it didn't seem like an hour and a half — more like ten minutes'; 'It created an effect of harmony around you . . . an almost unreal atmosphere'. There is also *sense of revelation*: 'It was a complete eye-opener'; 'It seemed a totally different form of Art.' Revelation does not just involve qualities within the art object — as Dewey indicated, it is also to do with something latent within us, albeit now recognized for the first time — 'molecules that were there dormant', or, in one young person's words, 'like a seed that was there — but it has to be triggered off'. *Inarticulateness* is the educator's nightmare! How can the teacher harness and build upon what a pupil does not even choose to divulge? However, Abbs has already emphasized that there is an important phase in the responding process of a pre-verbal nature, and in an atmosphere of mutual trust, important signs can be discerned, denoting that something of significance has occurred; this can mark the moment when response can naturally shade into evaluation. A further characteristic is *memory retention*; young people can often recall and describe the illuminating moment with unusual clarity of detail. The experience is so clearly remembered because it was emotionally arousing and hence disturbing. This poses the seeming contradiction that inarticulateness is complemented by a capacity to communicate with increased clarity and precision — hence the significance of these experiences to language development. The key element of arousal of appetite has already been touched upon; 'one simply wants the experience to continue or to be repeated, and this can be felt with considerable urgency'. Even in weaker versions of the experience 'there is still a lingering fascination which leads people to say that they felt "hooked" on the art object in some way'.

Arousal of appetite, being motivating by definition, can give rise to both added *commitment* and a desire for further *exploration*. In contrast to the idea that the theatre, art gallery and opera house are boring places, the young person so affected is now likely to want to revisit in order to repeat the 'buzz' already experienced. A sense of *discrimination* develops as one experience is gauged against another, particularly when this is allied to *background research* through reading, listening to records, etc. — a further outcome of the illuminating experience. Now, though, this is a discrimination born of responses of a powerful and personal nature, as opposed to being what others tell us we should or should not be liking, for whatever reasons. Hargreaves' adult informants indicate that a considerable timelag — sometimes amounting to years — can separate the motivating moment from the decision to read in order to further substantiate the experience. Provision of appropriate resources within the school context can help short-circuit this process, facilitating systematic approaches to research which might otherwise never take place.

Children cannot enter the aesthetic field unless the art of others is made accessible to them. Equally, their own practical engagement in the arts is crucial to the process. This duality of activities makes one further outcome, that of *heightened environmental awareness*, vitally important. Under the influence of powerful arts experiences, one can become unusually receptive to aspects of one's immediate surroundings and inner imaginative worlds. An art form with little educational history, that of film, is nevertheless one constantly experienced by young and old alike, in both the cinema and the home — and one not generally associated with boredom! The sculptor Giacometti provides an extraordinary example of heightened environmental awareness stimulated by a cinema visit made around 1945:

> I came out of the cinema, I looked about the surroundings, I came out and I was in the road, in a cafe; nothing happened, absolutely nothing happened. That is to say, there was no distinction between my view of the external world and the view of that which went on on the screen. One was the continuation of the other. . . . I looked around at the people around and all of a sudden I saw them as I had never seen them before. What was new was not what was going on on the screen: it was that which was happening beside me. . . . Everything was different, both the depth of space and the objects, the colours and the silence . . . because the silence counted, the film having been a talkie. . . . That day, reality became revalued for me, from top to bottom; it became the unknown, but at the same time a marvellous unknown.[13]

Film and television are relatively undeveloped art forms in school terms. Historically, a main impediment has been that of practicability, but the advent of video cameras and media studies centres has now opened up a whole new range of possibilities. Video makes it possible for children to study both the filmed imagery of others and actually to film themselves. The relationship which Giacometti highlights between seeing a film and a fresh view of the world is obviously important to the aesthetic potential of media studies in schools; for the first time it is relatively easy for children to become practically involved and to realize such connections tangibly. The implications for Giacometti's own sculptural and artistic practice are also too obvious to need labouring in relation to such profound evidence of an artist seeing the world almost as if for the first time, through another, albeit related, art form.

That the process is also pertinent to children of primary school age is made clear by the responses of a group of 10-year old pupils to the stimulus of Gerd Winner's prints of the London Dockland area and New York tenements displayed in Drumcroon, documented in *Educating for Art*. One example will suffice to illustrate the heightened awareness with which these pupils came to see their own urban environment — highly familiar, but now as if being seen for the first time; the mundane is transformed into something of wonder:

> A railway seeks its way through a smoky cloud. Suddenly a train shoots past making a hissing, clicking sound. As we walked it was like a never-ending town of houses, factories, warehouses and a labyrinth of roads. The main road was ominous. We went under a dark dismal bridge that carried trains over our heads. Lots of towering shops and broken-down factories, warehouses and mills. Iron bars in the lifting equipment were rusty and the water underneath was carrying away the rust.[14]

Though the initial stimulus was in the visual arts, the children's responses found expression not only in visual form — these were also of exceptional quality and range — but in creative writing of a vividly descriptive nature tinged with mood and atmosphere. Experiences in one art form can lead to heightened experience of the natural world, and can therefore find expression in *other* art forms within the school context. For added clarity, the characteristics and outcomes of the illuminating experience can be summarized diagrammatically:

ILLUMINATING EXPERIENCE =
CONCENTRATION OF ATTENTION + SENSE OF REVELATION
+ INARTICULATENESS + MEMORY RETENTION
and of particular educational significance
AROUSAL OF APPETITE.
These lead to, but not necessarily in discrete order,
COMMITMENT — EXPLORATION — DISCRIMINATION —
SEARCH FOR BACKGROUND INFORMATION
+ HEIGHTENED ENVIRONMENTAL AWARENESS,
an important bridging link between the study and practice of art.[15]

Because of their 'extraordinary power', Nicholas Davey maintains that we tend to see these aesthetic experiences in isolation 'rather than to see their cumulative power in the process of self-formation':

> What initially appear in themselves to be singular islands of meaning can begin to show themselves as an archipelago, to have a collective shape of their own, each new experience enabling a change or orientation to the whole . . . We are all desperately impatient to unravel the story that history and our own efforts have inscribed within us. To have a sense of that story is to have a sense of identity and to have that sense is to be both aware of one's distinctness but also of how one shares and is deeply implicated in the culture that has shaped one. The archipelago it turns out is invariably linked to a submerged *massif.*[16]

Ultimately, therefore, illuminating experiences have a crucial bearing both on our awareness of our individual uniqueness and of our relationship to the whole cultural cosmos of the arts as practised throughout time and across places.

An individual child can be captivated by a theatre or gallery visit which the majority have not enjoyed. One child might enjoy numerous experiences of this nature, to varying degrees of intensity, over a period of time. An important implication is that learning of an individual nature can emanate from them. It is therefore necessary for the teacher to address individual pupil needs, rather than insist that all children always do exactly the same thing. Proper preparation and appropriate support in the theatre or gallery can also lead to additional numbers being likewise affected, any teacher obviously wanting all to so benefit who can. Children should be actually taught to engage with all manner of art works so that they can spend time with them, discover their secrets, and learn to value and trust their own responses, observations and judgments. To this end, it is appropriate to return to the Content, Form, Process and Mood model to which reference has already been made.

The Content, Form, Process, Mood Model

This model is of practical value to children of all ages. It is empowering, enabling them to address all manner of art works from distinct standpoints, each aspect helping reveal different facets of an art work. In other words, it helps pupils *complete* the art work, as described earlier. In turn, children can come to a fuller awareness of a work as a whole and consider works for longer timespans; they can sense, unravel, contemplate. The model also comprises criteria which can help children make connections between their own work and that of others, with them as applicable to their work as it is to that of others. Each category can stimulate the use of distinct areas of vocabulary — essential to children acquiring the necessary language to negotiate about the arts and their arts experiences.

The structure was first set out in *Educating for Art*, as an aid to the classroom teacher rather than for its empowering use with children. Through its application teachers could, for example, make sense of original schools loan works. Even where available, such resources often remain underutilized because teachers often feel insecure, believing they lack the necessary knowledge to use them with confidence. In an ideal world, loan items would always be accompanied by relevant support material. Their absence need not lead to neglect, however; Taylor wrote in *Educating for Art*: 'Four fundamental areas all have teaching potential and should beneficially form the basis of any accompanying support information. They are relevant to all art and craft objects, though the emphasis on particular aspects will inevitably vary from work to work'.[17] The areas are:

1 *Content*: The work's content in terms of subject matter, how significant this is and how the artist has accumulated the necessary information, etc.
2 *Form*: The formal qualities of the work in terms of its arrangement into shapes, structure and colour organization, etc.
3 *Process*: The techniques, processes and methods — and timescales — involved in the making of the work.
4 *Mood*: The mood, atmosphere and feelings evoked by the work.

It will readily be seen that, with slight revision, the model can provide a structure applicable to all art forms. In essence, the four areas pose the following questions: What is the work about? How has it been ordered and arranged? How has it been made? What effect does it have on me and why? *Content* subsumes subject matter but implies far more. *Form* can lead to the consideration of parts as well as the whole. *Process* assimilates techniques, materials, all forms of preparatory work and every stage in the production — including the interpretation of music or play through performance. *Mood* can lead to analysis of how atmosphere or a particular range of feelings is conveyed, but most effectively elicits subjective responses stimulated by the overall 'feel' of the work. These categories are obviously interdependent. The debate about the relationship between content and form, for example, has taken place throughout time in relation to poetry, aspects of music, drama and the visual arts. Content obviously helps determine mood; it is unlikely that, unless in a spirit of irony, an artist would seek to portray a mood of calm contentment in a work designed to address the horrors of war. In turn, process relates to content and mood through the use of agitated brushwork or soothing rhythms, etc.

Children can make methodical use of the model, working singly or in pairs, maybe alternating between one posing pertinent questions, the other responding to them. A whole range of questions have been formulated relating to each area in turn (see Chapter 4). Many teachers encourage their children to make up their own, having first provided them with the criteria to formulate them. Because the arts engage feelings as well as minds, responses to vital stimuli can spur pupils to find precise but appropriately expressive words and phrases. As such, use of the model can significantly aid language development. In response to questions about content, children are likely to use *descriptive* language, questions about form can encourage use of more *structural* language, while in response to questions about process, children are likely to use *technical* language of a more subject-specific nature. Finally, mood can stimulate use of *evocative* language expressive of feelings. In subsequent chapters, the reader will note the relevance of this model to the primary sector from the examples of pupil practice used illustrating the range and depth of responses which can arise through its systematic application.

Contextualization

The model can also aid contextualization both within an art form and across the arts, each of the four elements providing means of establishing relationships. The pupils' practical work and any other works being studied can be linked to countless further examples, including ones so different in nature and form that they do not immediately appear to connect. By this means, children's understanding and awareness of art forms can be gradually and systematically extended and broadened. At a content level, the John Keane Gulf War paintings on display at the Imperial War Museum can provide a focus to open up the whole theme of war and conflict as depicted through all the arts: the *Bayeux Tapestry*, Uccello's *Rout of San Romano* and Goya's *Disaster of War* etchings. The Paul Nash paintings of World War 1, such as *We Are Making a New World* (1918) and the poems of Owen and Sassoon might be used comparatively. Britten's *War Requiem* and Tchaikovsky's *1812 Overture* provide obvious musical references. The possible examples are countless and can be drawn from contemporary and historical sources from any century. They can range across cultures for the theme is, unfortunately, a universal one. Newspaper photographs of the current strife in Northern Ireland, Bosnia and Iraq can be disconcertingly interchangeable once cut out and divorced from their captions and hence their specific contexts.

Passages from the Bible, the Koran, Shakespeare and Tolstoy, for example, can be introduced in uncontrived, related ways, the pupils becoming increasingly immersed in the theme or topic under scrutiny. Through process, the investigative procedures adopted by composers, artists and writers can be examined in relation to the children's own investigative activities. Through attention to mood, a wide gamut of emotions — fear, defeat, hatred, victory, compassion and forgiveness, humiliation, violence, etc. — can likewise be explored in practical ways in relation to the countless supporting examples drawn from a range of art forms.

The introduction of art and music as foundation subjects raised fears that attainment targets for AT2, 'Knowledge and understanding' in art and 'Listening and appraising' in music would lead to a divorce between theory and the practice enshrined within AT1, creating a retrogressive 50/50 teaching divide. This need not be the case. Both the Art and Music Working Groups scattered non-statutory but highly influential examples throughout their reports. However, the systematic use of content, form, process and mood can help any primary staff to construct courses which maintain a balance between the two attainment targets. Learning in one can constantly complement and affirm what is undertaken in the other. Pupils' knowledge and awareness can therefore develop harmoniously in relation to their practice, becoming ever more rich, deep and complex. The generalist primary teacher can draw upon personal enthusiasms and knowledge in relation to any art form, and then build upon them by applying clear criteria which can lead to further relevant examples, the teacher adopting investigative approaches similar to those required of the children themselves.

The Axes of Creativity and Some National Curriculum Requirements

In *A is for Aesthetic*, the second volume in the Library on Aesthetic Education, Abbs develops the thesis of two complementary axes of true creativity, the *vertical* extending inwards to the deeply personal expressive needs and the *horizontal* looking outwards, born of the recognition that art also grows out of art.[18] Both are essential to any broad and balanced education in the arts. In order to understand the vertical axis, Abbs suggests we turn to the phenomenon of the dream which 'creates the imaginative powers that are then extended to other conscious activities in the course of evolutionary development'. What was consciously hunted for 'rises spontaneously with the kinaesthetic sensation of water flowing'. The unconscious is a shaping energy which helps 'to determine the form of creative work'. The vertical axis has its counterpart in the horizontal, however, for in all culture 'there is a constant reworking of the established conventions, notations, images, narratives'. The artist, in other words, in seeking the form of the creative work, not only attempts to give shape to what rises spontaneously, but in doing so also draws upon a whole range of examples known to that artist through the history of the art form and, indeed, of other art forms. This applies to the innovative artist as well as to more traditional exponents. David Best, as we shall see in Chapter 3, argues that what might appear to rise spontaneously is, in fact, actually determined and only made possible because of our awareness of the art form itself.

The systematic application of content, form, process and mood as an aid to pupils' appraisal of their work and that of others and the relevance of the axes of creativity provide two related means of making sense of National Curriculum requirements. In art and music, for example, AT1, 'Investigating and making' and 'Performing and composing' respectively correspond closely to the vertical axis of creativity. AT2, 'Knowledge and understanding' (Art) and 'Listening and appraising' (Music) similarly relate to the horizontal. Concerns have been expressed with regard to how the two attainment targets might be linked in practice; the aware teacher can construct lessons consistent with the requirements of both attainment targets, by attending to both axes. In other words, while pupils are composing and performing in music through attainment target 1, they are also engaging with *related* examples of compositions and performances by others. The teacher, therefore, can consistently lead pupils into the aesthetic field of making, presenting, responding and evaluating, encouraging practice which is thus dynamic and interactive.

The form and structure of the National Curriculum risks marginalizing the arts. Primary teachers are also under constant pressure, enduring endless criticism and having to meet everchanging requirements as to what is to be taught and how. There are lobbies demanding a return to rote learning and formal approaches, based on an ever narrowing view of the curriculum. Nevertheless, the best primary practice remains vital and multifaceted. However simplistic the wishes of media, pressure groups and secretaries of state might be, primary teaching is a complex and refined activity, and must remain so. Michael Duffy observes how, in the present climate, the generation of excitement and response is being inhibited by dictate and imposition:

> It's as though the accountants have taken over, the bean-counters of education, the people who really believe that teaching is a simple matter of inputs and of outputs. Enthusiasts don't fall for that; they know that learning is more complicated and more fun, a sort of precarious conspiracy between the teacher and the taught.[19]

The kinds of excitement and response which exemplify good primary practice wherever that 'precarious conspiracy between the teacher and the taught' survives is evident in the material which illuminates the latter chapters of this book. The arts are central to this excitement, and will never be peripheral in schools which retain a positive educational outlook based upon pupil needs.

References

1 Read, H. (1943) *Education through Art*, London, Faber and Faber, pp. 223, 224.
2 The Gulbenkian Report, *The Arts in Schools: Principles, Practice and Provision* (1982) London, Calouste Gulbenkian Foundation, p. 49.
3 Abbs, P. (1987) *Living Powers : The Arts in Education,* London, Falmer Press; see Part I, 'Confronting the Crisis within the Arts'.
4 Clegg, A. (1971) *Revolution in the British Primary Schools*, Washington DC, National Education Association, pp. 10–11.
5 Abbs (1987) p. 54.
6 Hall, C. (1991/2) 'Mingei: The Living Tradition in Japanese Arts', *Arts Review*, Christmas/New Year, p. 635.
7 Berger, J. (1980) *About Looking*, London, Writers and Readers, p. 134.
8 Abbs (1987) p. 61.
9 *The Arts 5–16: A Curriculum Framework* (1990) Harlow, Oliver and Boyd, p. 3.
10 Hargreaves, D. (1983) 'The Teaching of Art and the Art of Teaching: Towards an Alternative View of Aesthetic Learning' in Hammersley, M. and Hargreaves, A. (Eds) *Curriculum Practice: Some Sociological Case Studies*, London, Falmer Press.
11 Taylor, R. (Ed.) (1991) *Mini-Drumcroons: Wigan School-Based Galleries*, Wigan, Drumcroon occasional publication.
12 Taylor, R. (1986) *Educating for Art: Critical Response and Development*, Harlow, Longman; see in particular Part I, Section 3, 'Illuminating Experiences', pp. 18–28.
13 Waddington, C.H. (1969) *Behind Appearances*, Cambridge, MA, Edinburgh University Press, p. 231.
14 Taylor (1986) p. 112.
15 *Ibid.*, pp. 27–28.
16 Davey, N. (1992) 'Aesthetics as the Foundation of Human Experience'. Paper presented on 1 November to NSEAD 'New Realities' Conference, Liverpool.
17 Taylor (1986) p. 181.
18 Abbs, P. (1989) *A is for Aesthetic: Essays on Creative and Aesthetic Education*, London, Falmer Press; see pp. 10–24.
19 Duffy, M. (1992), 'Flushing 'orses out of the woodwork', London, *Times Education Supplement*, 13 March, p. 120.

Chapter 2

The Major Art Forms: Their Recent Histories within Education

. . . the education we dispense falls into three fairly clear categories. In the first place, there are the loaves, that is to say the facts that the child has to learn: two and two make four, the Spanish Armada was defeated in 1588, a wild rose has five petals and so on. The character-istics of this kind of learning is that the child gets it right or wrong, and we can measure his [*sic*] accuracy. Then there is a category where the loaves and the hyacinths are mixed. A child learns the 'Ode to Autumn' or he dances a Highland Fling. He can get the words of the Ode right or wrong, and he can get the steps right or wrong, and this is a matter of loaves; but how expressively he recites or how elegantly he dances, the zest, the eagerness and artistry which he brings to these activities is a matter of hyacinths.

But in any good school there will be occasions when a child, prob-ably after a worthwhile and moving occasion, says what he has to say in a way in which he delights, and he can say it in writing, speech, paint, clay, movement, or any other medium of communication which is appropriate, and when this happens the hyacinths stand alone.

Sir Alec Clegg[1]

Preparing Children for an Unknown Future

'In the jargon we speak of the cognitive and the affective but in my view loaves and hyacinths makes the distinction clearer', adds Clegg. In reality, his hyacinths clearly represent aesthetic experiences. For 'hyacinths to grow', experiences of a feeling and sensory nature have to be catered for. This will invariably involve the arts. The arts must play an increasingly vital role in education in the coming years, for they encourage essential forms of under-standing of a lateral nature. They also help encourage mutual cooperation, respect for other viewpoints and empathetic links with nature — all of singu-lar importance to the present generation of pupils.

The world is changing at a dramatic rate, so much so that, if scientific estimates are correct, those being educated in today's primary schools will lead their adult lives in a world unrecognizable from that we know today because of a rate of ecological change no previous generation has even had to consider. Technological advances are also having dramatic effects on our lives — on occasions, compounding ecological problems in ways we fail to anticipate. Many children now grow up with a technological awareness and expertise adults have to strive to acquire. Few will enter jobs and stay in them for life. With the knowledge explosion, greater mobility, and the speed with which we gain awareness of what is happening around the world, there is no longer any consensus as to which facts and events are the ones to be learned and memorized. In this changing world, a necessity is that of educating children in ways that help them to become as flexible and adaptable as possible. The logical but linear thinking, which so dominated education in the past, needs to be balanced by approaches designed to encourage more imaginative and divergent forms of understanding and insight — entry into the complex web of the aesthetic field offers the most potent means of ensuring this.

In the current educational debate, however, the belief that today's children require a replication of the education our politicians received persists, and has staunch, vociferous — and highly influential — advocates; in many respects, the National Curriculum as initially conceived was a throw-back to the grammar and public school-type education of yesteryear: 'What was good enough for us must be good enough for them!' Education has always had to adjust to change, but never remotely to the extent that the requirements of today demand. The first of seven Wigan principles, states: 'Education must look forward and recognise that it is the means of preparing people for a future of which we have little or no conception'.[2] (The principles were formulated through involvement in the DES 11–16 Curriculum Project, set up in response to Callaghan's 1976 Ruskin Speech. The 'Great Educational Debate' followed — if education could not get its act together, a government-imposed national curriculum would be a probable outcome!) The first Wigan principle could conceivably have been written twenty years ago, but that would have been highly unlikely. Today, however, the speed of change is so irrevocable that it cannot be ignored. Ecological changes pose major world problems requiring collective action; the second Wigan principle states that 'Education must take place within an International context as opposed to the National context within which it has operated to date'.

The Gulbenkian *The Arts in Schools* made an important connection between now and the future, under the heading 'Living in the present':

> To see education only as a preparation for something that happens later, risks overlooking the needs and opportunities of the moment. Children do not hatch into adults after a secluded incubation at school. They are living their lives now. Helping them towards an independent and worthwhile life in the adult world of the future presupposes

helping them to make sense of and deal with the experiences which they suffer and enjoy in the present. The roles they adopt later and the employment they will seek will partly depend on what they be-come as individuals — what capacities and capabilities are developed or neglected — during the formative years of education. It follows that schools should enrich and broaden children's experiences through a broad and balanced curriculum. Literacy and numeracy are an important part of education. They should not be mistaken for the whole of it.[3]

There have always been educators, of course, who have been sensitive to changing future needs, taking account of them in relation to present requirements and concerns. Over a quarter of a century ago, Robin Tanner wrote,

> I like the notion that your aim as an educator is to fulfil the present, the immediate stage of growth, that through that fulfilment you are making the best preparation for the future. . . . In children, the far distant, primitive, elemental past, and the immediate present, and a future we adults will never see, all meet.[4]

This conviction led him to deplore much of what he saw happening around him in his old age, affirming his belief 'that in this Mass Age, it is nevertheless the personal qualities of the individual, the separate person, that count most and are the most vital force today'. In educational terms, this meant,

> . . . that the Arts are our most natural aid in the growth of our personal qualities . . . I believe in the absolute values which the Arts teach. I believe in the conception of the wholeness of life — rather than the diffuseness — which they demonstrate.
> I believe that the power of choice, discrimination, judgment that is inherent in the arts is a power that is of paramount importance for every one of us to cultivate to our fullest, if we are not to sink, to yield up human rights, and to be spiritually dead.
> I believe that the aesthetic sense and the ethical sense are one! I believe that the aesthetic test is infallible, even in human affairs.[5]

The Arts in Schools and Tanner both state unequivocally, therefore, that children can only be adequately prepared for the future when their education is broad, balanced and relevant to their *immediate* needs. Aesthetic dimensions facilitating the growth of hyacinths are essential to any such education.

The need for hyacinths in our schools has never been greater, but the time permitted for their cultivation is constantly being eroded. In *Living Powers*, Abbs argued for a third of curriculum time for the arts in the secondary sector on the basis that the aesthetic was one of the three fundamental means of 'knowing'.[6] Since that book was first published, the amounts of time available have diminished in the secondary sector. As art and music 'come on stream' as National Curriculum subjects, perhaps there will at least be a return to what was in terms of time. Within the primary context, however, it is possible — and indeed desirable — that the arts permeate and inform the whole curriculum, as well as specific arts activities warranting their own time. What Abbs proposes, therefore, could still be realized in this sector — but not without surmounting considerable problems, many of them with their precedents in history compounded by current 'core' curriculum thinking squeezing out essential experiences which, ironically, have this capacity to inform the so-called core subjects with greater meaning.

The Major Art Forms: Their Recent Histories within Education

Sir Alec Clegg frequently bemoaned that for too long we had denied children 'the right to learn by choosing and discriminating and forming judgments themselves. We created conditions in which it was impossible for them to make mistakes and then we congratulated ourselves because they didn't make them'.[7] There are currently strong pressures to return to such a spoon-feeding notion of education. Reflecting on his own initial acceptance of the *status quo*, though, he recalls an experience that was to influence him greatly, though he found it 'extremely embarrassing' at the time, for he wondered what on earth it had to do with 11-plus preparation. This usually comprised information being drilled into the children with punishment inflicted on those too dull to succeed — 'if they were dull the sooner they were made to face up to it the better'. In this school, though, children were painting on sheets of paper spread out on the cloakroom floor, while acting was going on in the hall, and the children 'were so engrossed in what they were doing that they paid no attention whatever to the Inspector or to me. . . . How, I wondered, did they get that degree of concentration . . .'[8]

Education has developed greatly in the intervening period, but there are still those who persist in seeing all creative approaches as the denial of all the more formal learning needs, whereas many teachers happily move from one to the other as appropriate, and organize their classrooms and related spaces accordingly. The arts frequently suffer through this polarization, teachers being made to feel that they are neglecting fundamental 'core' areas by devoting time to their practice. Clegg warned that 'so-called change can be brought about by imposing it on schools' but that the effects could be 'a lack of conviction, a lack of sincerity, and inert and sterile results', whereas teachers 'such as Montessori or Marion Richardson or Susan Isaacs find new ways of teaching, and the news spreads through the schools, changing both method and curriculum'.[9] The National Curriculum is a classic example of imposed change, and it is a tribute to teachers that they are still so positive in their attempts to prevent it from being sterile and inert.

More child-centred approaches throughout the age ranges developed from those pioneered in the 1930s infant schools, as noted by Clegg, but, with some notable exceptions, these only began to flourish in junior schools — albeit only ever on a patchy basis — following the widespread abolition of the 11-plus examinations. The 11-plus was extremely damaging to the arts, as it led to teachers teaching what was to be externally examined; this pressure has now returned with renewed vigour, in the form of testing at age 7 as well as at age 11. More simple paper and pencil tests are now to be introduced. It is certainly possible to formulate such tests. What their worth is, is another matter altogether, however. Once implemented, though, they will inevitably further skew the curriculum. The arts are likely to suffer by once again becoming more detached from the rest of the curriculum — that is in other than those schools with a steady nerve and sufficient conviction in their whole-school policies. This process is likely to be further accelerated by recent suggestions that children aged 9 and over should be taught by specialist subject teachers, in much the same way as appertains in the secondary sector; such a move would irrevocably reduce the potential of the arts to inform the wider primary curriculum, to the detriment of many children.

The place the various art forms already enjoy in the curriculum vary considerably, for a variety of reasons. Rather than divorce them from other curriculum areas, a high priority at both the initial and INSET levels should be to explore how they might more fully imbue learning as a whole throughout the primary phases of education. The recent history of each art form is succinctly summarized in *The Arts 5–16: A Curriculum Framework*, one of the publications contained within the NCC *The Arts 5–16 Project Pack*; the selection of points below focus on those with greatest relevance to the primary curriculum.

Dance

Dance is the least well-established of the arts in schools, usually relying on 'the enthusiasms of individual teachers' who supplement their teaching 'with BBC schools radio broadcasts of *Music and Movement* programmes'. Its developments within PE are due to the influential work of Rudolf Laban, whose theory of movement fitted well 'with the principles of child-centred education', for it facilitated 'dance as the creative and expressive aspects of PE'.

During the 1950s a division developed between educational and theatrical dance teachers; the first argued that emphasis on the strict conventions and disciplines of dance technique 'were inimical to children's personal development'. Performance and dance production 'were unnecessary, even irrelevant'. Rigorous training was seen as necessary by the dance and ballet schools, where spontaneity of movement was not encouraged. 'In the 1960s and 1970s these opposing views gradually forged a new conception of dance in schools'.

Educationalists came to accept the need for dance technique and the value of planning and controlling expressive movement. Pupils were encouraged to make dances and to present them to others, and teachers in schools have come increasingly to argue for dance to be seen as part of the arts curriculum in schools.

The evolution of British contemporary dance coincided with a growing appreciation of improvisation and experimentation in the theatrical dance world. Now well-established, contemporary dance has generated, over a twenty-five year period, new models of school practice. The work of dance companies within education has given added impetus to dance as a subject in the curriculum. The main examination issues are germane to the primary area as they pinpoint current concerns:

- to promote an understanding of dance as an art form;
- to develop expertise in dance performance and composition;
- to develop an appreciation of dance through observation and discussion of dance both in and outside school.

Contemporary dance has been an important influence, but is a limited form, historically and culturally; dance education should provide children with some insight into 'the many forms and functions of dance in the world'. There are few courses which train specialist dance teachers. 'All of these factors have perpetuated the low status of dance in the curriculum'.[10]

Drama

Prior to the 1950s, drama was thought of in terms of study and performance of texts, though from early this century progressive teachers had used acting and improvisation to explore the meanings of texts. Some had argued that these could 'enliven teaching and learning in all areas of the curriculum'. These ideas took hold of teachers 'on a large scale' in the 1950s. Slade, in *Child Drama* (1954), developed parallel arguments to those of Laban:

The real purpose of drama was to promote the personal growth of pupils through creative self-expression. Young children given only minimal help and direction by teachers generated their own distinctive dramatic forms — 'Child Drama' — which were different from theatre as understood by adults.

These precepts were developed in various ways in the 1950s and 1960s.

As a medium of creative self-expression, 'directions from the teacher should be kept to a minimum', and the objection to teaching technique and studying texts was that this 'interrupted the "spontaneity" and "sincerity" of free expression'. New approaches to directing and acting in the professional theatre influenced educational drama: 'It was the influence of the Method school of acting, for example, that led to popular caricatures, which sometimes persist still, of improvised drama meaning being trees — one of many exercises within the Method'.

Over the last fifteen years, a predominant emphasis has been that of using role play and improvisation to explore social and moral issues, with these processes used in other curriculum areas and to aid personal and social education. The debate about drama as a method of learning and as a basis for the study of texts, theatre and performances continues, with some teachers operating at each end of this continuum. Gavin Bolton (1980) and Dorothy Heathcote (1979) have both been influential through their 'explorations of the techniques of teaching in role', drawing on the forms and conventions of theatre, but emphasizing the exploration of issues across the curriculum. Critics like David Hornbrook (1989) argue that this 'has detracted from the importance of drama as an arts discipline in its own right'. (Hornbrook has written *Education in Drama: Casting the Dramatic Curriculum* for the Falmer Library of Aesthetic Education.)

In 1989, the Cox committee concluded that 'the inclusion of drama methods in English should not in any way replace drama as a subject for specialist study'. Main issues regarding drama at the present time involve:

- the status of drama in its own right;
- the relationships between drama methods in general teaching, and the study and practice of theatre.[11]

Visual Arts

The visual arts are 'the most securely established of the arts disciplines and have long been taught in all schools: in primary schools very often in association with craft'. As with dance and drama, there was a move towards the encouragement of the children's own creative and expressive work in the 1950s and 1960s. Child Art had been promoted by Franz Cizek as early as 1936; it had its own aesthetic forms and qualities as valid as those of adults' art, he maintained. Marion Richardson (1948) and others influenced both theory and practice, facilitating the introduction of 'simple, vivid materials — powder paints, thick brushes and so on — and the need for teachers not to impose adult techniques and standards on children'. Read (1945) argued for the principles of art education to inform the whole curriculum, helping considerably 'to consolidate the place of art in the education of all pupils'.

Issues of art in relation to design and of children's expressive work and its relationship with critical understanding of the art of others surfaced in the 1970s and 1980s. Design became 'a major area of development in the economy and is now coupled with technology in the National Curriculum'. Should the teacher promote art's relationships with design and technology, or press closer to the fine art traditions? These issues have implications for teacher training.

As in dance and drama, emphasis on the children's own creative work tended to 'replace the teaching of artistic traditions and critical appreciation. In the last five years, however, there has been a renewed interest in this area', through the CSAE Project (see Chapter 1). The project 'arose out of a concern that "the emphasis on practical work in many schools had become so dominant that the contemplative aspects of art education had virtually disappeared" and that there had been "a consequent reduction in the amount and variety of verbal communication in the art department"'.

> The aims of the project were to explore: the role and implementation of art history and critical studies in secondary schools [and the primary sector; see Chapter 1] and to link these to the use of external resources such as museums, galleries and art centres; the contribution which could be made within schools by visiting and resident artists and craftspeople, and by loans of collections of art and craft objects. Many of the principles and recommendations of the project have strongly influenced contemporary work in schools and the educational programmes of galleries and museums.[12]

Music

Witkin (1974) commented in a review of the arts in schools that 'music is apparently in the greatest difficulties'. Despite its long tradition, 'it repeatedly fails to obtain a general hold on the musical development of the majority of pupils' who see it as 'irrelevant to anything that really concerns them'. Through orchestras, bands and ensembles, music has 'made an enormous contribution to the culture of school and community life' outside the classroom, but this has involved the few; 'activities have been limited by perceived talent, numbers and facilities'. By the mid-1970s, primary school music comprised classroom singing and playing percussion instruments and recorders. Swanwick (1979) noted the 'elitism in our professional practice', the 'narrow definitions of music confined to Western classical tradition', and 'the inadequacies of our intellectual framework and teaching methodology'. Subsequent reappraisal over the last decade gained 'particular impetus by music specialists' planning for the introduction of GCSE'. Swanwick (1989) 'argues for a broader cultural base for music in schools', adding that 'the major distinctive contribution to musical development made by . . . schools and colleges . . . lies in the abstraction and practical exploration of clearly identified musical processes across a range of cultural "for instances" essentially in musical criticism'.

In part due to this, 'there is a new emphasis on the importance of practical music-making and composition alongside musical appreciation'.

It is now widely accepted that music education should give equal weight to the three aspects of listening, composing and performing. The conception of music has also broadened beyond that of the Western classical tradition to embrace all aspects of world music. These developments have been fuelled by technological innovations: practical music has been promoted by the availability of new instruments; the proliferation of recorded and broadcast music has brought new worlds of music within daily reach of the classroom. The central questions in music education now focus on content and on the role of the teacher in stimulating and sustaining pupil's own musical activity.[13]

Verbal Arts

This relatively new conception 'refers to any art form which is principally concerned with words, whether written or spoken'. There are three themes in current debates:

- the relationship of English teaching to the arts and between creative writing and critical appreciation;
- the growing interest in oracy;
- the need to recognize different cultural practices in verbal arts, including those that are rooted in speech not writing.

Creative writing has been a particular feature since the 1960s when it became valued as a form of self-expression, in keeping with the child-centred approaches of the time. By the late 1960s, though, 'English teaching began to centre on the social functions of language and of linguistics', and away from a key relationship with the arts. Abbs (1982) argues that the subject's intrinsic concerns are literary, expressive and aesthetic, though long obscured due to the unconscious absorption of habits from the classics from which it had emerged:

It was partly due to English being linked to literary criticism and the historical study of texts with the result that it became allied with the humanities and was seen, therefore, as being more akin to history or social studies than, say, dance or art. It was partly due to the demands of other disciplines which insisted that it was the task of English teachers simply to impart . . . the general skills of the language narrowly conceived.

The Verbal Arts Association was formed in 1983 'to reassert the relationship of English with the arts, with a particular emphasis on encouraging pupils' own writing'. The teaching of literature had for too long valued the capacity to criticize literature more than the ability to produce it; the study of texts overrode the development of pupils' creative abilities.

Verbal arts embrace spoken and written language. The *speaking and listening* profile component of the Cox committee recommendations (1989) 'confirmed the increasing importance that is attached to oral communication'. Talk promotes pupils' understanding and is an aid to 'evaluating their progress in all subjects'. The need to develop oral skills had been emphasized by the DES (1985), and these became a central part of pupil assessment for many through GCSE. The Cox Report specifically related 'the promotion of confident and articulate communication' to pupils' enjoyment of the arts 'as patrons or practitioners' (DES, 1989b).

> However, the relevance of the verbal arts goes well beyond the discussion and appreciation of literary forms. The concept of verbal arts helps to recognise that within many cultural groups, the arts are themselves rooted in oral rather than literary forms.[14]

Film and Television

One major art form is missing from the above brief review, of course, and it — not dance — is, in fact, the most neglected art form in education. *Film and Television in Education: An Aesthetic Approach to the Moving Image* by Robert Watson was a 1990 addition to the Falmer Library on Aesthetic Education. In the Preface, Abbs observes:

> There can be little doubt that of the six great arts which the Library ... is committed to defending and defining, film has been the most ignored in the curriculum of our schools. There is a grand irony in this for film is not only the one unique art form developed in our century but also the most unequivocally popular.[15]

To Gore Vidal:

> Movies are the *lingua franca* of the twentieth century. The Tenth Muse, as they call the movies in Italy, has driven the other nine right off Olympus — or off the peak, anyway. ... Today, where literature was movies are. Whether or not the Tenth Muse does her act on a theatre screen or within the cathode ray tube, there can be no other reality for us since reality does not begin to *mean* until it has been made art of.[16]

The influence of the 1963 Newsom Report led to some use of film in the classroom 'essentially as a kind of dramatic stimulus for discussion, or as illustrative material for project work; in other words, not as a profound art form requiring aesthetic response and creative engagement'. Recent Media Studies developments secured some space for film, television and video but under primarily ideological and discursive aims with them envisaged as part of a 'system of communication which had to be decoded in terms of ideology and contextualized in terms of power and control'. Though obviously important, '. . . the approach missed entirely the crucial aesthetic element, erased the difference between propaganda and art and failed to see the liberating creative powers of the camera when put in the hands of the learner'.

Watson advocates a 'highly practical aesthetic for the teaching of film, television and video', through an approach:

- which celebrates camera as eye, camera as pen, camera as accessible to everyone of whatever ability as an expressive tool with which to observe, record and create;
- which means sustained experience of making film; a purposeful and exacting apprenticeship with the medium;
- which provides initiation into the whole field of film, 'that vast international and interactive web of artistic traditions';
- which can and must extend the aesthetic of film to television and video, with it embracing all forms of popular entertainment;
- which must involve literacy in film, an understanding of the underlying artifice and intentionality involved in film processes; initiation into the grammar of film.[17]

From Formal to Child-Centred Approaches

It will be noted that three main trends have helped shape the major art forms in education as we know them today. They were initially taught in formal ways which were then challenged and sometimes replaced by the more child-centred approaches of the late 1950s and 1960s; these still manifest themselves today. In more recent times, strong political pressures have been demanding a return to more formal approaches allied to the conscious rejection of *all* 1960s values. But parallel with these pressures is the increasingly growing view that it is possible to 'marry' the more valuable aspects of *both* earlier formal and more child-centred approaches, providing a necessary rigour and enabling children to see their own art making within, and as part of, the whole cultural tradition. This latter view has informed the Falmer Library on Aesthetic Education. It is therefore necessary to look at some of the tensions which exist — and, indeed, previously existed — between these seemingly conflicting approaches to arts education.

Once established, the impact of Child Art was considerable. We have already traced, through Clegg's testimony, how its influence filtered into primary schools, initially via infant departments. Earlier approaches took little or no account of the child as an individual. Robert Lowe had introduced 'Payment by Results' in 1870. It was the most sweeping piece of centrally imposed education legislation prior to the 1988 Education Reform Act.

Teachers' pay was dependent upon how their children performed in the rigidly applied testing of 'basic' skills administered and monitored by government inspectors. Results determined the success or otherwise of schools. The influence and ramifications of payment by results extended well into this century, long after it had ceased, so pervasive was its impact. It produced a sterile education of imposition designed without regard for children's immediate needs.

The arts inevitably suffered, different forms entering the curriculum for a variety of reasons, but often enjoying only the most tenuous of footholds. They were valued not for their own sakes, but for ways in which they helped prepare children for the workplace. The art slogan, 'Skill of Hand and Eye', for example, was more concerned with 'the industrial magnate to whom skilled hands were of immediate importance'[18] than with cultivating and developing artistic sensibility as such. It was for functional purposes of this kind that art forms entered the curriculum, rather than for any intrinsic aesthetic worth they might possess.

The visual arts are the longest established, with an unbroken history of over one hundred years. Just how formally they were approached prior to the Child Art movement is graphically illustrated by R.R. Tomlinson:

> In the first place, children were taught to draw straight lines of different lengths, and trained not only to judge proportion but direction as distinct from the horizontal and perpendicular. This method, during the second half of the nineteenth century, was replaced by the use of the freehand copy. These freehand copies usually took the form of a symmetrical linear rendering of an architectural feature, the most popular being the Acanthus leaf. The skilled child was eventually allowed to draw, without mechanical aid, the Ionic volute — a fearsome task indeed.[19]

Drawing in tone eventually found a place in the curriculum, geometric forms like the sphere, cylinder and cone providing the basis for drawings focusing on mass without recourse to use of an outline. In turn, objects like fruit and flower pots found favour, the 'progressive innovation of the time' being the introduction of colour. Lettering was also introduced, so that script writing, developing into the illuminated page, became an additional subject. Plant form in line and colour 'latterly found favour, and the claims of industry, into which so many children found their way upon leaving school, called attention to design. So-called exercises in design took the form of the conventional rendering of plants and flowers', invariably arranged symmetrically in the flat.

In *Living Powers*, Abbs relates developments in modernism in the arts to progressivism in education, charting the reaction against such formal approaches born of the increasingly accepted belief that *all* children were *naturally* creative. He argues that the misconception about art as 'self-expression' was to 'badly distort the development of all the arts in the primary and secondary curriculum', particularly, he maintains, in dance and drama.[20] It can equally be demonstrated, particularly with regard to primary education, that the child art movement provided the essential impetus to demonstrate that the arts were central to learning, and not merely peripheral, as had previously been accepted. However, Professor Bantock provides persuasive support of Abbs' view that Child Art in general took insufficient account of the aesthetic field:

> One of the difficulties, however, has been the naive notion also encouraged by romantic progressivism, that 'creativity' was largely endogenous, a capacity with which a child was born and which needed only opportunity and encouragement rather than something on which to bite, whether technical or experimental. This also has tended to stultify progressive efforts to incorporate aesthetic elements into the curriculum — the consequent outpourings have been more remarkable for their becoming manifest than for their quality.[21]

The influence was considerable — on all arts teachers; Abbs records the impact it had on English teaching:

> In the 1960s many English teachers (myself included) genuinely thought in the name of 'relevance' and 'process' that one could discard the great literary inheritance of, say, Homer, Sophocles, Shakespeare, Wordsworth and Dante. What was valued was sincerity. What was largely overlooked was the need for a bed of culture in which feelings need to be rooted, to be given both *depth* and *connection*. In 'stimulating' feelings without sufficient reference to technique and traditional achievements, we tended to cheapen and exhaust the psyches of our pupils.[22]

That a separation of children's creativity from the cultural tradition can be associated with Child Art is undoubted, though there was certainly little or no such wedding in primary practice while the earlier formal approaches predominated. Rod Taylor points out, though, that Child Art's major pioneers often advocated that both aspects *should* be valued — it was in the hands of later followers that the divorce irrevocably took place. Marion Richardson, for example, sought to surround her children,

> . . . as far as possible, with reproductions of great pictures of all sorts. In this good company taste will have had the opportunity of developing unconsciously, and can prove an armour of defence. The children may not yet understand or even care for what is fine, but, as a pupil once said to me, 'It has an expression on its face'. She recognised it. This expression is the look of sincerity. In its own infinitely humble way, the children's work has it too, and they can dimly feel it as a broad and common denominator, the thing that makes their

own efforts more worthwhile than anything borrowed or second-hand.[23]

It was only subsequently that the strange argument gained credence that exposing children to the work of others was harmful because these works might then prove influential, thus affecting *spontaneity* and *natural* *creativity*. In turn, it developed an attitude akin to censorship — children *must* be kept in a state of ignorance regarding the art of others so as to avoid any possibility of influence. That the educational development most closely associated with liberal approaches should appear to embrace censorship seems a strange irony.

Child-Centred or Formal Approaches?

The recent questioning of many of the assumptions underlying Child Art has led to a variety of teaching approaches in which one frequently observes the child-centred and the formal brought together in various amalgams. Plummeridge observes: 'Amongst any group of educators who might be classed as either traditional or progressive there will be a number of opinions about the place of music in education and how the subject should be presented and taught to pupils'.[24] In similar vein, Taylor highlights three major visual arts developments since the 1960s: design education, visual studies and child art. The majority of teachers do not adhere rigidly to any one of the trends, with 'most syllabuses containing amalgams of aspects of each, and with "imaginative" and "expressive" lessons taught amongst those emphasizing objective approaches or the acquisition of basic skills'.[25] The advent of Child Art, therefore, brought with it a tension that affected all arts disciplines. It revolved around the problem of how much *directed* teaching should take place and how much the arts were *natural* means of expression for the realization of private concepts and ideas. Some teachers always remained sceptical about child-centred approaches, never deviating from their formal approaches; Alexander's analysis of primary classroom practice demonstrates that assumptions that 'modern methods' have led to a neglect of the 'basics' is, in fact, erroneous.[26] Even within the arts rigidly formal approaches continued to be practised, hence the inevitable tensions concerning different approaches.

Edwin Webb describes the resulting debate with regard to the content and philosophy of English as 'something like a running battle', with the history of its teaching 'characterized as a clash between "content" and "process", between "subject-centred" and "child-centred" approaches, and between a "literary" conception of English and that of a "language" concern'.[27] The terms of reference might change with regard to emphasis, 'but they are still there, explicitly and implicitly'. The 1975 Bullock Report *A Language for Life* 'reviewed and passed judgment on the matter of prescriptive grammar teaching'. In order to prepare pupils adequately for the future, we have already argued that it is essential to take proper account of *present* needs; Webb notes that:

At the same time as grammar teaching had its most forceful advocates there were voices not only raised against its usefulness but also the whole form and purpose of education which it symbolised. Such objections were accompanied by, and were in some senses a product of, a reaction against the view of children as raw material to be moulded to some ulterior, adult motive.[28]

Most arts educators will recognize parallels in their own disciplines with what Webb says about English. Similar polarities surfaced in every art form. Each had their advocates, with many teachers utilizing facets of each in their practice. Plummeridge, for example, while warning of the dangers of caricature, nevertheless acknowledges that:

We sometimes talk of a traditional approach to music teaching as one which is concerned with choral and instrumental programmes, skill acquisition (particularly literacy skills), 'academic' studies and the appreciation of the works of the great classical masters. Alternatively, there is frequent reference to the 'progressive' ideals of creativity and self-expression to be promoted through experimentation and the exploration of sound materials.[29]

Given this diversity, it is hardly surprising that a majority of pupils experience a lack of continuity, both in terms of the approaches to, and the content of their arts education.

These tensions manifested themselves in music later than the other arts. Marian Metcalfe suggests that Witkin's 'scathing attack on the content and methodology of their lessons' in *The Intelligence of Feeling* (1974) made many music teachers feel very threatened and defensive, and was further compounded by Ross's accusations of their 'narrowness of outlook' and 'deeply rooted inertia'.[30] Witkin believed that music teachers' main satisfaction was derived from the school choir and orchestra, with timetabled lessons often a necessary chore. Music as generally taught touched only a minority yet, ironically, profoundly affected children's lives *outside* school, with popular music and equipment for its making becoming ever more readily available. Music teachers were obsessed with the belief that skill acquisition had to precede the possibility of creative participation in music making. Only belatedly have progressive attitudes been accepted, argues Metcalfe, leading to a 'late flowering in music education', with 'proportionately more theories for revolutionizing its principles and practice' from the 1960s to the 1980s than at any other time in its history:

Indeed they have jostled behind one another so closely that in many cases teachers have not had time to examine and assess them all, and have simply given up the attempt and 'switched off'. At the risk of seeming simplistic it seems fair to say that there is still a sharp divide between the 'trads' . . . and the 'rads'. . . . However it is also fair to say that where they conflict most strongly it appears obvious that neither side has fully examined or comprehended the case of the other.[31]

The divorce between music appreciation and children's music making was often marked. Drama probably became the most extreme arts discipline in its advocacy of educational drama as separate from all other forms of drama, so wholeheartedly did its advocates promote 'child drama' and its potential to aid learning in *other* curricular areas. This has doubtless contributed to drama being subsumed within English in the National Curriculum. David Hornbrook 'challenges the idea that drama is best thought of as part of English and offers instead a new theoretical basis for drama as a subject and a framework for dramatic practice'.[32] In arguing that drama is an art form *in its own right* as well as being of benefit to others, he asserts that, 'the relationship between classroom drama and the theatre world outside has never been as close as it should have been. . . .' The desire for 'immediate spontaneity of expression ousted stylistic constraints — and hence, the formal possibilities — of inherited culture'.[33] Hornbrook believes that other arts disciplines 'manage successfully to combine attention to form with concern about content, and there is no reason why this should mean a retreat into elocution classes and lectures on theatre studies'.

> A dramatic curriculum which pays careful attention to theatre practice will allow drama teachers access to a subject framework within which they will be able to focus on the quality of the dramatic product as well as on the issues disclosed by it.[34]

Hornbrook sees the absence of theatre studies as a main reason why drama education elevated content — issues — above form. Taylor argues, conversely, that in visual arts education it is content that has been neglected through an undue attention to form and process, even though throughout time, 'the visual arts have provided one of the most potent means' whereby humankind has confronted major life issues and concerns. 'Any visual arts education that does not naturally accommodate these must be deficient', he insists with regard to National Curriculum proposals which initially only took account of process and form with regard to pupils' making activities.[35] These proposals were in keeping with long-held attitudes in art education.

Teachers had rejected art appreciation lessons as inappropriate but had failed to devise alternative critical studies strategies. This led to an undue emphasis on making alone. Here, too, the tension between Child Art and more prescriptive approaches was long apparent. Both often sat uncomfortably side by side within the same course, at both primary and secondary levels, though it was in the transfer from primary to secondary school that the greatest disruption in what was taught and how invariably occurred. Where the Child Art emphasis on natural creativity and spontaneity characterized the primary phase, it was likely to be followed by a basic course in visual studies designed to teach pupils an art vocabulary. Exercises in colour, line, tone and texture, allied to observational drawing, 'the "object" being the environment', would now be the order of the day. Taylor argues, though, that — however diverse these elements — 'the one powerful unifying factor bringing them all together was the overriding concern with making alone'. Critical studies was the missing element, essential for full access to be provided to the aesthetic field.

What Art, Which Artists?

In our complex modern world, the notion that children should have access to the aesthetic field inevitably gives rise to the question, but what art and which artists? Each art form does not have but one history, it has *many*, providing a multiplicity of perspectives, some seemingly conflicting with others. Should the emphasis be on the European tradition or on a world perspective? Should it be on traditional values or take account of current race, gender and special needs concerns? Does an irreconcilable conflict exist between 'high' and popular art? That children must be taught Shakespeare and GCSE boards not set questions about popular television 'soaps' is currently a political issue generating heated debate. In the interplay between the art of the past and the addressing of the major concerns of today, arts education can reconcile these diverse aspects but can be challenging and provocative in the process. Eric Bolton warns against the desire to restrict and sanitize education in order to make it more conducive to pencil and paper testing:

> The arts must be invited to sit at the curriculum table. But they must and will come as they are. We cannot expect them to have perfect table manners, nor to be unfailingly polite to authority and supportive of the way things have always been done. They will be irreverent and decidedly not politically correct.[36]

The Library on Aesthetic Education, in its entirety, presents a tantalizing picture of just how rich, broad and diverse the aesthetic field can be, and how the seemingly irreconcilable can be brought together, each aspect assuming its rightful place, if children are to be genuinely empowered to make essential links and connections within a challenging environment in which they, too, have voices.

In *Film and Television in Education*, Robert Watson recognizes a bond which unites the television programme *Blind Date* with Ulysses, Aeneas, Jason, Perseus, Jane Eyre, the Ancient Mariner, Captain Ahab and others:

> *Blind Date* deals facetiously with the matching and mismatching of couples. But if we ask, 'What is it about?' doggedly enough, most classical narratives will give up a kind of generative essence which does link them to *Blind Date* and its ilk.

> A protagonist has a goal but may not reach it directly. The goal
> is a prize which may be won only after certain tasks have been per-
> formed successfully (or ordeals endured, or obstacles dealt with). The
> prize may be the love of a lady, laurels of victory, the securing of
> peace in the realm, social hegemony, finding the Holy Grail or Golden
> Fleece, spiritual or material wealth. . . . The obstacles may be monsters,
> distracting and destructive temptations, threats, or riddles.[37]

And so on. The important thing is that the classical hero emerges 'with his
identity absolutely unchanged'. Likewise, gameshow contestants

> tend to emerge from their trials unchanged: they are ordinary at the
> outset and ordinary they remain. The paradigm is not used to effect
> transformation, simply to entertain, as it has been entertaining people
> for thousands of years. Programmes such as *Blind Date* are not so much
> a debasement of the formula as an under-elaborated repetition.

It is preferable that the teacher harness programmes like *Blind Date*, not
as ends in themselves but because children are likely to be familiar with them.
It is preferable to help them recognize that such connections exist, than to go
down *another* government-imposed censorship road. The recognition of such
contexts is also important as an aid to discrimination, as pupils learn to gauge
one thing against another through their understanding of these relationships.
The appreciative aspects of arts education can then evolve naturally, for
countless other works will likewise fit into a category, meaning that it continuously expands and broadens as more and more works are 'discovered'
which fit into it. Children can then locate themselves within at least an aspect
of the cultural tradition and a climate is created in which critical debate and
comparison is encouraged. To progress from the known to the unknown is
an educational process adopted by sensitive teachers from time immemorial.
By acknowledging the existence of *Blind Date*, teacher and pupils need not
remain there nor neglect works of more profound artistic significance. *Blind
Date* and facets of Shakespeare can exist at different ends of the same continuum; recognition of the continuum and its various constituents is important,
for the boundaries between so-called 'high' and popular culture are contest-
able, not fixed.

Peter Brinson emphasizes this point in an intriguing opening chapter
called 'Is There a British Dance Culture?' in *Dance as Education*: 'To talk about
dance is to talk about you and you and me'. He maintains that today the
British are 'leaders still in dancing':

> They are the reference point in international ballroom dancing. Scottish
> dance is vibrant. . . . They dance still the sword dance in north-east
> England, the clog dance in Lancashire, and the Morris and other
> traditional dances in the Midlands, the south and in Cornwall. In the
> culture of our young people dance is linked closely with making and

participating in popular music. Our youth dance companies and student companies are welcome visitors in Europe, south-east Asia and the USA. Our disabled and elderly are devising their own choreographic forms. We are embarked on the great adventure of exploring and learning the dance cultures of citizens from Asia and the Caribbean just as we have done over centuries with dance forms from Europe.[38]

He adds that as many tickets are sold each week for dance halls and discos as are sold for football matches and the cinema, further illustrating the degree to which any art form is multifaceted and organic in the ways in which it manifests and shapes itself as part of our culture. This culture draws upon and grows out of the past, but is vital and alive and not irrevocably 'fixed'.

In one section in the *Visual Arts in Education*, Rod Taylor focuses specifically on the need to take account of cultural diversity and gender issues and women artists. He cites Judy Chicago's assertion that her female students' work often goes through an awkward stage because of their attempts to articulate feelings 'for which there is, as yet, no developed form language':

'As the women develop as artists, they build skills that are relevant to their content. Their work improves and they become sophisticated, but that sophistication is built on a solid foundation and is not the result of imitating existing art modes'. In the process, women artists often find themselves occupying previously unoccupied territory, broadening the scope and range of artistic endeavour for the ultimate benefit of all artists, for there are many male artists as well who fit uncomfortably into 'prevailing art modes'.[39]

Artists like Rose Garrard consciously draw upon hitherto neglected women artists of the past — Artemisia Gentileschi, Elizabeth Vigee Lebrun, Judith Leyster — opening up issues concerning women's roles in society past and present, and the need for the woman artist to have her role models, too; the woman artist can easily feel divorced from tradition, as if working in a black void, when alone in the studio. The range covered by these examples indicates something of the breadth of the material contained within the Library on Aesthetic Education. All have a legitimate place in the context of the aesthetic field, with its implications for pupil response and practice. The arts are rich, multifaceted and complex, and children should be provided with an equally rich and ample view of them, both in terms of their past histories and development and as they manifest themselves in society today.

The Aesthetic Field and the Individual

The tensions between the desire for a rigorous arts curriculum on the one hand and concern for the child as an individual can be reconciled through teaching approaches which take full account of each aspect of the making, presenting, responding, evaluating cycle of the aesthetic field. All pupils should be systematically introduced to the breadth and variety of every art form so that their knowledge and understanding can constantly grow and be extended. For this to happen within the aesthetic field, however, the process must take place in creative and dynamically interactive ways which also take account of the practical aspects of children's art making. There is an onus on the teacher to help pupils acquire knowledge and understanding of all the arts in ways which are personally relevant to them and their needs. In the cycle of making, presenting, responding and evaluating, the activity of making then becomes more generous and expansive in its scope:

> The appetite — the impulse to expression — animates the specific medium of the art-maker . . . and in the encounter between appetite and medium the art-work begins to take shape. . . . The material also carries with it a history, a repertoire of previous uses, of working conventions, of established connections and meanings, both covert and hidden. In engaging with the material the art-maker thus engages both consciously and unconsciously with tradition, with the forms already used and the modes and techniques those forms have employed and passed on. Indeed, sometimes, the art-maker in the process of composition will actively study other artists' work. And so art does not come solely out of appetite but also out of other art.[40]

The excesses of Child Art sometimes led to over-indulgence, but a return to the formal methods of the past is surely unthinkable, given the levels of motivation and personal expression and communication achieved in the best of child-centred work. Issues concerning individual personality and temperament are not without controversy, however. It is important that some attention be paid to this matter to understand more fully why some children within any age group are particularly responsive to certain art works, and others to completely different ones. Through such awareness the two axes of creativity can be brought together in tandem on a more consistent basis, creating the fertile climate necessary for the cultivation of those hyacinths so dear to Sir Alec Clegg.

References

1 Clegg, A. (1980) *About Our Schools*, London, Blackwell, pp. 17–18.
2 *Red Book 3: The Wigan Chapter* (DES 11–16 Curriculum Project), Wigan LEA.
3 The Gulbenkian Report, *The Arts in Schools: Principles, Practice and Provision* (1982) London, Calouste Gulbenkian Foundation, p. 4.
4 Tanner, R. (1989) *What I Believe: Lectures and Other Writings*, Bath, Holborne Museum and Crafts Centre, p. 10.
5 Tanner (1989) p. 4.

6   Abbs, P. (1987) *Living Powers: The Arts in Education*, London, Falmer Press, p. 209.
7   Clegg (1980) p. 14.
8   *Ibid.*, p. 4.
9   *Ibid.*, p. 41.
10 *The Arts 5–16: A Curriculum Framework* (1990) Harlow, Oliver and Boyd, pp. 10–11.
11 *Ibid.*, pp. 11–12.
12 *Ibid.*, pp. 12–13.
13 *Ibid.*, pp. 13–14.
14 *Ibid.*, pp. 14–15.
15 Watson, R. (1990) *Film and Television in Education: An Aesthetic Approach to the Moving Image*, London, Falmer Press, pp. x–xi.
16 Vidal, G. (1992) 'In love with the movies', *The Observer Review*, 22 November.
17 Watson (1990): points summarized from Series Editor's Preface, pp. x–xi.
18 Tomlinson, R.R. (1947) *Children as Artists*, London, King Penguin Books, p. 10.
19 *Ibid.*, p. 11.
20 Abbs (1987) p. 44.
21 *Ibid.*, p. 45.
22 *Ibid.*, p. 45.
23 Taylor, R. (1992) *The Visual Arts in Education: Completing the Circle*, London, Falmer Press, p. 23.
24 Plummeridge, C. (1991) *Music Education in Theory and Practice*, London, Falmer Press, p. 14.
25 Taylor (1992) p. 25.
26 Alexander, R.T. (1984) *Primary Teaching*, Eastbourne, Holt, Reinhart and Winston, p. 11.
27 Webb, E. (1987) 'English as Aesthetic Initiative', in Abbs (1987) p. 69. Webb is also author of *Literature in Education* in the Library on Aesthetic Education.
28 *Ibid.*, p. 109.
29 Plummeridge, 1991, p. 14.
30 Metcalfe, M. (1987) 'Towards the Condition of Music: The Emergent Aesthetic of Music Education', in Abbs (1987) p. 107.
31 *Ibid.*, p. 109.
32 Hornbrook, D. (1991) *Education in Drama: Casting the Dramatic Curriculum*, London, Falmer Press, p. 2.
33 *Ibid.*, p. 2; Hornbrook is here quoting Abbs, see *Living Powers*, p. 44.
34 *Ibid.*, p. 2.
35 Taylor (1992) p. 34.
36 Ward, D. (1993) 'An ex-inspector calls foul', *The Guardian*, 7 January.
37 Watson (1990) p. 100.
38 Brinson, P. (1991) *Dance as Education: Towards a National Dance Culture*, London, Falmer Press, p. 3.
39 Taylor (1992) p. 158.
40 Abbs (1987) p. 57.

Chapter 3

Towards a Psychological Basis for Arts Education

We know that young babies explore their immediate world in a direct, sensory way. Initially they grasp and suck, respond to sounds and the presence of the mother. Gradually, as limbs grow and become stronger, they probe and touch, enjoying or developing sensation or withdrawing from it. We can observe how this establishes patterns of action and reaction in the baby and can infer that physical patterns which can be seen reflect hidden patterns in the mind of which they are evidence.

Keith Gentle[1]

Essential Sensory Explorations and Experiences

Gentle chooses to begin *Children and Art Teaching*, a book concerning the 5–13 age group, with the moment of birth. The French obstetrician Leboyer, he explains, believed that greater sensitivity was required at birth than is customarily the case, when the delicate senses of the baby are subjected to 'bright lights, a harsh, clinical environment and almost immediate separation from the mother-support by the cutting of the umbilical cord'. By contrast, he ensured that 'the transition from womb life to outside' took place in a softly lit room with the child then 'laid on the mother's abdomen, and not until the umbilical cord ceases to pulse is it cut, and then the child is laid in a bath of blood-heat water, where it is gently supported'.

Why does Gentle choose to begin here? Because, in discussing 'the needs or shortcomings of any particular group of students or pupils it is not unusual for teachers to refer, often disparagingly, to what should have taken place at an earlier period'. Dissatisfaction with the achievements of earlier upbringing and schooling is not uncommon, he suggests. This then provides justification for 'wiping the slate clean', allowing each new teacher simply to commence where the syllabus starts without feeling any need to take account of the crucial formative experiences that have so far informed the children's lives and shaped their personalities. Leboyer obviously believed that entering the world to a blaze of glaring, harsh lights or into a gentle, more conducive environment were important psychological determinants for good or bad.

Another obvious justification for tracing back to the earliest moments is that children have learnt more by the age of 5 than they will do throughout the whole of the remainder of their lives. Most of this learning emanates from direct sensory experience. Gentle sees the exploration of sensations as 'fundamental to the development of young children and, beyond this, as being an essential ingredient to the development of visual, tactile and spatial imagery in older children and adults'. Had he been writing about the arts, rather than art, he would doubtless have included the development of the oral and aural senses, etc. Denied from birth of all opportunities for direct sensory exploration, nobody who saw them can possibly forget the expressionless, dull-eyed faces of the Romanian children, all looking remarkably alike, who were discovered in orphanages and filmed on the fall of the Ceausescu regime.

Given the crucial importance of aesthetic experience in infancy and childhood, the lack of any government commitment to nursery provision seems strange. There should obviously be emphasis on providing a wide variety of opportunities for direct sensory exploration during this important formative phase. Perhaps that is why there is such indifference, for then to decree that all such exploration should cease once statutory schooling begins would be deemed unthinkable. The demands and requirements of testing at age 7, and the competitive climate in which testing has been introduced, are already leading to reduced opportunities for play and the cultivation of sensory experience. Given children's early learning capacities, allied to the vastly differing experiences children have already had, plus the variations in age at which they start school, it seems odd to test children at 7 without having first assessed them by agreed procedures on their entry into school.

Sensory experience both grows out of and gives rise to play. To Gentle, play is very important but, within educational contexts, he emphasizes the need for adults to understand it fully in order to build upon and utilize it properly:

> A child's play can create a world, for however brief a time, in which he [sic] makes the rules and always wins; in which he feels secure and confident to play out his experiences of the real world around him. The enrichment of play is one of the most significant teaching jobs that a parent or teacher can do but it requires the knowledge gained from the careful observation of children and an acceptance of their level of activity.[2]

How different it is, suggests Gentle, 'for most children who experience the pressures of having to grow up and come to terms with formal learning, increasingly leaving behind any opportunity to play, to explore in their own way and their own time or to follow through their own ideas and investigations'. There may well be many adults who, in reflecting on their lives, 'will recall that somewhere between five and seven they felt they lost something of the magic of childhood', having to grow up, take responsibility and 'somehow lose that innocent and timeless wonder of childhood where so many things seemed to be waiting to be discovered'.

At the age of 80, the artist Michael Rothenstein can still consciously draw upon qualities inherent in his childhood works, vividly recalling that 'innocent and timeless wonder of childhood'. In the process, he provides a potent illustration of Herbert Read's thesis of how the arts grow naturally out of play with the unity of 'the harmoniously developing personality':

> . . . when I was four . . . the drawing was a fairly automatic overspill from the things one found dramatic and exciting to imagine or think about. To some extent mime action and sound accompaniment went with the drawing. A lot of growling and crouching when you drew lions: the noise of jabs and slashes, with ouches of pain, when you were doing battle scenes. At the battle-scene phase I needed so much red, for blood — in splashes, drips and pools — that this colour was always used up first in the paint box.[3]

Drawing was an essential aid if his lead toy soldiers were to actually come alive:

> I drew these figures because I liked them so much, and the liking spilled over from the excitement in one's head onto the spread whiteness of the drawing book. It made them more real. I wanted to make them march, fight, or stand in line on the outspread page.

Water: A Medium for Exploration in Play and Art

To advocates of formal learning, play is equated with 'messing about', and the sooner it is eliminated or marginalized the better. That their views are currently in the ascendancy is to the detriment of countless young children's growth and development, for they are being denied proper opportunities for play, even at age 5. Advocates of play go back a long way; in the early years of this century, Caldwell Cook saw play 'as the natural focus of a child's interests', inevitably opening his philosophy of English teaching to attack:

> . . . for 'play' can be seen as purposeless, a free exercise of time demanding no discipline. If seen, however, as that process by which a child experiments among alternatives, directed to specific outcomes — in the course of which 'discoveries' are made — then Cook's outline is perfectly consonant with an accumulation of findings from child psychology. For what Cook had identified was a programme of work based on the needs and interests of his pupils, and achieved through

the processes of talking, reading and writing. By these means of engagement with their experience, children were the more ready to enter the created worlds of established writers in imaginative inter-play.[4]

Gentle likewise believes that adults should be sensitive to the opportunities constantly provided by play, for 'it embodies patterns of activity and non-activity and rhythms of learning that are peculiar and essential to the learner' — and just as applicable to the *older* child, too. Water, sand and clay are essential materials to explore while playing, but if a child 'naturally spends time playing with these basic materials they must have educational potential and be worth a closer study and thought by the teacher'. Water, for example, has special characteristics well worthy of consideration:

> Water flows, settles, makes things damp, runs and bubbles. You can see your breath bubbling down a tube into it or frothing in soap suds. Things float or sink, fill up or drain out; you can colour it and see the light through it, splash and dribble it. Although a child may have experienced water many times, the fact of its being provided in a transparent bath with all kinds of things to try out in it and with it focuses the child's awareness of water as a substance. Here, in these simple experiences, are the beginnings of scientific enquiry, the language for discussing and comparing, the observations which stimulate the memory and aesthetic expression.[5]

Water sometimes imposes itself on the child, at others the child on the water. Controlling water by exploring it can make one more alert and aware of the sensations it produces, so that games and experiments with water become more complex and inventive as the child gets older; 'the kind of learning which enters the child's pattern of understanding at this stage is an important foundation for later learning'. So it is with other basic earth materials like sand and clay.

Such play can lead to curiosity about water in all its forms. Rothenstein describes how his childhood drawings of fish and aquatic forms originated 'from my staring into streams and ponds around the house':

> I found that to crouch peering into a pool at the varnished brown and olive green of gravel and stones and the electric greenness of pond-weed was to look into a crystal clear mirror of a magic and mysterious world. Suddenly, as you watched, a water-beetle would streak across the water's surface, or an armoured caddis worm lumber across the gravel down below. The other source of this imagery was a large square glass aquarium shared by my two sisters. It contained water snails, sticklebacks, minnows and newts: creatures that came and went in continual movement.[6]

For many years, primary schools automatically provided vital first-hand experiences of this type, now unfortunately being displaced in favour of what must be tested at the ages of 7 and 11. Yet the curiosity Rothenstein possessed as a child grows into subtle awareness, when properly cultivated. Andy Goldsworthy is a mature artist who, it can be argued, still plays games in and with water. He illustrates the extraordinary levels of complexity and insight which can be developed when direct sensory experience is cultivated over many years to a heightened degree, providing sophisticated testimony to Gentle's assertion that scientific enquiry can develop out of play through what, in his hands, has become a profound and complex variant of play. Witness his leaf constructions, hanging from trees or in flowing water, with the artist working outdoors, without recourse to tools or equipment, using only the natural materials immediately to hand. He seeks out the most subtle nuances of nature, to which most people are oblivious:

> Every so often I see colour in leaves, maybe a red or a yellow leaf, and then out of a sense of curiosity I start collecting the colours to see how many colours are there, to see the range of colours. The tree, or in this case the bramble bush, becomes like a paint box that I am dipping into. In my work, often the most simple things can be the most profound. Just to know the colours that are there is very important to me — to know what colour a leaf changes to in autumn, because I really don't know until I actually start looking, and looking for those colours. It's like when I make a range of colours, I can see a red leaf and a green leaf and a yellow, and I make a line to follow those colours through. There may be one colour missing — but I know it is there. I know that colour is there somewhere, and that forces me to find that colour, the missing colour. For me that is a lesson about nature.[7]

Returning to a spot where he has previously constructed lines of leaves in a river, he notes that:

> To make a line in summer and to make a line in autumn is to make two entirely different lines. The colour is different, the river is different, the place has a different quality in autumn that I am made more aware of because I am making a similar work. Ideas travel in the same way that the line travels down the river. Ideas are not static, and they can develop and grow and each add another layer to the work in process. The last time I made a leaf line was in summer and the river was low. I released the leaf lines and they fairly gently went down the river in comparison to how the leaf lines went this autumn . . . there was much more power in the current and it just tore the line apart. That in itself was interesting and it has just made me more aware of the differences, because there was only an inch or so in difference

between the levels, but what a difference that foot or so has made in the energy of the river.

The parallels with a child's enquiry into water as proposed by Gentle are clear and are also in keeping with John Dewey's observations regarding the developments which take place in play:

> There is also a gradual transition, such that play involves not only an ordering of *activities* toward an end but also an ordering of materials . . . Past experiences more and more give meaning to what is done . . . Play as an event is still immediate. But its content consists of a mediation of present materials by ideas drawn from past experience. This transition effects a transformation of play into work, provided work is not identified with toil or labor. For any activity becomes work when it is directed by accomplishment of a definite material result . . .[8]

He continues, 'In art, the *playful* attitude becomes interest in the transformation of material to serve the purpose of a developing experience. Desire and need can be fulfilled only through objective material, and therefore playfulness is also interest in an object'.

Goldsworthy's playfulness is always apparent, yet he plays very serious games by making artistic statements of profound ecological relevance at the present time: 'When historians look back I hope they'll see the art of people like me as the result of the time when we reassessed our relationship with the land, and began to value it in a way that it hasn't been valued for a very long time'.[9]

His art has attracted wide attention, arousing interest among adults who do not generally regard themselves as art lovers. Children, too, are most responsive to his work (see Chapter 7, this volume). In the process, a focus of the type which Read saw as leading to the coordination and development of play can be stimulated. It will be recalled that this growth led, in turn, towards drama, design, dance and music, and craft — 'four divisions into which primary education naturally falls', providing a basis for an education in which direct sensory experience is cultivated. 'Getting to know the world should, therefore, include responding to images and finding the source and nourishment for image-making in their own looking', argues Gentle, recommending that children should also talk with artists and craftworkers to heighten perceptions and extend their range of visual ideas — in other words, even the youngest children should be provided with systematic access to the aesthetic field in all the arts.[10]

Subjectivity and the Arts

The Child Art emphasis on 'free expression' at the expense of communication and appraisal led to an assumption that the arts were about forms of feeling but not reason. It was subjectivity that was prized — all children were naturally creative and had personal concepts and ideas to which they could naturally give expression, given encouragement and a favourable ambience. However, Goldsworthy reveals an extraordinary awareness of the subtleties of natural phenomena made known to him through his constant explorations utilizing a particular range of artistic methods. It is these, in turn, that then enable him to visualize a range of further possibilities within a work or in terms of future ones. Gentle emphasizes the importance of getting to know the world through exploratory approaches which facilitate experimentation, but in contexts which provide clearly identifiable learning experiences to be built upon and Dewey traced the resulting developments. Without consciously providing these kinds of exploratory experiences, the 'creative process' as we normally speak about it is, perhaps, not even possible. In *The Rationality of Feeling*, David Best argues that a public medium, like music, 'is not merely the convenient but extraneous means of expression. If there were no such medium there could be no such experience. Thus it is only by learning the discipline of the medium that an individual can *have* such an experience.'[11] Hence the full extent of the tragedy of those Romanian children in the state orphanages, without access to either sensory stimulus or awareness of any relevant forms to give shape to experiences, however limited these experiences might be.

Best therefore feels able to assert:

> . . . it is a direct consequence of my argument, by contrast with subjectivism, that if, for instance, there were no art form of music, the respective experiences would not be merely inexpressible, but, more important, *they could not intelligibly be said even to exist.* Moreover, the *individual* could not have such experiences unless he [*sic*] had acquired some grasp of the public discipline and objective criteria of the art form of music.[12]

In the relationship between the two axes of creativity, therefore, the vertical axis may depend for its very existence on its horizontal counterpart — hence the importance of critical studies approaches in the classroom with regard to *all* art forms. A futher implication must therefore be that no art form is a substitute for another in educational terms:

> Thus the existence of the art form, and the learning of its techniques and criteria, are necessary preconditions of the possibility of individual experience and development. This clearly exposes the pernicious subjectivist fallacy that freedom for unrestricted personal development depends upon the *avoidance* of the disciplines, since, on the contrary, the freedom of the individual to experience the relevant feelings necessarily *depends upon* his [*sic*] having learned those disciplines.[13]

Variations of Temperament and Personality: Implications for Learning in the Arts

It will have been noted that child-centred approaches manifested themselves in most of the art forms within education, but that recent reappraisals in all the arts have led to attempts to bring children's art making into tandem with the study of the art of others. The post 11-plus child-centred developments provided a natural target in the 1970s for the *Black Paper* writers, especially through their recognition in the influential Plowden Report. Plowden sanctioned too much freedom for children, they argued, and such freedom breeds 'selfishness, vandalism and personal unhappiness'. The values of the *Black Paper* authors are still very much in evidence today in the many sweeping changes currently being made in education. In reality, much of Plowden emphasized the need for rigour and for children to be exposed, for example, to a wide variety and forms of literature. *Black Paper* writers however, emphasized rigour through a return to external examinations, streaming and more formal approaches.

In *Black Paper 1975*, H.J. Eysenck also expounded the thesis that much of the educational debate to date had focused on intelligence and much less on personality. He argued that pupils are attracted to subjects 'which are in some way geared to their personality'.[14] He focused on the two general personality groupings of introverts and extroverts:

> Discovery methods work with extroverted children, who enjoy the process and do well; it does not work with introverted children (of similar IQ), who do not enjoy the process, and do not do well with it. It is impossible to make any general statement about the success or otherwise of these new methods; they work with some but not with others . . . machine teaching is appreciated more by introverted children . . . extroverted children prefer, and do better with, orthodox teaching by teachers. Introverted children are more easily motivated by praise, extroverted ones by blame. Making examinations more stressful improves the performance of stable children, but worsens that of emotionally unstable ones.

There is a need for 'different approaches, different methods of teaching, and possibly different subject matter' based on personality. Taking account of personality, he argues, leads to acceptance

> that there are no universal truths which apply to all children, but that all conclusions apply only to some types of children, and not to others. It seems quite likely that extroverted children like, and do well, in the new 'open' schools, whereas introverted children probably prefer the old-fashioned 'class-room' type of school.

Both types of schools should therefore continue to be built:

> This would enable parents (and children) to make intelligent and in-
> formed choices, rather than submit to the tyranny of architects and
> educational authorities. . . . The facts of human inequality demand
> different types of education for different children. . . . Human diver-
> sity is the one fundamental and obvious fact which is basic to educa-
> tion. . . . Equalize the environment as much as we like, we will never
> reduce human diversity very much from that we observe today.

There are some seeming, and extremely important, contradictions in this paper
— it states that extroverted children prefer discovery methods *and* orthodox
teaching *and* the new 'open' schools. (There is presumably a misprint; could
this have led to some children finding their way into the 'wrong' schools?)

It is interesting that this essay should have appeared in a *Black Paper*
context. It is, of course, arguing for parental choice in ways all too recognizable today, but the practicalities of choosing between two types of school
determined by layout and design allied to whether one's child is introvert or
extrovert are vast — especially if the interests of all children, rather than just
those with assertive parents, are to be considered. Imagine the problems of
selection by intelligence — so dear to the hearts of *Black Paper* advocates —
(attempts to revive selective schools determined by results at 11-plus are now
resurfacing) combined with selection according to whether a child is introvert
or extrovert! Imagine whole schools full of one type or the other, with never
the two coming together and mixing or sharing from the first days of schooling! Interestingly, prior to open-plan schools, there was no choice in this
respect; all had conventional classrooms with rigid rows of seating and formal
teaching approaches with all children usually working on the same task at the
same time. Presumably, in Eysenck's terms, extrovert children equally suffered unduly for many years due to this absence of choice. The argument
should not be about building one of this type of school and one of that, but
of flexibility within each. Eysenck skews the issue, however, and shows his
bias by introducing his categories as the 'stable introverts' — they become
university students of mathematics and philosophy — and the 'unstable extroverts' — they become sociologists, whose exploits lead to 'student unrest
and militancy'!

Properly taught, the arts, with their emphasis on individual modes of
expression, communication and response, and of children working together
in cooperative ways, naturally bring a diversity of teaching approaches and
flexibility into a school. In this respect, it is worth turning to Plowden and
what the report *actually* said about the discovery methods to which Eysenck
refers:

> A word which has fairly recently come into use is 'discovery' . . .
> The sense of personal discovery influences the intensity of a child's

experiences, the vividness of his [*sic*] memory and the probability of effective transfer of learning. At the same time it is true that trivial ideas and inefficient methods may be 'discovered'. Furthermore, time does not allow children to find their way by discovery to all that they have to learn. In this matter, as in all education, the teacher is responsible for encouraging children in enquiries which lead to discovery and for asking leading questions.

. . . What is immediately needed is that teachers should bring to bear on their day to day problems astringent intellectual scrutiny. Yet all good teachers must work intuitively and be sensitive to the emotive and imaginative needs of their children. Teaching is an Art, and as long as that with all its implications is firmly grasped, it will not be harmed by intellectual stiffening.[15]

Eysenck argues that not enough account is taken of personality, yet it was those who incorporated aspects of discovery into their teaching, taking account of more child-centred approaches, who realized the significance of the arts in relation to personality because they sought to encourage more individual responses and approaches.

Herbert Read's matching of the study of psychological types with children's art work was structured around eight temperamental categories: extrovert and introvert types in each of the four areas of thinking, feeling, sensation and intuition.[16] We have noted that he also links these areas to particular art forms, with each developing out of play. In any one class there will obviously be all manner of blendings of these categories, but Read seeks to uncover more about why there is such variety within a class, and hence the range of responses to be expected. Eysenck's crude over-simplification in *Black Paper 1975* could easily mislead conscientious parents seeking to do their best for their children and lull some teachers into accepting that generalized teaching approaches can suffice.

Like Read, Tanner also believed:

Every child has gifts and qualities that are unique. No two are alike. Each one is a very distinct personality. Children cannot therefore be seen as a mass: the need of one may not be the need of another. . . . The art of teaching is the art of discerning in children, of protecting, and of promoting all kinds of hidden graces.[17]

It is important to further qualify 'child-centred' in Tanner's terms, for to him it did not mean placing children in a protective bubble, divorcing them from the wider world and all its influences. He goes on to emphasize: 'Children learn through firsthand acquaintance with what is good. . . . Above all, children learn by emulation. They need opportunities to watch the painter, the potter, the workman [*sic*] at work. In this way they catch a sense of standard.' In other words, they are only freed in terms of their own creativity through the wider range of possibilities opened up by being allowed to enter fully into the aesthetic field. In the light of recent critical studies developments, the evidence of young people recognizing something dormant within themselves being brought to life for the first time through illuminating experiences, and of Dewey's notion of the viewer 'completing' the work of art, it is worth turning to another facet of Read's argument. It is one he fails to develop fully and some might now question the Jungian premises upon which the argument is based. However, had he followed it through, it might have led to essential links commensurate with critical studies practice and the concept of the aesthetic field informing arts practice many years before this was envisaged as a possibility — other than in all too exceptional cases.

Children and Art History

Read relates aspects of modern art to Jung's four function-types. Realism, embracing naturalism and impressionism, relates to the *thinking* type; superrealism, 'reacting from the external world towards immaterial (spiritual) values', relates to the *feeling* type; expressionism relates to the *sensation* type; constructivism, finally, relates to *intuition* — it embraces cubism and functionalism, and indicates a preoccupation with inherent 'abstract' forms. Read cannot think of any aspect of modern art which does not fit into one or other of these four categories, most of which have parallels or equivalents in other art forms. There has been considerable conjecture about which types of art children respond to best at what age. Read provides a basis for anticipating the *variety* of art forms to which children in any group are likely to relate at any stage, the *variety* of art work which can arise, and the developments which might then take place in relation to their engagement with one multi-faceted art work or artistic experience.

Read does not develop these implications. In consequence *Education through Art*, a cornerstone of child-centred approaches, has equally become associated with the debit side of the Child Art movement: that of denying children access to the art of others on the grounds that natural creativity will be impaired. As a consequence, teachers frequently felt unable to teach in positive ways, some becoming essentially providers of materials while offering encouragement, praise and a pleasant working ambience. One result was that Child Art turned in on itself, becoming repetitive and predictable, whether in art, drama or creative writing forms. Respect for a child's particular stage of development proved insufficient on its own to ensure proper continuity and development without regard for other factors, as Alexander writing prior to his involvement in the 'Three Wise Men' report highlighted;

> . . . it is noticeable that in student essays, as in professional discourse and teachers' books and curriculum materials, the stages as such feature more prominently than the stage-independent theory, despite the fact that an understanding of the latter is essential to using the undoubted insights of Piagetian theory to promote or accelerate

learning. A Piagetian approach to HMI's concept of 'match', for example, would demand that children encounter learning tasks which are slightly, but not excessively, more complex than their present understanding, and that without this element of 'stretching' the disequilibrium necessary for learning will not be produced. Where students or teachers perceive development in terms of stages rather than processes they will tend to wait for learning to occur 'spontaneously' and 'naturally' rather than seek as teachers to advance it, on the grounds that the child has to be 'ready'.[18]

It is salutory to note, therefore, that towards the end of *Education through Art*, Read makes an observation which, if fully substantiated, could have led to at least a tentative linking of the past and modern art forms he lists and the temperamental types he identifies in children's art, offering a basis for 'stretching' children in the arts. A quite different future for Child Art might then have developed in all the arts disciplines, given the widespread influence of the book!

> Children should, of course, be shown the work of mature artists, both of the past and of the present (and preferably not reproductions), but these again should be treated with respect, and shown in an appropriate setting. But it should always be remembered that the school is a workshop and not a museum, a centre of creative activity and not an academy of learning. Appreciation is not acquired by passive contemplation: we only appreciate beauty on the basis of our own creative aspirations, abortive though these be.[19]

By associating the various categories of modern art to temperamental types, the children's 'own creative aspirations' could have gained added momentum and clarity of purpose through the potential afforded for entry into the whole aesthetic field. Might these connections provide a clue as to why certain children appear to be irrevocably drawn to particular art works? Once identified and systematically made accessible to them in relation to their own practice, might these then act as catalysts for the children's own creativity, in terms of both stimulus and affirmation? By combining two of Read's diagrams,[20] and associating the eight psychological categories to each, these connections become immediately apparent:

Realism	= thinking	= extrovert	= enumerative
		= introvert	= organic
Superrealism	= feeling	= extrovert	= decorative
		= introvert	= imaginative
Expressionism	= sensation	= extrovert	= empathetic
		= introvert	= expressionist (haptic)

Constructivism = intuition = extrovert = rhythmical pattern
= introvert = structural form

Using the series of drawings 'The Trees Stood Stately and Tall', reproduced in *Education through Art*, Read classifies each according to his groupings, the use of words like 'organic', 'structural form', 'rhythmical pattern', 'expressionist' etc., suggesting further potential links between children's assumed temperaments, their artistic creations and the range of prospective art works to which they are likely to respond.

He goes much further, also surveying the art of the past, explaining the variety of forms it takes in relation to these psychological groupings: 'if we take the whole history of art into consideration, from prehistoric and primitive art down to the present time, all its diversity can be explained, and to a large degree ordered, by reference to corresponding psychological types'.[21] He suggests that there have always been artists who, because of their function-types, have worked outside the prevailing style of the time; these examples probably most forcefully illustrate the thesis. The *extroverted thinking* type finds expression in a naturalistic style, so is to be found in most ages, though in Arabic art 'the type has been entirely suppressed'. Impressionism epitomizes the *introverted thinking* type, as do artists like Constable and Delacroix, and Chinese cave painting.

The *extroverted feeling* types project their feelings onto the object to such a degree that the two fuse together. This type is found naturally 'among the art of primitive peoples' but 'is much rarer in civilized epochs'. Jung notes that examples 'are almost without exception women', though presumably works like Van Gogh's chair and much of Munch's output naturally fit here. With the current reappraisal of women's art of the past and the higher profile and presence of women artists generally since *Education through Art* was written, models now exist for an extra 50 per cent of the school population — girls — with whom to associate directly! Women need *their* role models too; Virginia Woolf considered 'taking sentences from great writers and expanding them', but acknowledged that, for the woman writer, 'the very form of the sentence does not fit her. It is a sentence made by men; it is too loose, too heavy, too pompous for a woman to use'.[22] The *introverted feeling* type 'has produced some of the greatest art known to the world', for this is the type 'which gives feeling-values to transcendental ideals, such as God, freedom and immortality'. Here we find the builders of the Gothic cathedrals, William Blake and Odilon Redon. German Expressionism of this century and, in medieval times, Grunewald, belong to the *sensation* types. El Greco and Rubens belong to the *extroverted* aspect of sensation, Piero della Francesca to its *introverted* counterpart.

The *introverted intuitive* type is identified by Jung, Read notes, with the 'fantastical' arist. This artist reveals 'extraordinary, remote things . . . which in iridescent profusion embrace both the significant and the banal, the lovely and the grotesque, the whimsical and the sublime'. Read finds this a not very precise definition, and suggests that had Jung been more familiar with modern types of abstract art, he could have provided illustrations of a more definite nature — presumably the metaphysical art of Kandinsky, for one:

> The fact that such art has rarely been recognized as a distinct form of plastic expression . . . is perhaps accounted for by the fact that in music it is the *normal* mode of expression. Music can, of course, express the other function-types but it finds its normal and most profound development in the expression of the introverted intuitive mode of expression.[23]

Read observes that 'Jung generally seems indifferent to the evidence provided by the art of music'. The visual arts, perhaps because they are tangible and easily reproduced, frequently provide examples to illustrate propositions which have relevance to the arts in general, hence a further significance in the quotation with which Chapter 1 opens; feeling, sensation, intuition and thought embrace drama, design, dance and music, and craft, and provide the basis through which all subjects can be addressed at the primary phase. Children need regular access to every art form in any balanced education, though inevitably in the primary sector they will weave in and out of the curriculum, as already indicated, while some will enjoy more pre-eminent positions in certain schools because of staff enthusiams and strengths. The notion that some of the arts should be being practised all of the time in every primary school has already been highlighted.

The association of each art form with one of Read's types might be why some children seem naturally drawn to, and excel in, one art form and not another. It provides a basis for structuring learning in all the arts with children able to find precedents and equivalents in the art of the past and present with regard to any art form and across art forms, major developments within one invariably being manifested in others; the thinking introvert drawn to impressionism in art can find equivalent examples in music, and so on. It therefore provides a firm basis for children to engage with a wide range and variety of art forms as an essential aspect of their education. They must be given opportunities to locate themselves within the whole cosmos of the arts as practised throughout time and across places and cultures. In the perhaps surprising hands of Read we find a model which gives added emphasis to the significance of the aesthetic field; he provides criteria whereby children can be be introduced to works likely to be of specific interest to them through qualities to do with style and content, paralleling with their temperaments and personality.

The Axes of Creativity and Individual Temperament

The vertical axis, it has been noted, relates to our deepest expressive needs, extending to 'movement between the conscious and unconscious'. Its horizontal counterpart, in contrast, is to do with the notion, that art creates art, that science creates science, that theory creates theory; that, in all culture, there is a constant reworking of the established conventions, notations, images, narratives; that, at nearly all times in the creation of new art, new science and new theory there are constant acts of plagiarism and theft, acts which are redeemed by the further adaptation to which the stolen material is deftly put before it is stolen again and cast, yet again, in another shape, always in part derivative, always in part potentially new. Creativity, in brief, cannot be understood without reference to the symbolic field in which it takes place . . .[25]

Child-centred approaches invariably put emphasis on the vertical axis to the exclusion of the horizontal — hence Read's failure to develop what he had hinted at — and music and art appreciation lessons as traditionally taught emphasize the horizontal, divorcing the study of both art forms from contact with the vertical axis, essential to true creative activity. In emphasizing the personality types which one might expect to find in one class and relating those types to the whole history of art, Read had provided the clue as to how child-centred approaches could be enriched through essential relationships with the historical and cultural dimensions. Had he pursued this argument, links between children's practice in one art form leading to a wider web of interconnections across art forms, connecting literature, music, film, art, drama and dance, might have been envisaged years ago. A child's creative acts in one discipline could have led to initiatives in other art forms, with potential to generate work in those where it did not otherwise occur, as well as indicating further possible developments within the initiating form. His emphasis on child-centredness caused Read to neglect the horizontal axis and to emphasize its vertical counterpart. The complex web of making, presenting, responding and evaluating, allied to the need for all young people to acquire a critical vocabulary commensurate with their age and stage of development, and to know about art as well as making it, emphasizes today that both the vertical and horizontal axes are of the utmost relevance.

First-Hand and Second-Hand Source Stimuli

The Child Art emphasis on innate creativity masked the need for essential resources in both primary and secondary schools essential for the wedding of the vertical and horizontal axes. It was neither deemed necessary to take children out of school to exhibitions and performances or to bring resources into the school. Because art gallery, opera house, cinema and theatre are the natural arenas for the illuminating experience, engagement with art works in the original is of prime importance. Within the school context, however, many invaluable uses can be made of second-hand stimuli. They can acquaint children with aspects of all art forms of which they might otherwise remain unaware. Second-hand source materials, skilfully used, can also help anticipate and substantiate children's first-hand arts experiences. Schools which have built up these types of resources have amply demonstrated their worth. However, generally speaking, the traditional emphasis on child-centredness has led to their neglect in a majority of schools. With regard to National Curriculum requirements, these schools must now start building up resources in relation to prescribed areas of study from scratch.

It is helpful to be fully aware of the variety of first-hand and second-hand sources now available. The following provides a useful check-list of what is already in use in a school and what might fruitfully be added to provide pupils with greater access to the horizontal axis of creativity, without which important links with the vertical cannot be facilitated:

1 *First-Hand Sources*
    a) Out-of school art experiences in theatre, art gallery, opera house, cinema, studio, arts centre, workshop, etc.;
    b) School-based art experiences through loaned works or school's own original collection, books, visiting residences by theatre or dance groups, resident artists, film and video, etc.;
    c) Study of texts, scores and manuscripts produced by authors, composers, etc.;
    d) Statements made by artists or performers about their work (including comments made during workshop and performance sessions), published or broadcast interviews, letters, manifestos, etc.;
    e) The practice of other pupils in the arts;
    f) The practice of the school's own teachers in the arts.
2 *Second-Hand Sources*
    a) Art works reproduced in the form of photographs, video, records and cassettes, slides, film, postcards, books, etc.;
    b) Monograhs, critical or appreciative studies in books, or on film and video;
    c) General background documentary information which places artist's or performer's work in a social or historical context, including reconstructions or fictionalized accounts of their lives, methods of working, etc. in books, film or video;
    d) Catalogues, programme notes, synopses, etc. provided to aid gallery visit or theatre performance.[26]

There are inevitably important overlaps; what is reproduction in one art form constitutes an original work in another context — film or video constitute primary source material when used in their own right, whereas a film or video of a dance, music or drama performance comprise a second-hand form. Books dealing with poetry and literature are regarded as first-hand material, whereas books about art or music are secondary — authors' manuscripts be-come collectors' items yet the multiplicity of published versions are not re-garded as secondary sources, making them an especially interesting category!

All these first and second-hand sources have their place and usage in any school context. In a school conscious of the pupils' creative art making in relation to that of others, there will inevitably be a range of secondary sources, as well as first-hand stimuli on which to draw. For others, however, the National Curriculum poses important resource implications, and the process of acquiring a basic range of essential resources for arts teaching has to be a top priority; children must be given access to the aesthetic field as active participants if the knowledge and understanding requirements stipulated by the National Curriculum are to be realized other than in those arid ways which Clegg saw as the outcome of imposition by governments from above.

Resources are therefore vital if education is to take account of children's individual needs as determined by personality and psychological outlook. An over-emphasis on the so-called 'basics' risks ignoring the use of resources as an essential stimulus. The National Curriculum and the obsession with testing have become intertwined, but the English Working Group felt compelled to admit: 'The best writing is vigorous, committed, honest and interesting. We have not included these qualities in our attainment targets because they cannot be mapped on to levels'. One primary headteacher believes:

> It is time to look harder at the ways in which children appropriate knowledge. In its present form the National Curriculum is unsuited to this task. Its predominant concern for testing places the emphasis on exercises rather than on compositions. Its orthodoxy resists the novel, the personal and the unexpected. It is a curriculum for those who still believe that education is a matter of learning to speak with-out having anything significant to say. That may satisfy the Govern-ment, it ought not to satisfy teachers or parents. Least of all should it satisfy children.[27]

The Library on Aesthetic Education provides a clear rationale for approaching the arts within the National Curriculum in vital ways, but these arts issues are having to be addressed at a time when existing patterns of INSET are break-ing down without adequate structures being in place to replace them. Aspects of the National Curriculum also threaten to undermine the already fragile ground of the arts at the initial training level.

References

1 Gentle, K. (1985) *Children and Art Teaching*, Beckenham, Croom Helm, pp. 2–3.
2 *Ibid.*, p. 55.
3 Rothenstein, M. (1986) *Michael Rothenstein: Drawings and Paintings aged 4–9, 1912–1917*, London, Redstone Press, pages unnumbered.

4   Webb, E. (1987) 'English as Aesthetic Initiative' in Abbs, P. (Ed.) *Living Powers: The Arts in Education*, London, Falmer Press, p. 73.

5   Gentle (1985) pp. 58–59.

6   Rothenstein (1986).

7   *Two Autumns* (1992) A Lightyears Films production for the Arts Council of Great Britain in association with Border Television, Channel 4 and Tyne Tees Television.

8   Dewey, J. (1934) *Art as Experience*, New York, Capricorn Books, pp. 278–9.

9   Taylor, R. (1992) *Visual Arts in Education*, London, Falmer Press, p. 116.

10 Gentle (1985) p. 78.

11 Best, D. (1992) *The Rationality of Feeling*, London, Falmer Press, p. 80.

12 *Ibid.*, p. 80.

13 *Ibid.*, p. 80.

14 Eysenck, H.J. (1975) 'Educational Consequences of Human Inequality', *Black Paper 1975* (Edited by C.B. Cox and R. Boyson), London, Dent, p. 40.

15 The Plowden Report (1967) *Children and Their Primary Schools*, London, HMSO, p. 201, paras 549–50.

16 Read, H. (1943) *Education Through Art*, London, Faber and Faber; see Chapter 4, pp. 73–107.

17 Tanner, R. (1989) *What I Believe: Lectures and Other Writings*, Bath, Holborne Museum and Crafts Centre, p. 10.

18 Alexander, R.J. (1984) *Primary Teaching*, Eastbourne, Holt, Rinehart and Winston, p. 92.

19 Read (1943) p. 298.

20 *Ibid.*, pp. 97, 147.

21 *Ibid.*, p. 100.

22 Abbs, P. (1991) 'From Babble to Rhapsody: on the Nature of Creativity', *British Journal of Aesthetics*, **31**, 4, October, Oxford, Oxford University Press, p. 295.

23 Read (1943) p. 101.

24 Peter Abbs (1989) *A is for Aesthetic*, London, Falmer Press, see pp. 10–22.

25 Abbs (1989) p. 17.

26 This is a modification of a diagram used in Taylor, D. and Taylor, R. (1990) *Approaching Art and Design*, Harlow, Longman. We acknowledge a debt to Andrew Mortimer, who formulated the original version.

27 Armstrong, M. (1992) 'Dull, dull, dull . . .', *Times Educational Supplement*, 9 September.

Chapter 4

Educating for the Arts:
Implications for Training

The Reform Act gives us a vision of a broad and civilizing education for all our children; an education which offers them the opportunity to grow spiritually, morally, emotionally and intellectually; which opens their eyes to the enormous pleasures which the arts can provide; and which helps them to understand the values and traditions which inform the society in which they live . . . an education which takes spiritual, moral and cultural development seriously, an education which pursues goals beyond the immediately utilitarian, balancing knowledge, skills and understanding, is a true preparation for life.

David Pascall[1]

The National Curriculum and Some Initial Training Implications

How welcome it was to at last hear somebody in a key political position arguing that the arts are central to any broad and balanced curriculum! Similarly, his warning that the case for a civilizing curriculum cannot be taken for granted was much needed in the present climate:

There are many in positions of influence today who, as Bernard Williams once put it, see the arts as a vaguely civilizing luxury which it is agreeable for some people to have (rather, as he suggested, like a leather blotter from Harrods). The case for the importance of the cultural dimension and the civilizing power of the arts for all our children needs to be put.

Welcome though his words undoubtedly are, they nevertheless come somewhat belatedly, for the 'vision of a broad and civilizing education for all our children', as presented in the 1988 Reform Act, was seriously eroded once its form was irrevocably changed by art and music being made optional at key stage 4, meaning that the stipulated core and foundation subjects to be studied throughout a National Curriculum did not include a single stipulated aesthetic discipline other than English — and it is too often taught without regard for its aesthetic aspects, a disregard which is likely to intensify, not diminish, as its structure is modified to put greater emphasis on punctuation, grammar and spelling as ends in themselves.

All secondary schools in England and Wales were invited to respond to the questionnaire on art and music being made optional, the issue perceived as only being of concern to that sector — but the implications for the future of the arts in the primary sector are dramatic. Dance, too, is optional within PE but in the event, perhaps not surprisingly, this aroused less controversy. The problem, though, is that as a consequence of these decisions, the prospective primary teacher can be opted out of *all of the arts* at the age of 14 and then undergo a higher education training in which they barely feature. This perpetuates a long-standing problem which then affects the teaching of the arts in the primary sector. Further, making art, dance and music optional at key stage 4 has sent unmistakeable messages right through the system; they are seen at ministerial levels as being of only minor significance to learning *at all stages of education*. The added clout which other disciplines now enjoy will inevitably lead to a further weakening of the place of the arts in college of higher education structures, at a time when all primary teachers nevertheless *do* have to meet art, music and dance requirements by law. At the same time, there are murmurings from those who appear to influence government thinking unduly that the drama dimensions within National Curriculum English and activities like speaking and listening, desirable though these might be, take up essential time which should be devoted to 'the basics'. A recognizable *Black Paper* scenario is reasserting itself through the right-wing Campaign for Real Learning, 'A return to traditional teaching methods could double standards in schools'; 'Dr John Marks urges a switch to whole-class teaching, streaming by ability and replacing coursework with rigorous exams' (*Guardian*, 22 June 1992). It is worth noting that, as a member of *both* the Schools' Examining and Assessment Committee and the National Curriculum Council, Marks is able to exert considerable political influence.

Yet it only takes a brief look at the arts in teacher training in recent years, to recognize their long-standing neglect on the altar of the so-called basics. It was central to the *Black Paper* thesis that colleges of education shared a large part of the blame for declining standards. There should be more emphasis on the teaching of 'the basics', i.e. reading and mathematics, and on formal approaches to them. Modern methods, as promoted by colleges, were at the root of the problem. In reality, of course, these so-called modern methods have yet to see the light of day in many primary schools. As Alexander points out, on the basis of those who have made a close study of primary schools, 'the combined message . . . is that primary rhetoric and primary reality can be a long way apart. The accusations of the *Black Paper* authors (Cox and Dyson 1971) of the 1970s and of Rhodes Boyson, still, in the 1980s, over the supposed neglect of reading and mathematics, were a long way wide of the mark: the basics have received consistently high priority — it is the rest of the curriculum . . . that should give most cause for concern.'[2]

> The Cockroft report on school mathematics (DES, 1982b) and the Gulbenkian report on the arts in schools (Gulbenkian, 1982) both made powerful cases for their curriculum areas in terms of both social utility and the child's educational needs. A rational observer might expect the two reports to be treated with equal seriousness: indeed, if anything, the case made for the arts as a central 'core' element of the curriculum was the more powerfully made. In fact, as might have been anticipated, not only have the reports had unequal impact at school level but many teachers appear to have not even heard of Gulbenkian. Cockroft was commissioned by the Secretary of State, Gulbenkian by an independent foundation. Cockroft dealt with an area of existing priority; Gulbenkian did not. Cockroft has become the new orthodoxy for initial and in-service courses and indeed for the everyday professional vocabulary ('As Plowden says . . . As Cockroft says . . .'). By such means the 'reactive' approach to educational change tends to confirm rather than question established curriculum assumptions and priorities.[3]

In order to rectify this imbalance, considerable changes must take place at the initial training level. *The Arts: A Preparation to Teach*, produced by the NFER in 1986, paints a bleak picture of the widespread inadequacy of arts preparation at the initial training phase, especially as the research grew directly out of concerns about the arts expressed by classroom practitioners.

> The need to examine initial training in art, music, dance and drama was brought sharply to the fore during observations carried out as part of earlier NFER research in primary schools. Teachers frequently expressed the view that they lacked the confidence and the expertise to provide adequate arts experiences for their pupils.[4]

Compulsory course time allocations, for example, make interesting reading, especially as the report cites evidence of decreasing amounts of time between 1979 and 1986, a decline which has subsequently accelerated, if anything. 'The shortest courses were found in the PGCE programmes, some of which provided arts courses of as little as two contact hours' duration.'

> On the whole, compulsory arts courses tended to be quite short; the majority were under 20 hours and some were of only two hours' duration. There was a tendency for courses in art to be more substantial than the other art forms; over half the art courses were between 21 and 70 hours in length. The majority of music and dance/

movement courses were under 20 hours in length. Drama courses tended to be shorter still; no drama course was over 20 hours long and many were of less than 12 hours' duration. Ten of the 14 combined or integrated courses covered all four art forms. The majority of these courses were between 40 and 77 hours in length.

When it is considered that many students cease to have any dealings with the arts by the end of their third year in secondary school, the problems besetting many primary teachers with regard to the teaching of the arts, in their own right and as aids to wider learning, become immediately apparent. The recent decisions to make dance, art and music optional at key stage 4 ensure that this vicious circle will continue into the next century; in addition to negative signals regarding government perceptions of the importance of these subjects, the inadequate school experience of many will continue to lead on to inadequate college preparation. Making the only named foundation arts subjects optional at key stage 4 will further defer the overdue reappraisal of the time required for the study of the arts in colleges, especially as this is compounded by drama being subsumed within English and dance within PE. Core and more favoured foundation subjects — now being referred to as 'extended core subjects' — will, if anything, claim even more priority and, therefore, time.

It is still unclear at the time of writing whether changes in secondary initial training, requiring two thirds of training to be undertaken in schools, will also be applied to primary training, but additional school-based training also brings its particular problems in the arts. NFER found that inadequacies of time allocation were further compounded with regard to *existing* teaching practice placements. '"Good" arts teachers were not easy to find' and many tutors 'pointed out that opportunities for students to observe good arts teaching' could not be guaranteed, as examples of good practice 'were considered to be "still rare in primary schools"'.[5]

Rather than the 'basics' being neglected, it would appear that there is a pronounced need for increased amounts of time in arts education; it is hardly surprising that teachers dithered over *how* to teach when Child Art was so much in vogue, for many only had the most superficial initial experience on which to draw. Such deficiences regarding time allocation at the initial training phase have inevitably led to the relative absence of hyacinths in schools at the present time, further emphasized but not necessarily rectified by the introduction of the National Curriculum! When it is added that opportunities for in-service beyond the confines of the school have also been dramatically reduced, it will also be appreciated that the possibility of teachers developing the necessary skills for arts teaching post-initial training has likewise diminished — a pertinent issue, for the National Curriculum certainly poses new challenges for the teaching of the arts, particularly with regard to their critical studies aspects and the aesthetic field.

To practice the arts adequately, all primary teachers must obviously possess reasonable practical skills. The arts are, by nature, practical disciplines and, throughout the primary sector, offer countless means for children to learn *in* and *through* them. Where these skills are lacking at even the most basic of levels, students are required to demand of children what they themselves cannot do — creating obviously educationally unsound situations. Essential skills can only be acquired if reasonable time is provided for their acquisition; the time allocations cited above do not even provide scope for students to understand the role and significance of the arts to children's learning even at the *theoretical level*.

A further major contention of the Library on Aesthetic Education is that it is not sufficient for children to simply 'make' in the arts — their making must be seen within the overall context of the aesthetic field of making, presenting, responding and evaluating. The rich benefits which can then flow obviously have subject-specific and cross-arts implications, but are equally enriching to the whole curriculum — for example, dynamically interactive critical studies approaches to the arts aid the acquisition of an extended vocabulary relevant to *all* learning. Initial training must, therefore, provide all students with a basic knowledge of the essential characteristics and nature of each art form as epitomized by its major practitioners, both past and contemporary. These must obviously be valued and used in their own right to further arts education but can also provide invaluable pointers for the enrichment of history, science and environmental studies teaching, etc. In addition, the teacher of the future must possess more specific knowledge about the arts, their major practitioners and where they belong in history, for children must now acquire this knowledge as a requirement of their education.

It is a further contention of the Library that learning in the arts has too often suffered from partial concepts in the past. These have frequently led to them being taught in fragmentary ways, with their full aesthetic potential not addressed and unrealized. *All* students of primary teaching should therefore, of necessity, receive a training which provides an overview of how and why each arts discipline entered education and has subsequently manifested itself in the classroom. Students will then more fully appreciate the demands and rigours of arts teaching and its vital role in children acquiring the necessary practical skills to form and give expression to personal feelings and thoughts. Children can then be led to understand that artists, past and present, have addressed concepts and used means relevant to their immediate needs — sharing, perhaps, psychological characteristics not dissimilar to their own. Such artists provide a vital source of reference and response, to be enjoyed in their own right *and* to inform the children's own practice. By such means, the vertical and horizontal axes of true creativity are brought into tandem.

In order for future teachers to be effective arts practitioners, therefore, the Library on Aesthetic Education proposes the adoption of a range of fundamental concepts and classroom strategies with which they should be equipped as a direct consequence of their training. Applicable across the whole spectrum of the generic community of the arts, this ranges from the kind of the aesthetic intelligence outlined in these chapters, through the notions and implications of the aesthetic field — with its four phases of making, presenting, responding and evaluating — and the illuminating experience — and the forms of revelatory understanding it discloses — to such practical day-by-day measures as the systematic application of the content, form, process, mood model to help children engage with art works at both the objective and subjective levels necessary to develop artistic knowing. But what of those teachers who are already in post? Do the principles and practical implications of the Library on Aesthetic Education help them to make better sense of the many and conflicting demands currently being made on them? Part II looks at these implications from the perspective of both child and teacher.

References

1 Pascall, D. (1992) *The Cultural Dimension in Education*, a speech to the National Foundation for Arts Education (NFAE) at the Royal Society of Arts, London, 20 November.
2 Alexander, R.J. (1984) *Primary Teaching*, Eastbourne, Holt, Reinhart and Winston, p. 11.
3 *Ibid.*, pp. 179–80.
4 Cleave, S. and Sharp, C. (1986) *The Arts: A Preparation to Teach*, Slough, The National Foundation for Educational Research (NFER), p. 5.
5 *Ibid.*, p. 11.
6 *Ibid.*, p. 35.

Part II:

Practice

Introduction

Into this dynamic field we would wish to place all the expressive arts
in the curriculum. The implications are as complex and momentous
as they are urgent and necessary. . . . We can bring the aesthetic field
to each arts discipline and ask crucial and wholly practical questions.
*How much making? How much presenting? How much responding? How
much evaluating?* It gives us a coherent way of looking, it provides the
conceptual elements of a unified aesthetic.

Peter Abbs[1]

Knowledge and Skill Requirements for Teachers

We have now reached the stage where it is appropriate to consider the above
implications through actual practice. What will actually happen in a primary
school if the above questions are applied and considered by a whole staff
working cooperatively together? Whatever the problems that confront the
primary teacher of the future, the demands being made on teachers *now* — in
every curriculum area — are considerable. Many subjects are in a state of
constant flux, being altered and modified even before teachers have had a
chance to come to terms with them as originally specified. Further, each new
requirement has to be assimilated at a time when existing patterns of in-
service training are breaking down without adequate alternative structures
replacing them in a climate in which teachers are under closer scrutiny and
subject to greater criticism than at any time in living memory.

Many schools are having to address new requirements on their own,
with little opportunity to draw upon outside expertise or to share with other
teachers from diverse backgrounds, but confronting similar problems and
issues. Nevertheless, if continuity, progression and coherence are to become
realities in terms of children's *actual* experience, the days of individual teachers
attending to their own practice in isolation, without regard for what has taken
place previously or is required next, are over. There is therefore a requirement

that every school staff meet together regularly to formulate and develop a whole-school approach to the curriculum. For children to acquire ever-growing and worthwhile knowledge and understanding in the arts, to have constant access to the aesthetic field, and for the arts to inform learning across the curriculum, a school policy for the arts is an essential feature. Though one teacher might assume responsibility for the actual writing, it must be formulated by the staff *as a whole*, with even the most reluctant teacher of the arts being an active participant in the process.

One Specimen School as Exemplar

To illustrate the benefits of this process to both staff and pupils, case-study material drawn from one single form entry combined infant and junior school in Wigan has been used in all the subsequent chapters to help relate theory to practice. This material spans the period from early 1981 to late 1991 while Glennis Andrews was deputy headteacher at the school. Rod Taylor was also art adviser for Wigan throughout this time. Much of the material was fully documented because of Wigan's involvement in the SCDC Arts in Schools Project, from its commencement in 1985 to 1990. During this period, the school consolidated and further developed its already rich arts practice by formulating a whole-school policy for the arts, ensuring that it continued to work from existing strengths while attempting to widen its practice so as to embrace all the arts by systematically taking account of the principle, 'some of the arts all of the time'. Formulated by the Wigan Arts in Schools Primary Working Group, this principle acknowledges that, though it might not be possible to teach *all* art forms *all* the time, it is nevertheless possible for the arts, in one form or another, to permeate the life of a primary school constantly by being practised on a regular daily basis, in their own right and to inform and enrich learning across the whole curriculum.

A school policy of keeping pupil work and constantly utilizing it afresh in new contexts ensured that an unusual wealth of pupil practice was available, not simply as end products but as essential components within dynamic and organic teaching contexts. Children's art work all too often disappears once its *immediate* useful life has been served, being returned to the pupils and even destroyed. There was such an abundance of work and documentation of projects in all arts disciplines that the constant problem was what to select and what to leave out; equally worthy examples could have been used throughout as alternatives to those used in the following chapters, for the quality of the pupils' writing in each project extends in-depth through the work of whole groups.

Half the school staff — two infant and two junior teachers — have contributed to the writing of this book by providing written and tape-recorded observations and comments, ensuring that a multifaceted picture is presented. The school also has a notable history of working in close cooperation with a wide range of local authority services, thereby providing unusually rich stimuli for its pupils and developing important partnerships with agencies outside the school. Consequently, we have been able to draw upon the knowledge and perceptions of a wide range of artists, performers and educators from the support services, with each able to offer a clear perspective on a particular aspect of school policy and practice.

These wider involvements have enabled the staff, all generalists, to continuously — sometimes imperceptibly — extend and develop their arts skills and expertise, with them all fully aware of the vital place and role of the arts in education. In the final chapter, our approach illustrates how a committed staff working together can periodically bring *all* the arts together in celebratory ways that encompass the full aesthetic field and involve *all* their children. It is, however, necessary to first consider some specific aspects of primary arts education, beginning with how the arts play an essential role in establishing a desirable school ethos, thereby creating that positive community in which all children can flourish and advance:

> All the arts offer special opportunities and a rare capacity for pupils to study and learn at heightened levels of involvement. What they are doing is seen by them as being of personal relevance, having a direct bearing on their own lives, drawing upon their experiences and histories.[2]

References

1 Abbs, P. (1987) *Living Powers: The Arts in Education*, London, The Falmer Press, pp. 62–63.
2 *The Arts in the Primary School: Some of the Arts All of the Time* (1990) Metropolitan Wigan 'Arts in Schools' Primary Working Group publication, p. 13.

Chapter 5

The Arts and the School Environment: Establishing an Ethos

The whole quality of the school environment, its mode of organisation and display, can enhance or actually inhibit learning and can build or erode the child's understanding of whether his [*sic*] work is valued or of little real importance. It is an opportunity to set the scene for consideration and care of the environment and the things within it. If our own organisation and presentation is poor we quickly communicate to children a lack of pride in what we do and an acceptance of low standards. It is not an overstatement to say that this often leads to carelessness on the part of the child or even to thoughtless vandalism.

Margaret Morgan[1]

Environment can and does have a profound effect . . . upon the form which conceptions take. It is therefore of great importance that children should be made acquainted with the world's great art and craft in addition to well designed things of modern manufacture, and that they should live and work in as suitable and beautiful surroundings as possible.

J.J. Tomlinson[2]

Whole-School Environments

When the arts occupy their rightful place in the curriculum, their impact affects the whole school, for a feature of the arts is that they naturally enhance the environment. In a genuine artistic climate, the work produced is, by definition, individual and distinctive, so each child's contribution can be valued in its own right. Such schools invariably have the problem of insufficient display areas, rather than that of what to display — a constant headache for some. The statements quoted above were written over forty years apart, showing that the appearance and nature of the school environment has long been regarded as of importance.

The nature of the school environment strikes the visitor immediately on entering. However subconsciously, one rapidly forms opinions and makes judgments about a school, before even speaking to anybody. Feelings of well-being or otherwise are quickly engendered. As Morgan emphasizes, the child who spends large amounts of each day in the school is being likewise affected, for good or bad. Though a conducive environment is beneficial to every aspect of school life, the arts — in particular those of art and literature, lending themselves so naturally to presentation in this manner — inevitably have a vital role to play. Every art form benefits, of course, for each has opportunities to flourish when the ambience is appropriate to creative and imaginative endeavour, with the children's own creative products obviously valued.

The creation of attractive environments is not entirely free of controversy, however. Some argue that stimulating display is 'distracting', sometimes even extending to teachers papering over windows to prevent children seeing outside, or making them work facing blank walls to encourage better concentration. During a secretary of state's recent fact-finding mission to Japan (it is always assumed that other countries have the educational answers while we fail to capitalize on our own models of good practice) a description of one school visited was as follows:

> The school is supposed to be one of the best in Tokyo — but it looks like a prison camp. The buildings are in a square with a sand sports pitch in the middle. It had been turned into a sea of mud yesterday by heavy rain. The classrooms are grey with no decoration. Many of the windows are opaque so the students cannot see outside. The long, echoing corridors are drab and cold.[3]

Surely few would wish such a regime on the children of this country. Robin Tanner, for one, envisaged an education in which 'the place you live in will be all-important. I hope there will be general agreement here that nothing need be ugly . . . I want a sweet, dairy-like place where children can live, and I want a place where children can grow.'[4] However, many high schools, though possessing areas of visual delight, because of their design, scale and sheer size, and the logistics of movement around them often convey a somewhat barren overall appearance. A constant problem is that, though some staff take care of particular provinces, large tracts remain anonymous with nobody accepting responsibility for them. By comparison, most primary schools are extremely attractive because all staff *do* accept a responsibility for the environment as a whole, in addition to caring for their own teaching spaces or areas.

In some schools — of modern and traditional design — there is, of course, the complaint that the design of the building does not naturally lend itself to considered and attractive presentations of work or related stimuli. Even so, Morgan emphasizes that 'with ingenuity much can be done'.

A working party of members of staff viewing the buildings and its environs with a fresh eye can often generate ideas for development. A disciplined approach, somewhat like a 'Time and Motion' study, which takes into consideration the nature of the work, the philosophy of the school, and the 'fixed points' (toilets, sinks, dining areas, etc.) is a useful start. If an overall plan is then drawn up and costed, it can be systematically put into practice as finances permit (although it is surprising what can be done with very little outlay in many instances).[5]

The function can extend, she suggests, to school grounds. 'Playground equipment or play sculpture may be installed . . . Sculptural forms (free-standing or relief) designed and made by the children, or purchased by the school from artists and craftsmen [sic], can also be introduced.' She points out that the support of regional arts and parent–teacher associations have both been successfully enlisted on occasions. Until recently it was the norm to see only children's work displayed in and around schools. Only rarely was there evidence of mature artists' work, except perhaps reproductions of famous paintings provided when the school opened, or through a circulating loan service.

Introducing the Art of Others

Tomlinson wrote *Children as Artists* in 1944. He emphasizes that adult work, too, has a part to play in the creation of attractive spaces in which to educate children. Many education authorities, 'have formed circulation collections of pictures for their schools'.[6] These collections were of reproductions, and he notes that children, 'when given the opportunity to choose their own pictures for their classroom, invariably choose modern examples, work of the post-impressionists in particular'. Maybe children are not yet capable of apprehending the 'sustained emotion' of the old masters, he conjectures. Through use of more recently devised and tested models like that of content, form, process and mood, there is growing evidence to suggest that children can engage with a wider variety of art works and forms than was previously assumed.

Loan collections of original works also exist in a number of authorities now and, by definition, are of contemporary works. They denote a now widespread acceptance that it is more valuable for children to 'know' works in the original, even though not as 'great' ones as are available in reproduction form, valuable, too, though the place of them is in everyday school usage. Tomlinson goes on to make an observation of particular pertinence today, given the design and technology concerns teachers must now address:

Much good can yet be done, however, by giving children the opportunity of seeing well-designed things of everyday use as well as paintings. It is therefore to be hoped that a circulation collection of well-designed articles will be formed for this purpose in the near future.[7]

Local authorities provide the most effective means of acquiring and circulating such objects, but with local management of schools and the ever-diminishing powers of local authorities, this is an issue schools will increasingly have to address on their own — or on a local consortia basis, if that is not too at variance with competition, so fundamental to the hearts of those committed to local management principles.

Any school, though, can form its own mini-collections of functional everyday objects — cups, kettles, spoons, umbrellas, ties, whatever — with the help and support of staff, children, parents and friends. Children can then compare and contrast, freely handle and use, and consider relationships between form and function of the everyday objects that surround them. Some items will, doubtless, not be particularly attractive or well designed but, provided good examples are also obtained, such displays and their use can aid development of children's discriminatory powers with regard to objects which will always feature prominently in their lives. Perhaps variations in quality are essential for children to learn to distinguish between the good and bad, and more fully understand important relationships between form and function.

However, few schools will achieve on their own what authorities like Leicestershire did through a systematic purchasing policy over many years born of a conviction that exposure to original works of art should be an essential part of all children's entitlement. Andrew Fairbairn, as Director of Education, wrote,

> I have always thought schools, where children can spend at least five hours a day, five days a week for thirty-six weeks in the year, ought to be places which offer experiences of contemporary art, not just in the art rooms, but in different parts of the buildings and outside in the grounds themselves. So often, however, schools are bare places, occasionally relieved a little by rooms with different colour schemes, which reflect more the atmosphere of the barracks . . .[8]

Of course, every art form has a significant part to play in establishing the ethos and communal vitality of a school. For example; in the music volume in this Library on Aesthetic Education, *Music Education in Theory and Practice*, Charles Plummeridge writes:

> Concerts, plays, productions and other artistic events, usually prepared during out-of-school hours, have always been valued for their contribution to the general style and ethos of the educational institution. These celebrations bring with them the magic of the arts for all to share; they permeate and animate the life of the school in a very

special and powerful way. Arts presentations are particularly appreciated by parents and members of the local community. Indeed, without such activities schools would be very different and almost certainly poorer places.[9]

Shaping the Environment through a School Policy for the Arts

Perhaps in some ways we are not at too far a remove from that Japanese school in the rain, with things certainly worse in this respect than when Fairbairn worked in Leicestershire. Many schools are suffering by not being adequately maintained and decorated over many years. The environment within our Wigan school is a somewhat special one, yet the building has many features usually considered to be disadvantageous. Nobody can enter the school, though, without being immediately affected by its rich and extraordinary environment, whichever way they turn. This can come as a considerable shock — seen from outside, the two storey red brick 1912 building in a somewhat depressing-looking area, seems to epitomize school buildings of a previous era quite unsuited to modern educational requirements yet, as one parent explains,

> When I first got the opportunity to see the school from the outside, I wasn't very impressed — very drab, dull looking from the outside. But once I actually got through the door, and saw the amount of art work and the interest in the school, I was very impressed. . . . I believe that art is a part of their whole education and not just a specific thing, and that it helps the children to find excitement in everything they do, which they show very well in this school.[10]

— a parental view in accord with the philosophy of both dedicated staff and the headteacher. In her view, we are 'only fully developed as people if we have the full range of the arts available to us'. In the primary school context, of course, this invariably has to be achieved without recourse to specialist arts teachers but the school capitalizes fully on enthusiasms fed through partnership with the authority's resources and expertise in many arts areas. Utilizing these in relation to a school philosophy which fully embraces the arts, staff are constantly developing in terms of confidence and expertise; 'we try between us to give the full span to the children, and we just think that education is so much more exciting, so much more vital, and the challenges are there through the arts that wouldn't be if we just spoon-fed them information.'[11] She recalls the day of her appointment, and a senior education officer, later to become Director of Education, taking her to a window and, looking out across the bleak landscape, saying, 'They've got nothing much out there, have they? Give it to them in here!'[12]

Attention paid to the overall environment is therefore, in part, in mitigation against the immediate bleak surroundings, but is also an educational necessity in curriculum terms, not just mere top dressing. Staff devote long hours attending to the appearance of their school, the displays relevant to present and future learning needs rather than being simply a record of past achievement. They have demonstrated to their satisfaction that the educational benefits, in arts terms and in informing the whole curriculum, make the considerable effort involved worthwhile.

The Environment and Children's Learning

The school is not just an unusually attractive place, therefore; the whole environment is the positive working out and reflection of a carefully formulated philosophy shaped and honed over many years:

> There is an attempt to weave the thread of the arts through all cross-curricular work, from reception through to fourth year junior. Most work plans used by teachers include a translation through the arts, an exploration through dance, visual art, drama, music or writing. The approaches and the work in these areas give a deeper understanding, a richer dimension and a long term hold on a 'Theme'.
>
> Whatever the 'form' used, it will allow reflection, helping children to identify and articulate their own learning processes. At each return to the arts in our teaching there is a need to 'scribble' a little — through discussion, music, movement or through drawing, time and space for new starting points is vital, to allow for the full use of 'making' and 'responding' possibilities. It is here that children 'grow', a growth that cannot be accommodated by instruction or direction alone.
>
> The growth of the individual is encouraged in many ways. Children are encouraged to become confident in ways of communicating both their needs, and their understanding. They are encouraged to be aware of themselves in relation to others, seeing themselves as part of a greater whole.[13]

The whole school environment makes this philosophy manifest, with the children unusually aware of and able to communicate about their surroundings. This both generates new work and reflects a set of values which determine the central role of the arts in learning, with an emphasis on engaging with arts experiences through original works, performances and visits. Equally, every attempt is made to provide the children with opportunities to work alongside artists and performers, seen as an essential part of their entitlement. The Year 2 teacher vividly illustrates the significance of this environment to her practice and her children's awareness:

Taking from it is very easy. You can take from all the displays, all the work, and get the children's opinions of it, which is very important. You can use it all the way across the curriculum, from looking at maps and pathways for history, geography, science — a lot of science from the materials that are around. Getting an idea of other people's work, an empathy, which is something that is very difficult in a barren environment.

Because their work is on display, it gives children a particular sense of pride — you've bothered — and they communicate much more easily. Walking down that coridor, they look at the work, the structures made with the artist, Anne-Marie, and I know only six children have had the main input in that, apart from the making of the paper, but that belongs to our class — it's ours. Everybody who walks past is told that it's ours — even total strangers! This is very important to the younger children, the fact that it is theirs and they have done it with Anne-Marie.[14]

The environment also extends the children's working space beyond the confines of their classroom in important ways:

I've noticed the confidence they've had to go out and work on it themselves, out on the corridor — which is a long corridor, is sometimes ill-lit, and they've been going backwards and forwards collecting the materials. They've had a fantastic self-confidence to do that, which I don't think they would have had without the art input, because of the nature of it.

This philosophy, emphasizing the significance of presenting, requires the help and support of many people and can only be consolidated through active partnership between teachers, children, parents, governors, and the school and the wider community.

The Environment as a Focus for Issues

The environment is a challenging one, however, being not only attractive but reflective of educational attitudes towards fundamental life issues. 'We work through an examination of key concepts, such as interdependence, conflict, similarity, difference, cause and effect and change. Within this framework issues of gender and cultural significance can be addressed in a positive way.' The impact of the environment is visually striking, therefore, but also underlines work which addresses vital current issues — the rainforests, the ivory trade, conflict and strife in areas of the world today, our life-styles and values in relation to those of the third world. The children are conscious of the significance of the environment in this respect, as well as it being valued and cared for in its own right.

To aid this process, the school makes use of many outside agencies, particularly those of the local authority, an unusual 'provider of rich resources, particularly in the Arts'. The school uses these to the full, 'but not just in a consumerist sense':

> There is an expectation that an experience will be built upon in a way that enriches and expands the original stimulus, so that ways of working and attitudes are developed that can be transferred across the curriculum. Excellent resourcing in school and a 'flexible response' to timetables are added contributory factors to a more successful development of the arts.

Systematically Building upon Strengths

Complex ideas of a thematic nature are therefore worked out over considerable timespans rather than just through single workshops, in the immediate wake of stimulus brought in or of visits out of school. As has been emphasized, the school has no arts specialists: 'We have no "specialists" or "experts" apart from our expertise as primary class teachers with an understanding of child development and appreciation of entitlement'. In describing the work of one school, its strengths in particular arts disciplines are inevitably reflected, but so also is the extent to which, in addressing entitlement needs, steps are being taken to develop confidence and further expertise. All the arts play their part in the practice of the school today. There are clear timescales involved in the development and evolution of each art form, the process beginning in the visual arts — its growth paralleling with that of the Drumcroon Education Art Centre, set up over a decade ago and articulating a set of principles which, with inevitable modifications according to contexts and circumstances, have proved transferable to any situation:

> Our work in Visual Arts originally grew out of Environmental Studies, and the use of our local environment/community — a way of looking and recording that has developed over the last ten years into all areas of the curriculum, and also provided a way into World Studies. The work in Visual Arts has also broadened out into the Performing Arts, exploring attitudes and concepts that maybe otherwise remain inaccessible. We are also developing a musical tradition/ vocabulary, which is translated into the wider context of understanding social interaction and consequent cause and effect.

The arts do not take place in every class all the time, but 'there is a consistency that means that at any time some class will be developing some arts form', at times as a vehicle for other work, at others as a 'vital part of the curriculum in its own right'. Allied to an open communication between staff, this allows developments in one art form 'to be transferred into the introduction and development of another, so capitalizing on each new experience'.

All these concerns contribute to a shared view that the school environment as a whole is vital to the children's development. This can be achieved in an old building as effectively as a modern one where care has been taken over provision of appropriate surfaces and areas facilitating the presentation of work. Old buildings, however, do have advantages to be fully exploited:

> Classrooms open up off long narrow corridors and it certainly was not built to accommodate the display needs of a primary school. But there is the advantage of large rooms, spare areas, and the possibility of nailing, stapling and generally 'sticking up' in any way we can. . . . The general environment plays a very important role in the 'ethos' of the school, it maintains and influences a standard of presentation, gives access to a variety of source material, recycles and presents past work as reference material, reflects current work, offers a variety of textures and media, and challenges and stimulates new departures for staff and children. It is intended as a working environment, not an untouchable display, nor as a fixing of old glories or just wall decoration. It is an environment for everyone to interact with . . .

No one simply tends 'their patch'. On many an evening, staff will stay to work together on an area of corridor, a sharing reflected when children show visitors around the school. They reveal an understanding and insight into their whole school, rather than simply of the particular bit in which most of their education takes place — an understanding of 'the where, how and why of it', and of 'the development of work'. All the children are expected to have an opinion, '. . . and it is only through their own making, responding, searching for clues and use of evidence in a supporting environment, that they can develop an informed one. One that has been enriched by their exposure to, and use of, the arts'.

Presenting and Recycling as School Policy

Presenting therefore represents a crucial dimension of school policy, but the making, presenting, responding and evaluating cycle applies not only to the children's work, for extensive use is made of the Wigan Schools Loan Collection of original art works. Contacts are also made with artists, and many readily loan works. Allied to periodic commissions and gifts, there is now a central core of works the school owns: a donated screenprint; a large embroidery panel contextualized by text and reproductions of Islamic architectural motifs which inspired its form; two pig sculptures by the late Ted Roocroft, commissioned by the school and usually displayed with photographs of children observing him at work, for some of the carving took place in the school.

Particularly significant is the body of work made by various artists who have undertaken residencies in the school — pieces with special meaning for children who have worked alongside them, gaining insight into their ideas, concepts and working methods in the process.

A Michael Rothenstein running cockerel woodcut from the Wigan Loan Collection hangs opposite the children's version, made during a Drumcroon workshop the artist attended. Both adorn the school library, which contains files of all Drumcroon and Turnpike Gallery catalogues. Those from exhibitions groups have visited regularly find their place as contextualization within displays — an enlarged section of photocopied text often highlighting a key aspect of a display. Loan works are changed at regular intervals as the authority's officer replaces them with works appropriate to planned themes and projects. She is aware of these project many months ahead, giving her time to bring the works together. When pupil work and contextualized material is changed it is not thrown away, as is usually the case; it will have relevance to some future context. Consequently, pupils understand that their work is specially valued; it, too, will have further use, supporting future children's needs. This policy has paid rich dividends, creating an extensive resource and in breeding respect for all the children's work, past and present, among the pupils.

Bold pupil images bring glowing colour, floor to ceiling, to areas of the corridor, large-scale group pieces travelling around doorways, completely covering wall surfaces. One such series, stemming from an in-service course run at a nearby school by the artist Susan Ross at the culmination of her residency there, was attended by the reception teacher. It had a profound impact on the teacher — like children, teachers, too, can be subject to the illuminating experience!

> It struck an immediate chord in me. . . . I said, 'Yes! I've got to pass this on to somebody else.' . . . that three days changed my way of working . . . it supported the way I wanted to work and gave it more meaning. It gave a backing to what I thought, but wasn't quite sure of. It gave me a lot of enthusiasm for that way of working, but now I felt I knew what I was doing and I was justified, in a way. I was able to say to other people, 'Why not try it like this?' Because they'd show me a piece of work and say, 'Oh! I don't know what to do with this'.[15]

The 'ethos' is by no means determined by just the purely visual. Music can frequently be heard emanating from classrooms, and Pitprop Theatre and Ludus Dance value close working relationships built up with the school over many years. Ludus enjoy such relationships with many Wigan schools, each new production being initially performed in a number of them, prior to touring. Each residency is 'tailored to the individual school, to its expectations, both of staff and children. A contract is made between the company and the school'.[16]

The performance of any Ludus programme provides an exciting combination of live music, dance and theatre. It is a full performance with theatrical sound and lighting equipment. It is professional. The programme's theme provides scope for the development of cross-curricular work, allowing the dance to be a natural and involved part of the school's ongoing work and not an isolated stimulus allowed no further than the fringes of the curriculum.

Communication on a Shared Basis for All

When Ludus performed *Crying Out Loud,* a group of primary teachers involved in the Arts in Schools project wrote the teachers' notes, applying Wigan arts policy document principles, also set out in a complementary primary publication, *The Arts in the Primary School: Some of the Arts All of the Time.* Making, presenting, responding and evaluating were therefore fundamental to these notes, providing a major element in their construction: 'Much primary practice demonstrates that there is no one "correct" way to enter into this sequence. The importance is the interaction of the parts as used by both the child and the teacher in relation to the work'.

The performance explored communication, the notes identifying English as the core 'communication' subject through its elements of speaking, listening, reading and writing, providing 'a set of processes that are crucial to the development of language skills across all subjects at a functional level'.

> Within each level of attainment the individual pupil has the opportunity to use a number of language skills in the context of their developing knowledge and understanding.
>
> As pupils mature, the range and sophistication of language skills expected increases appropriately.
>
> . . . most communication takes place in speech, and those who do not listen with attention and cannot speak with clarity, articulateness and confidence are at a disadvantage in almost every aspect of their personal, social and working lives.

The notes provided teachers with a cross-check to relate knowledge and tasks, skills and concepts, attitudes and the various National Curriculum programmes and attainment targets to the areas of learning and experience (the aesthetic, communicative, technological, scientific, mathematical, etc.). Making, presenting, responding and evaluating provided ideal structures for this project, communication involving the passing and accepting of messages and cooperative sharing of them, with one important diagram in the notes tracing them outwards from the child, through social factors to national and international contexts.

Ludus was based in the school for the first week of a spring term, performing *Crying Out Loud* to four junior classes, a group of top infants and all the staff (made possible by the head supervising the rest of the infants). Governors and parents who help in the school attended one performance, and two neighbouring schools brought pupils to another. In spite of the disruption to dinners, the school benefited enormously from these performances taking place within it:

> The children had the opportunity to see part of their environment transformed by the set, and every child in school watched, totally absorbed for about fifteen minutes, as dancers did 'class' before the performance. Three and a half days of the week were then used for dance/music workshop sessions in the three schools, with a sharing of work on the Friday afternoon. These cold facts of course give no indication of the richness and excitement of the experience: 'I felt all funny inside with enjoyment' (top infant).

The school's evaluation of the residency did not set out to show how to 'do' a residency, but offered 'a case for the partnership ideal between schools and Ludus to be an entitlement for every child in Wigan'. The school returns time and again to the T.S. Eliot lines,

> What we call the beginning is often the end.
> And to make an end is to make a beginning.
> The end is where we start from.

Planning was on a dramatic timescale, for some of the spring term Ludus experience built upon the content of the junior Christmas Service of some months earlier. Work for this programme started in the November, around the general theme of links.

> The planning for this demanded a great deal of discussion between staff, which was influenced by the knowledge of the Ludus visit and the theme of the show. Many ideas presented by each class at the service are communicated through dance, music, drama, words. The processes of making, presenting, responding and evaluating are readily used by groups of children developing an idea, and finally the whole thing is evaluated. Because of the common experience of working together for the Christmas performance it was felt that all four junior classes should share the experience of the Ludus residency.

The *Crying Out Loud* topic was approached from five standpoints, all built into the teachers' notes: technological communication, that of a sensory nature, cooperation and communication, discovering new ways of communicating and communication breakdown. The residency and its theme were consciously used:

. . . to elevate the principles of 'Partnership' and 'Sharing'. The whole school, not just the four classes, benefited directly from the residency, prepared for the visit, and worked on some element of the 'communication' theme. The environment around school was prepared to welcome Ludus, but also to give them some insight into work that had been going on before their visit.

The Year 4 teacher wrote:

A partnership between the school and Ludus offered a very special 'all round' experience to children, integrating dance into the curriculum in a very real sense, giving the Junior department an opportunity to work together to some depth and to take a whole school approach to the theme of communication.

For one pupil, 'Working with Ludus made me feel serious and important', the project not being just about dance and music but of sharing their school and work as part of the whole experience.

Timescales and Reflection through Presentation

There is an important time element involved in children accessing material they are provided with so that they can use and re-use ideas presented to them. They can only make proper use of experiences and information when they have time to reflect and respond in their own terms. A lot of planning time is spent in finding ways to link and weave things together; the more successfully this is done, the greater the scope for pupils to internalize experiences — leading to potent responses like that of a Year 6 boy, making a notice for a display about the working of the brain, linking work done in science to the content of the Ludus dance (originally sequenced vertically):

Head, Interlocking, Each piece fitting to another A powerful system, with hundreds of thoughts and ideas. Thoughts, important, unimportant The system controlling predators, An overlord of an organic line Its power is strong, but still unknown It has a beckoning yearn for knowledge. It feeds on input.

Ludus provided a common stimulus, but one capable of stimulating a wide variety of pupil responses, illustrated by further rich fourth year pupil responses:

Inside my head there is a red fire Liquid bubbling around, it won't stop Inside my head there is also a major control centre, A vital element. Without this element I could never survive This control centre knows when it's happy loud music will be playing And it will ask to be improvised. It's hard to resist What powers it, it's unknown to me The control centre is made of dense layers of tissue Of nerve endings and veins Its power is so great It's like the 8th wonder of the world You can build a picture of what you could look like If you were not what you are. The immensity of the thoughts it holds is inconceivable.

. . . the 3rd path is memories that ebb and flow like the tide over dry sand A long stream running and bubbling Cascading over rocks. My brain being changed into a binding river washing away the sands.

. . . I ponder over my future, and there are things I wish to change about my past. My whole head is a delicate masterpiece. A work of art . . .

Each of the four classes focused on different aspects — control systems in the body, structures, newspapers and the Look and Read programmes, 'Machines and me' — but all held together because each related to broad aims explored in the Ludus show. Each junior class linked with an infant one, so as to communicate to others what they had done, were doing, planned to do, and why. Year 6 have a responsibility for the general environment of the school, the spaces affecting everybody as they move around the building, but they also produced a beautifully illustrated written book to be subsequently used by Year 3 children.

Finally, all the participants in the Ludus residency made presentations to each other in the school hall. A Year 4 pupil commented that it was 'something like we do at Christmas, when we think of a "theme" and then each class does something about the theme, and we all share our work'. Another child emphasized the importance of the initiative in terms of art growing out of art: 'It is important and interesting that we all know what each class did with Ludus'. The Ludus residency, it can be seen, had a direct and dramatic bearing on the school environment in terms of conventional display while the whole junior department and many infants were conscious of an interactive stimulus informing the school's work for a sustained period of time.

Individual performers also work periodically in the school, a whole tradition of puppet-making emanating from two puppeteers visiting on a number of occasions. It is commonplace to find these artists working with small groups in quiet corners around the school. Alongside displays of children's and artists' works, beautiful natural and made forms are also to be seen and handled. One visiting student, feeling it would be a privilege to own these objects, asked a child showing him round if many got stolen. The pupil responded, 'Stolen! What do you mean? Of course not!' To ensure maximum access, the musical instruments also feature prominently in displays as attractive objects, but with pertinent questions also posed to draw attention to their function — inevitably, they constantly move in and out of displays in relation to usage.

A School-Based Gallery and Its Residencies

Emily, Year 6, thinks it 'important that work by artists is put on the wall because it helps us to remember what we did'. These works give her 'different feelings'. However, she then draws attention to a relevant but unusual feature of the school: 'When I am in the Murphy Room I remember things that have happened. We are lucky to have a room to go into for quiet and enjoying the pictures'. The Murphy Room is the school's own art gallery, accessible to all its pupils. Like his peers, Duncan knows how the room got its name; its creation and evolution to its present state have developed throughout his time in the junior department.

> The Murphy Room is named after Ian Murphy. The link between Ian Murphy and the Murphy Room is that Ian worked in here a lot more than anywhere else in the school because this was his studio. We have made the room like this because it's peaceful to work in it. It attracts people a lot more than any other room in the whole school. They get attracted more because of all the different kinds of art work.

The Murphy Room is founded upon the values and principles of the Drum-croon Education Art Centre. It was the first Wigan school-based gallery, all of which are termed 'mini-Drumcroons'. As regular use is made of Drumcroon, pupils are fully aware of the close ties which link the Murphy Room to Drumcroon, as Claire illustrates:

> It is important to have a Murphy Room because you can come and look at different displays. When I come into the Murphy Room it is so much like Drumcroon, different pieces of work by different artists. When artists come to our school different classes work with them and learn their techniques. My favourite piece of work in the room at the moment is 'Reflected Buildings' by Brendan Neiland. When we show visitors around I look forward to showing them the Murphy Room because I think it is the best room in the school; it is quiet and peaceful and full of interesting art work. I enjoy explaining about the different pieces of work and what they are linked with. If we didn't go to Drumcroon or the Turnpike Gallery we wouldn't know about the different artists, and wouldn't have the things in the Murphy Room or in the school.
>
> I am looking forward to seeing the new exhibition at Drumcroon. The best exhibition I've seen at Drumcroon was the Amanda Faulkner. Amanda has different styles than other artists I have seen. It takes a while to understand her work, but it's worth it. The work from Drumcroon is linked with our Murphy Room because each exhibition we go to we always do work about it.

Claire provides insight into the knowledge of contexts and relationships. Sometimes teachers can understand these without helping pupils to make sense of them in their terms. In making these connections, Claire begins to see how work arising out of different situations can still relate in an overall sense. Another pupil, Lynn, is likewise aware that, 'The link between the Murphy Room and Drumcroon is that the Murphy Room is like a thinking place, they are where you get new experiences'.

Ian Murphy is a member of the Artists in Wigan Schools Scheme, administered from Drumcroon, and was in residence at the school 1986–87. A painter concerned with landscape, light and atmosphere, his works are darkly dramatic in the moods of nature they convey with his use of a glowing light source around which rich, dark areas, redolent with mystery, revolve, a recurring feature. Early in the residency, he accompanied Year 6 pupils to Hinning House, an authority residential centre in the Duddon Valley, Cumbria. In this setting, children experienced the vastness of landscape and atmospheric qualities also discernible in Ian's work. Groups visit each year, and each Year 6 week generates a volume of significant work. Their writing vividly communicates the sense of wonder these urban children experience in this contrasting world of sky and mountains. Inevitably, these dimensions fed into corridor and Murphy Room displays. Art works and writing frequently combine, and it is a pleasure to linger in front of them, to absorb what the children have written. Inspired by his Duddon Valley experience, Alan wrote:

It was rough
Rocky and wet.
Views from above,
Scenery,
Colours.
Damp, muddy and fresh.
A waterfall dribbling down the slimy rocks.
Grass blowing with the wind.
North, West, East or South?
Trees rustled,
Leaves gently caressing.
Nothing like Tyldesley.
Listen!
Silence.

But a struggle to climb the steep stony mountain.
Weary,
A tired group
Going up the hill.
Gazing over at the misty mountains,
Feeling nervous.
The little matchboxes moving up the hills,

The little doll's houses are for real people.
The earth is patched,
Fields stitched by stone.

The children's writing often captures the profound feelings aroused by the infinite landscape they now inhabit, as Joanne conveys;

The night peace,
Only the sound of flowing rivers.
Ghostly grey skies.
Mist creeping over protruding mountains.
Wind whistling through the trees.
Mossy ground, soft and spongy,
Animal sounds in the night,
it's all like a dream.
Strange flowers growing peacefully on the mountain sides.
Night comes,
The mountains seem to be the sides of a hole
with everyone and everything at the bottom.
The sky slowly changes colour with the position of the sun.
The sky is pink, and then it changes to yellow mixed with pinky
    greys.
The horizon line is untouchable
you seem to be there but you never are.
You can just see the profiles of the mountains through the grey mists.
When morning comes the sky turns yellow,
but still the mist.
It never rains continually,
it rains, then stops, rains then stops altogether.
The sky changes,
the landscape seems to vanish,
and another world of mountains appears,
even more beautiful.
It's a wonderful view,
A place to be treasured.

Ian's residency also led to the production of a whole series of drawn and painted studies, an equivalent of the students' writing in artistic media. Written material and photographs taken by the pupils backed up their on-the-spot studies. On their return to school, the children embarked on an ambitious series of landscape panels designed to create a corridor 'environment'. Large in scale, extending from floor to ceiling, and irregularly shaped to fit changing corridor levels, the pupils built up the surface of these panels, layer by layer. An unusually impasted and heavily textured surface was achieved. Leaves collected in the Duddon were embedded in marvin-laden paint, giving added drama to their waterfalls cascading down mountain sides. The experience was stimulating to artist as well as pupils. He found their 'reaction to oils and impasto blatant', and their creativity 'only bettered by their enthusiasm'. His fears that his trademark 'atmosphere and scale' might be too much for them proved unfounded, and he was delighted by 'their awareness of evaluation and constant change'.[17]

The panels were displayed on the corridor; when the studio became the Murphy Room, they naturally formed the inaugural exhibition. Ian describes a transition from studio to gallery in which,

> . . . the spiritual air remained, the appearance of the studio altered dramatically, cracks and splattered walls were rejuvenated and the oil paint scrubbed away. . . . My palette became a focal point alongside reproductions of Turner, Constable and John Martin. Instead of the studio the room became the gallery, a room, now a private and quiet area to read, study and contemplate . . . but my essence lived on. The Murphy Room was now born.
>
> Tranquillity is the essential ingredient in the Murphy Room now, a foundation for current and future projects . . . an integral nerve centre to initiate plans and stimulate fertile writing and drawing . . . six years on, the recognition is still alive, younger children who I have never met are aware of my contribution and the bond between us is just as strong . . . I am just pleased I played a part in laying the initial foundation.[18]

Glennis Andrews describes the process of establishing a school-based gallery[19] as one of lurching, guessing and plotting. It was a few years before all teachers gained sufficient confidence to take full account of the resource in their thinking, and for the school to produce appropriate exhibition support material to encourage informal pupil, as well as structured teacher usage. Nationally, falling roles have been perceived negatively, leading to school closures, staffing reductions and invaluable resources being taken out of commission. This gallery epitomizes the constructive opportunities it presented, and is a model worthy of replication on a wider scale — appropriate spaces are plentiful, the main requirement being that of vision.

Like her peers, Vicki makes clear the connection between the Murphy Room and Drumcroon, but goes a stage further by describing actual strategies for engaging with the works on display:

> Both the Murphy Room and Drumcroon make me feel I have been involved in the paintings. I feel I know a lot of information from the pictures even if I have only been there ten minutes. I look at these pictures by carefully looking at what the picture contains, the mood that the artist felt and what I feel, and the process, how the picture is made, and what materials were used.

She has absorbed the Content, Form, Process, Mood model, briefly described in Chapter 1. She has made it her own and can now approach art works with confidence, in the sure knowledge that she can make sense of them by asking herself crucial questions.

Content, Form, Process and Mood in Operation

When Ian's work was featured in the Murphy Room exhibition *Sticks and Stones*, it was in combination with Ken Cottam's *Treescape* paintings, Loan Collection Lesley Yendell's sculptures and the pupils' own work. A school-produced catalogue and brochure contained statements by and about the artists and a brief passage entitled 'Looking at the Exhibition':

> It is hoped that when working in any of the Arts, children will have the opportunity to experience the following processes,
> [Making]   [Presenting]   [Responding]   [Evaluating]
> To accommodate responding and evaluating children need to be taught more than just evaluating their own art. They can respond to and evaluate the work of others, and establish a broader context in which their work takes place. To help give structure to the 'reading' of someone else's art, the fourth year looked at the exhibition thinking about:
> Content — in terms of subject matter, its significance.
> Form   — its arrangement, its formal qualities.
> Process — how it has been created.
> Mood   — the atmosphere or feeling evoked by the work.

There was a passage by Louise on Murphy's painting *Eruption*, displayed in *Sticks and Stones*:

> Rushing and racing.
> Rocks and water.
> Full of excitement.
> Ripped up paper thick with paint.
> Marvin, making it look like water colliding with the sharp
> jagged rocks.
> Fragments of blue and black.
> Vertical, horizontal, rugged and sharp.
> Rapid and swift.
> Rocks leading to others,
> Making you carry on the picture,
> Even when you've ended the picture on the frame.
> Your imagination carries on thinking,
> What will come next?
> From massive giant rocks, to tiny segments of slate.

The catalogue included another informative passage about Lesley Yendell's sculpture, *Climbers*. Written by a group of pupils working together, it reveals 'inside' knowledge about the artist and her work. Yendell's sculptures feature strange half human, half lizard-like figures clinging to rock faces. A rock climber herself, they are based on sketches made while rock climbing. When her work was shown at Drumcroon, the Centre staff built a climbing wall in one of the rooms, and children observed and sketched each other clinging to the wall by rope; a Drumcroon catalogue statement provided important information for *Sticks and Stones*.

> Lesley Yendell watching the figure climb.
> Sketching a stick form.
> Designing this strange figure, expanding its body form.
> Lesley Yendell made the creature out of welded metal,
> leather and ceramics.
> One of the climbers is reaching for water, the other is
> climbing a cliff and slipped, but is clinging on trying
> to save itself.
> The white bits are bone because there is a drought.
>
> Lesley Yendell got the idea for the climbers from the
> climbers on mountains.
> She sketched people on a climbing board to get a closer
> look at the tension of the body.
> The climbers look as if they were stretched like elastic
> bands. They look alive as if they are still climbing.
> The climbers give a mysterious feeling, as if you were
> on your own.
> It looks as if it's reaching for a certain treasure or a
> power of immortality.
> So near, yet so far, it is near but cannot reach. It is
> trying to extend its arms, but still it cannot reach.
> It still tries to steal its treasures, but all is in vain.

In Chapter 6 of this book, attention is paid to the teaching strategies which enable pupils to consistently produce writing with depth of meaning and expressive form. These qualities are apparent in the above passages, but it is particularly important that the children's empowering use of the content, form, process, mood model is noted at this stage.

First set out in *Educating for Art*, with a view to supporting teachers insecure about their knowledge of art, this model has proved an invaluable aid to learning when put directly into the hands of children themselves. These pupils make confident use of it, producing notes in their own gallery, discussing works together, maybe as a group but frequently working in pairs, with each posing crucial questions to the other. Drumcroon catalogues and teachers' notes are displayed alongside work around the school, likewise constructed with attention to the four areas, affirming pupil usage of it in relation to their thinking. Drumcroon and Turnpike Gallery catalogues are also displayed in binders in the school library, to be studied at leisure by teachers and pupils alike, further affirming these underlying principles and structures.

To aid this work further, Drumcroon staff formulated a range of questions for each of the four areas. Teachers lacking confidence in their skills in this area frequently surprise themselves at their ability to analyze Schools Loan works during in-service sessions, and the power and quality of their writing in response to first-hand stimulus. A common response is, 'I didn't realize I had such skills!' — an important realization if they are to recognize and cultivate similar skills in their pupils. The model has relevance across the arts, children applying it with equal success to Ludus residencies, for example. A short extract from a Phoenix Dance Company review further illustrates its relevance to dance contexts:

> It is for two men and two women, strikingly costumed . . . in black and white and takes its title, Subject Of The City, and its theme from the idea that people react, and in their dance make structures, which reflect changing city scenery. The dance is short, dimly lit, introspective, and contains unexpected, imaginative contacts, lifts and balances.[20]

This is a brief, almost shorthand, reference to the different dimensions of one dance amongst many reviewed in the course of the article. Nevertheless, the reviewer has indicated — even if only in one word — all the areas.

There are, of course, contemporary art works and a body of music possessing little or no obvious content. The areas have been chosen to embrace fully all the dimensions of art works, of whatever types, and with this small contentious area it is helpful to think of the form as subsuming the content — a familiar notion to most musicians. There are also functional artefacts, worthy of study — cutlery, tableware, furniture and the like — which likewise possess little obvious content, but which can be thought of as fitting into a function/content continuum. In Chapter 6, it will be seen how children's imaginations can be stimulated by a wide variety of art works, with the model standing them in good stead across the breadth of the arts.

As an aid to engaging fully with these works, it is helpful to consider questions of the following types, rephrasing them as appropriate according to age and stage of development of particular groups, so as to help them engage fully with art works, and to value their own responses, views and judgments — a virtually lost art, according to Neil MacGregor, Director of the London National Gallery:

> What has got lost is the idea that, when you look at a picture and you don't know what's going on in it, in a sense it doesn't matter whether you get it right or wrong. We should have the confidence to construct the narrative and decipher it in terms of our own experience.

It's a confidence we've all lost. In our secularised post-classical, post-Christian culture, it has been undermined by changes in education and a certain kind of highly formal art criticism that is intimidating.[21]

The questions we pose are designed to help rectify this deficiency. They are not definitive — children will happily coin their own as they gain confidence in their use of each area:

1 *Content*: What is the work about, what is its subject matter? Is this incidental, or does the work address religious, social, moral or political concerns? Was the subject matter experienced directly at the time of composition, or was it imagined or remembered? Has it been rendered with a concern for accuracy, or has there been distortion or exaggeration? If so, why? Is the subject matter surface deep or are there hidden, less immediately apparent, meanings alluded to through use of symbol, metaphor or analogy?

2 *Form*: What is the overall shape of the work? Is this in keeping with the content; does it contradict or affirm the content? What organizational scheme in terms of rhythm, texture and colour has been used? Is it harmonious or one built around contrasts and clashes? Does one colour, textural quality or rhythmic sequence dominate or are other elements equally as significant? Are you conscious of one overall structure or do you sense interrelating sequences of form, sound and shape? How do recurring elements of this nature contribute to the overall form of the work? Does the work have variety of structure and shape? Does it hold together as a unity or is it only satisfying in parts?

3 *Process*: How was the work made and with what? Through what stages did the work proceed from initial conception to final realization? Might there have been supporting studies — notes, sketches, scribbles, jottings, maquettes, photographs, preliminary workings out, improvisations, notations — or was the work created directly? Do you think the work took a long time in its composition, or was it produced rapidly without much need of refinement or modification? Was it produced on location, or in a studio away from the initiating stimulus? What skills must the artist have required to produce such a work?

4 *Mood*: How does the work affect me? Does it capture or convey a feeling, mood or emotion which I have already experienced in my own life or through art? Does it convey feelings about life or nature? Can you envisage the artist's state of mind at the time of creation? Is the work quiet/noisy, soothing/disturbing, happy/sad, relaxing/jarring, etc. in the mood it conveys and feelings it arouses? Is your mood simply the one of the moment, or has the artist directly affected you? If so, can you identify the specific means employed by the artist in order to so affect you?[22]

A major new National Curriculum requirement is that children of all ages acquire knowledge and understanding about art forms and their practice by others. 'Child-centred' work was made in isolation, divorced from the history, contexts and meaning of the art form in any wider sense. This separation is now no longer acceptable, time having emphasized the emptiness of much of the resulting work. Content, form, process, mood is an invaluable aid to joining practice to wider contexts and meanings, providing both teacher and pupil with a means to engage with, analyze and respond to a wide variety of art works.

A Model for Pupil Empowerment

At the primary level, the first premise must be that of children learning how to respond to works of art on their own terms. Reasoned conjecture is preferable to children learning second-hand facts and data about works, devoid of all response. In the wake of felt personal response, though, children often want to find out more from books, video, etc. Only now are they able to gauge their responses in relation to those of others — fundamental to genuine artistic appraisal. The relevance of contexts now also becomes apparent, whereas a diet of facts and others' opinions at the outset can be alienating. These only assume special significance in the light of their own 'reading' and interpretation of the work.

Let us therefore return to Vicki. Initially she used the words representing the four areas as headings under which to organize her thoughts. Soon she made the model her own, now writing freely, knowing she was fully capable of taking account of all four areas. She admired Anne-Marie Quinn's pastel paintings on the theme of mother and child, displayed in the Murphy Room during the artist's residency. While Vicki acknowledges all four areas, she chooses to focus with loving care on the content and mood of one of these intimate pastels:

A delicate look passes between people.
Central to the picture is the loving relationship between mother and
  daughter.
There is a delicacy in the hidden adjectives behind the tissues,
which lie upon layers and layers of marvin.
Some meaning is to be seen, but others not revealed.
Is the artist too timid,
or are some things not just for casual observers?
Patterns, signs, signals, secrets,
Waiting to be discovered.
Mother and child holding, wrapped in each other.
It is hard to think of one without the other.

The mother protecting.
Thoughts, loving and gentle.
They are both intrinsically linked. One to the other.
A strong bond that survives each parting.
Behind all the colours and tissues there are both disturbing and sat-
    isfying thoughts.
In storage places nobody knows about.
Only the mother, the child,
playing, enjoying everything.
What could be going through their minds?
Could they be passing on old memories?
Passing thoughts,
that will help the child through her life?

Like her colleagues (see Chapter 6), she could observe the artist at work unsupervised, providing further insight into the liberating use of this model; it now completely her own. In a passage remarkable in its concepts, her writing takes wing. The model can help all children to structure their thoughts more clearly. It enables Vicki to move into extraordinary realms in the process, willingly drafting and redrafting until a complex layering of ideas is fully conveyed. The previous passage focused on content and mood. With the privilege of being able to closely observe an artist at work in her school, she now focuses on process, revealing many of its facets, confidently conjecturing where appropriate, to produce this beautifully sustained passage:

Anne-Marie takes great care in her work, she makes sure every little bit is satisfactory. No bit of detail is left out. Sometimes she will stop to see if she has placed something appropriately, or to see if she needs to add more colour or collage to make a better texture. When I see her working I feel inside she is pushing herself to work until she finally gets it right, but I don't think she pushes herself into depression, not so far that she gets all worked up inside. She lets all her feelings out onto paper, I can see this in the types of strokes and colours she uses. Also in the gentleness of her hand. Sometimes Anne-Marie spends quite a while on just one area of detail. She will concentrate on just one part until she finally got it to look just as she expected it to look. The look in her eyes makes me think of the picture that is hanging over the sofa, you can't see the mother's eyes, but that is how I would expect them to look. Interested, hard at work, loving, involved and caring.

Sometimes Anne-Marie will take some masking tape and stick a little to a piece of collage and put it on the place where she thinks it will fit. She steps back and looks at it, and if it's not right she can take it off and put it somewhere else.

Anne-Marie gets her art work to look almost 3D, because when you are doing art you like to see all the different angles, exposing all the different bits of detail. She includes every line, it is very rare that she misses slight detail. I like the way she uses her colours by blending them into each other so they run off, and go into their own secret passage way, then maybe make their own way back joining the rest, blending in, making an undiscovered colour. The colours mix in with different textures, making different surfaces by putting chalk pastels over other materials, making them either harder or softer, or even the same but with a different appearance. The colours are mainly skin colours, pinks, whites, light and dark shades of purple, oranges. The colours stretch out over the paper to make it look larger.

Anne-Marie looks at her work critically and thinks what's needed in a certain place. She spends quite a while thinking hard and concentrating so hard you can almost hear her thoughts, and sometimes you are waiting for her thoughts to go down on paper. The music helps quite a lot, because it is soothing and helps you to relax, so your hand isn't tense and that means you can do a lot more loose work, freely flowing over the page.

Anne-Marie works until she is satisfied. She will not leave her work alone until she is happy. She may go home and wonder whether she should have changed that one piece. She will be working on one thing and then without warning she will move onto another piece, just while she thinks a little more. I think some of the movements used when she is drawing are because of the music. Some of the music is soft and that means she uses soft strokes, and the louder faster music means she uses little harder strokes. When Anne-Marie looks at her photographs she doesn't just use what's there, she looks at what is beyond the image and sees the sort of things she could write to symbolise her thoughts.

Having dealt with the school environment in general terms and its importance to learning in and through the arts, the emphasis has shifted to individual pupil responses to art works within such an environment. These responses illustrate the profound impact environment can have on children's artistic insights, empowering them to give expression to thoughts and feelings about art which extend both language and concepts in significant ways. Jerome Bruner maintains that we see the world differently through our use of language, which reorders our experience: 'the limits of my language are the limits of my world.'[23] The content, form, process, mood model enables children to engage with art and art works in significant ways, and to communicate their analysis and responses by verbal and written means. All schools utilize strategies aimed at developing vocabulary and language skills. The next chapter examines some of these in detail, specifically in relation to the use of a wide variety of arts stimuli.

References

1   Morgan, M. (1988) *Art 4–11: Art in the Early Years of Schooling*, Oxford, Basil Blackwell, p. 126.
2   Tomlinson, J.J. (1944) *Children as Artists*, Harmondsworth, Penguin, p. 27.
3   'Clarke silenced in class' (1991) *Daily Express*, 28 May.
4   Tanner, R. (1989) *What I Believe: Lectures and Other Writings*, Bath, Holborne Museum and Craft Study Centre, p. 9.
5   Morgan (1988) p. 126.
6   Tomlinson (1944) pp. 29–30.
7   *Ibid.*, p. 30.
8   Fairbairn, A.N. (1980) 'An Essential Ingredient', in *Growing Up with Art*, catalogue of the Leicestershire Collection for Schools and Colleges, London, Arts Council of Great Britain.
9   Plummeridge, C. (1991) *Music Education in Theory and Practice*, London, Falmer Press, p. 112.
10 *The Education Programme* (January, 1988) BBC 2. This programme focused on arts provision in Wigan and its underlying rationale in relation to National Curriculum Consultation Document, Summer 1987, and the view of the arts as presented there.
11 *Ibid.*
12 From a statement made by the headteacher to a primary teachers' meeting held in the school, 1987.
13 From an unpublished school document following a 1988 staff meeting addressing the arts entitlement of all pupils and the formulation of a whole-school arts policy. The meeting summarized discussions that also arose out of previous ones conducted during the course of the National Arts in Schools project, in which the school was an active participant. There is a long-standing school policy of documenting and summarizing what arises through staff meetings and school-based INSET; this material is freely drawn upon throughout this and the following three chapters which likewise utilize the practice of the school.
14 From a recorded interview between Liz Surman, the Year 2 teacher, and Glennis Andrews, October, 1991.
15 From a recorded interview between Jean Nicholson, the reception teacher and Glennis Andrews, October, 1991.
16 Andrews, G. (1990) 'Ludus in Residency', *Wigan Arts News*, Bulletin 12.
17 Taylor, R. (1987) 'The Murphy Room at Tyldesley County Primary School', from the Drumcroon brochure celebrating the opening of the Murphy Room and unveiling of the 'Four Seasons' murals in the Wigan Children's Library, 9 September.
18 Murphy, I. (1991) 'The artist's perspective on the Murphy Room', *Mini Drumcroons: Wigan School-Based Galleries*, Drumcroon occasional publication, p. 6.
19 See Andrews, G. (1991) 'Lurching, Guessing and Plotting Intentions', *Mini-Drumcroons: Wigan School-Based Galleries*, pp. 3–4. As well as its obvious value, the article also illustrates timescales involved in fully wedding an invaluable, but unusual, resource into the planning and thinking of a school as a whole.
20 Clarke, M. (1991) 'On hallowed ground', *The Guardian*, 11 October.
21 Marks, L. (1992) 'Tops of the postcard pops', *The Observer*, 27 December.

22 See Taylor, R. (1992) *The Visual Arts in Education: Completing the Circle*, London, Falmer Press, in particular, Chapter 4, 'Four Necessary Categories for the Teaching of Art: Content, Form, Process and Mood', in which the significance of the four areas is fully explored in relation to the teaching of the the visual arts, the questions posed in a more subject-specific form. Chapter 5 focuses upon work with teachers utilizing the four areas, and the next on two student case-studies showing its relevance to their study and practice of art. (Its significance in terms of student empowerment permeates the book as a whole.)

23 *Ibid.*, p. 26.

Chapter 6

The Arts and the Creative Use of Language: Stimulus, Strategies and Realization

Spoken language plays a central role in learning. Parents in talking to their children help them to find words to express, as much to themselves as others, their needs, feelings and experiences. Through language children can transform their active, questing response to the environment into a more precise form and learn to manipulate it more economically and effectively. The complex perceptual-motor skills of reading and writing are based in their first stages upon speech, and the wealth and variety of experience from which effective language develops. Language originates as a means of expressing feeling, establishing contact with others and bringing about desired responses from them; these remain as fundamental functions of language, even at a more mature level. . . . Language increasingly serves as a means of organising and controlling experience and the child's own responses to it. The development of language is, therefore, central to the educational process.

The Plowden Report[1]

The Creative Use of Language and Heightened Environmental Awareness

Involving the senses in heightened ways, the arts have a crucial role to play in the development and use of an extended vocabulary. Some educators even had the courage to capitalize on this richer use of language through the stimulus of arts involvements during the constraining days of the 11-plus. The Plowden Report (1967) sanctioned this work by articulating what underpinned their practice. In the process, it provided a vital springboard for further developments in other schools. Though the *Black Paper* writers cited this proliferation as a major reason for declining standards, the truth is that these approaches were never adequately developed or practised in the majority of schools.

Ironically, it has taken the introduction of the National Curriculum to legitimize such a creative approach to language in schools which have remained determinedly conservative in the face of obvious need for change — ironical in that the person who chaired the English group was none other than one of the initiating editors of the *Black Papers*. Where these methods had taken earlier hold, children's use of language was frequently richer and more imaginative, to the point where it often became a potent force in the expression of a wide range of ideas and concepts, as well as aiding their negotiations of a more prosaic nature. The benefits were consequently felt in all areas of the curriculum.

Sybil Marshall is one of the educators whose practice anticipated Plowden and she maintained that, though she established a considerable reputation as an art educator, English was always her first love. At a formative stage in the development of her imaginative approaches, she reflects that 'English, religious education (call it what you will), and art became inextricably linked with each other', with history, nature study and geography similarly intermingling with them.[2] This work eventually found its fully fledged form in what she described as her 'symphonic method'.[3]

> The 'symphonic method' allows for second subjects, bridge passages, variations, differences of tempo and, indeed, wholly separate movements; yet the term's work, like a symphony, is only completely satisfactory as an entire whole. . . . In this method the separate subjects are analogous to the different sections of an orchestra, playing in concert for full effect every now and then, but between these moments, first one and then the other taking up the theme. This theme occurs and recurs, but the entire symphony is not one endless repetition of the melody. Though all the work is in some way related to the theme it is not tied to it or limited by it . . .

Teaching a whole class throughout the course of a year for most aspects of the curriculum, the primary teacher has always accepted responsibility for the whole child, but sometimes for only one year of his or her life. In recent years, the development of whole-school policies — though not yet in enough schools — has facilitated greater coherence and continuity of learning and increased pooling and sharing of vital information among all the teachers within a school. Awareness of the implications of language across the curriculum has also led to children using language in a greater variety of ways and away from rigid, but often meaningless, approaches to the teaching of grammar and vocabulary in a subject vacuum. Many teachers have demonstrated that, within this generous framework, increased numbers of children can develop a love of language and use it as a creative and expressive tool in a whole variety of contexts ranging across the full breadth of the curriculum.

Again, the role which the arts have to play in this process is an extraordinarily rich one; various teachers have devised numerous means of effectively harnessing them.

Sybil Marshall's 'symphonic method' was so named because it arose out of her use of Beethoven's *Pastoral Symphony*, henceforth providing her with an invaluable model for linking the whole of the primary curriculum together in a meaningful way. For all the virtues of the 'project' and 'centre of interest' methods, she was concerned that these 'various subjects have been made to fit into the chosen theme, whether they would or not, or else entirely neglected because they were too far away to be tied to it, however clumsily'. Those teachers with a concern for the education and development of the whole child, while coming to terms with the statutory requirements of the National Curriculum, can still find constructive ways ahead through a study of Marshall's approaches practised some thirty years ago.

On the morning she first introduced the class to the *Pastoral Symphony*, one child said ecstatically at the completion of the second movement, 'Isn't it SMASHING!' A whole term's work grew out of that morning's listening experience, and it embraced the whole primary curriculum. Many natural ways into learning were discovered, for when she was unable to visualize ways forward with regard to a particular subject, the children's responses invariably provided her with the right pointer. She sometimes had to sit up late into the evening, though, preparing herself by finding out more about a subject in anticipation of the children's questions she knew were sure to come. The use of relevant stimuli was crucial to the processes of enquiry that were generated. Children invented their own dances in response to the peasant merrymaking of the third movement and produced 'symphonic' paintings from the allied stimulus of music and dance. Though country children, they went out into their Cambridgeshire landscape with which they were so familiar and tried to see it as a stranger might, just as Beethoven had successfully communicated a person's feelings on first arriving in the countryside from the town.

Following the making of a 'cooperative collage' inspired by these heightened experiences, the children went out into the landscape again and again, and their poetry and prose illustrate how sensitive they became to their all too familiar world through the music of Beethoven and their related artistic endeavours. Jill, aged 11, wrote:

> The wind whistles across the fields of many colours. There are all sorts of fields: fields where the sheep graze, the field nearly matching the colour of the sheep: the fruit fields just coming into blossom, silvery-white: and fields where the green shoots of corn are just appearing.
>
> Away on the undulating horizon the trees show dark. Some are almost black, others brown and green. The feeling in the country is so free, for one can see for miles around.

> The sky looks just like a large blue basin, upside down; the clouds of all different shapes, sizes and colours float silently into different patterns. The whole countryside is full of fields, sky, and quietness.[4]

Many chose poetry as the most effective vehicle for their ideas, as Sarah, aged 10, illustrates:

> The feathery clouds sail silently by,
> Like cotton wool in light blue dye.
> On the horizon a heap of snow
> Breaks into bits to dance gaily below.
>
> A big black rain cloud comes into sight,
> Making the other clouds seem pure white.
> The edge of the clouds is dark and grim
> Except on those with a silvery rim.

Angelo, aged 10, clearly carries the sounds and sequences of the merrymaking peasants into his writing, based on that musical passage, as one extract makes clear:

> The first piece of music was merry and light, but after a little while it became heavier, and louder than ever: then a merry tune came in again, which was a young shepherd playing his pipe, under a spreading oak tree. All the people twirled round and round, and kicked their legs up, and then they went off in a long line, and I knew that the dance had ended.

The storm, in particular, caught the children's imaginations, with nature conspiring beautifully with art to enhanced effect, as Marshall explains:

> As any one familiar with 'The Pastoral' will know, there is no break between the merrymaking movement and the storm. And so it proved, for on the Friday afternoon . . . the sky, which had been practically cloudless for a month, suddenly grew heavy and lowering, and the children were sent home early to avoid the coming storm. They had, however, had the second side of our record played to them that afternoon, and had listened to the orchestral storm with interest. . . . The storm did not come that afternoon. . . . They need not have worried, for the Saturday evening brought the worst storm of the year, a whole night of violence and brilliance to which no orchestra or paint brush could ever do justice. Monday morning brought the children back at school filled with the experience of watching and listening to nature's roarings.[5]

The children were inevitably full of the storm and of the practical use they intended to make of it: 'I got out of bed and watched it for a long time'; 'I kept thinking how we could make a picture of it'; 'There's a piece of gold string in the bit-bag that would make a lovely flash of lightning'. Here, indeed, is rich evidence of children investigating, as proposed in the *Art for Ages 5 to 14* National Curriculum document. This is a world away from the 'today we are going to do . . .' approach. The children produced a group painting of their village 'in the grip of the storm', the church and several cottages in accurate detail. A vivid flash of lightning utilized the gold string from the bit-bag, and it was set in a dark, windswept sky.

Feeling, perhaps, that poetry 'could not do justice to the spectacle', they all elected to convey the drama of that night in prose. Beverly, aged 11, wrote:

> The thunder rolls across the black, inky sky, softly at first, then growing to a deafening roar, which makes the very earth tremble.
>
> Flash. A streak of lightning zig-zags, brightening up every swaying tree. Shadows appear, making frightening visions. A mother passes with two children huddling against her skirt. They stared with big wide eyes at the dark trees towering over them. A dog lies cowering under a small bush, where it whines at the whistling wind.
>
> Crash. An uprooted tree leans drunkenly against a sturdy oak. In the houses people shudder and dive under the bedclothes hardly daring to breathe. They peep out like timid mice to blink at the thunderstorm.

Jeffrey, aged 10, wrote:

> The lightning streaks and flashes across the sky, shaking trees and sometimes striking them down. You can actually see the streaks of forked lightning in the sky.
>
> The deafening, crashing thunder rumbles through the sky, and then — flash. The lightning springs again like a wild yellow beast. Then you can see the blackish dark blue, and you can smell the thunder.
>
> Then it happens; the rain comes pelting down, making brooks high and cornfields flat. As the rain pours down, the rushing winds blow the raindrops down towards each other, like a wall of rain as it beats on the ground and then suddenly the rain dies off, and you can hear it going away.

There is an abundance of extraordinary work, all stimulated by arts experiences relating directly to those of their own lives. How often do children come into school on a winter morning entranced by the transformation in the landscape brought about by last night's snowfall, only to be told to open their books at page 35 as if nothing had happened? The arts, being rooted in the senses, demand that the teacher, too, should be alert to those moments of heightened sensuous awareness. It must be added that music was the stimulus and, though Marshall had no musical expertise through her own training, she acquired violins and recorders for the school and, of course, the symphony led back into music making as well. It was the practice of teachers like Marshall who anticipated Plowden. Here, surely, are the abundant fruits of discovery methods; Plowden notes that, 'The best writing of young children springs from the most deeply felt experience'.[6]

Some teachers still express suspicion of children's writing when it becomes so rich and vivid: 'Primary children cannot write like that! — I have been teaching for X years and have never come across anyone so fluent! — who are these children?' It is an irony that those schools who pride themselves on their teaching of 'the basics' invariably produce children who can write 'correct' sentences, starting with a capital letter and finishing with a full stop, but it is surprising how little is usually written and how lacking in content it is. Sybil Marshall tells the story against herself of the time when, as a young teacher, she asked a class of juniors to write about 'The Milkman'. This was before she had worked out how to draw profitably upon essential stimulus. One girl wrote, 'The milkman brings the milk, milk, milk, milk, —' 153 times![7] She always sought to develop calligraphic skills in her children: 'Good handwriting is an asset and an art which can give pleasure, but a beautifully written page saying nothing is a complete waste of time; reading is a wonderful skill to possess, and comprehension greater still, but what is read and its bearing on life is the important thing.'[8] She rejected formal exercises, finding them 'a complete waste of time'. This did not mean that her pupils wrote instinctively without any knowledge of essential techniques and skills — quite the contrary.

Children, Their Use of Language and Audiences

She sought to close the gap between talking and writing, for there was an assumption that talking was what was done out of school, and writing was what was done inside; initially, the children had 'no idea that talking and writing and reading bore any relation to each other'. They soon began to realize that a good discussion 'was as exciting as any other sort of contest', but that they had to obey the rules of good conversation, 'which meant listening while others talked, keeping to the subject under discussion, and saying only those things they were prepared to back by further argument if necessary'.[9] These are all skills sanctioned by the National Curriculum, presenting a new set of challenges to some schools. There are many ways of introducing them so that they generate a richness of content. Providing children with access to the aesthetic field is vital if these aspects are to be fully cultivated, and this dimension was certainly not lost on Marshall:

To believe in their potential for creativity was for the children the first half of the journey towards being educated beings. The other half could be completed only when they could see their lives surrounded, sustained, and indeed explained by the general experience of all humanity. To be able to approach the classic works of art without fear, and with pleasure, interest, understanding and love is to be able to tap the inexhaustible well of past human experience.[10]

An Experiment in Education (1966) was written shortly before the curriculum development 'explosion' took place, but it is as relevant today as when it was written. In 1975 *The Bullock Report* was published. It noted that: 'In much of the writing that takes place in schools, the pupil's first attempt is expected to be the finished article; there is not enough encouragement of the idea of a first draft to be followed by a second, more refined production'.[11] Running simultaneously with the Arts in Schools Project was the 1985 Schools Curriculum Development Council National Writing Project, which was to have considerable influence, with many of its ideas finding their way into the National Curriculum. An initiative which gained widespread currency was that of writing for audiences. One benefit of the two SCDC projects running in parallel was that the ideas of one were also cultivated and developed through the other. For example, the Wigan Arts in Schools Verbal Arts group practised and helped disseminate this notion of writing for audiences.

Junior children writing for specific infant children was one model. One child describes writing for Gemma, aged 4. Initially, a group of about six upper juniors wrote a questionnaire:

The questions were something like this: Does someone read to you at night? What's your favourite story? We thought some of the questions might be too difficult for a 4-year-old child to understand so we had to simplify the words. For instance I was going to ask a child what is your favourite character but I changed it to what people do you like?

She asked Gemma the questions, 'and she answered them confidently, quite near the end she got a bit bored and wanted to play', but when asked what she wanted her story to be about, 'Gemma said that she liked teddy bears and Care Bears she also said that she wanted them to have a party in Spain. I decided that the bears could have a party on the beach'.[12]

When I started the story I didn't quite know what to write but when I got going I found it quite easy. I tried to put interesting words in the story so that the listener would not become bored, for example zoomed and bumpity bump. I quite enjoyed writing for a younger child and would recommend it. When I started to make the book I was very nervous in case I made a mistake. First I wrote the writing in my own handwriting and then did a picture. I did the two things alternately so as not to get bored. I stuck the pictures and writing onto white card. The book was taken to the library to be bound and laminated. When it came back I was very pleased with it.

The pupil had to get four opinions on her work. The next door neighbour wrote, 'A very well written and illustrated book easy to read and easy to explain through the pictures to very small children. An excellent attempt, Karen!' The child was delighted at the comments she gathered. Next, Karen was able to take her book to the new children's library, where she read it to two young children from another school:

> I read to Zoe first and she was really interested and joined in talking about things in the story. Michelle was very fidgety and looked at everything else but she listened. Near the end all the children sat down in a group and Zoe put her hand up and said that she would like everyone to hear my story, so I sat on a chair feeling very nervous because I was the first one to read in front of everyone.

Even this was not the conclusion, though, for the children were filmed on video so that other library childhood visitors could participate further. Here we are a world away from the pupil writing for the teacher's red pen to correct what has been done, with grammatical errors assuming greater significance than relevance and content. An audience was crucial to the concept from the outset, and Karen had the opportunity to present her work to a variety of audiences in a variety of ways. In the process she gained access to the aesthetic field, involving others in the evaluation of her work, and taking account of a 4-year-old's literary preferences.

In the National Curriculum speaking and listening are given consideration alongside reading and writing. Evidence might include 'reference to the way in which they talk in small groups, as well as brief transcripts of talk; tape recording and videoing children', and 'children's writing about their speaking and listening', in order to help build a picture of their perceptions of their achievements.[13] Karen provides sound evidence of these dimensions through school work in pre-National Curriculum days.

Though reluctant to teach meaningless exercises, Marshall evolved a system of assessing pupils' work on a purely formal basis, with attention paid to grammatical correctness, etc. but with the whole class then participating in a further assessment based on content — she was always impressed at the fairness of her pupils' appraisals of each other's work in this regard. At our Wigan school a two-prong attack is likewise used today so as to ensure that children's language skills are systematically developed, but in relevant ways related to creative and expressive needs. The vast majority of the nation's teachers have always accepted a professional responsibility with regard to the former. Unfortunately, far fewer have taken as full a responsibility for the latter, though the evidence that one enriches the other is overwhelming.

In her use of the *Pastoral Symphony*, we have already seen how Marshall persuaded her pupils to see their environment as strangers. Jeff lives in the urban environment of Tyldesley, and his response to the rural landscape of the Cumbrian Duddon Valley, experienced during a school week at a Wigan residential centre, potently illustrates how a child's use of language is enriched through the search for appropriate words to convey powerfully felt and experienced sensations. His school had constantly introduced him to a variety of written forms through poetry and stories. The resulting imagery transposes the experience into pure poetry. Marshall defines her children's work as poetry when it says 'something that could not have been said in any other way', and the last line of Jeff's piece is extremely moving as he communicates the town child's sudden awareness of silence encountered within the immensity of nature;

> Towering fells, high in the sky,
> Touching the clouds.
> Enchanting, ghostly feeling
> Passing through my mind.
> Pink blazing sky enlightens all.
> The magic feeling
> of the tune of the flowing water of the river.
> Beauty lies in every crack and corner.
> The tough Herdwick and Swaledale ewes
> browse for a second
> and listen for danger.
> A shooting star cruises the moonlit sky.
> I hear my heart beat.[14]

Reference has already been made to the need for audiences, and the school's children meet a more than average number of adults through the visits undertaken and the policy of bringing outside agencies in; the children's skills in informing others about their school environment have already been noted. Letter writing in real contexts is another beneficial outcome of these approaches. In writing to Ludus Dance, two girls convey a great deal about the wide ranging arts activities which can flow from a visit by a dance company:

Dear Ludus,

I thought the show was great! After watching it we decided to do a book based on Crying Out Loud.
  First of all we did a story on what we thought Crying Out Loud was about and what happened. We then read our stories out to the rest of the class to get more ideas for the book. The next stage was for the storyline to be written. We decided to do 25 pages 1 page for each person but somehow it didn't turn out like that.

Then some illustrations got underway. Now the illustrations and text was being done. Even now it was looking good especially when we started to put the writing onto the ones that were finished. We used lots of reference material. To get the right colours and shapes we used photographs and pictures.

We called all of the characters their real names except for the robot which we called Robyte. We called it Robyte because there are bytes in computers and the robot came out of the computer. The book is an infant book, an illustrated story book, like the ones they have in their classrooms. The writing has to be easy and clear for the infants to understand. When all the illustrations were done we put them together and decided to put a spiral spine on then it would open easily.

Some of Miss Surman's class watched the show. Miss Surman is going to read it to them so we will get their opinion on it. We are going to do a colour photocopy and some black and white copies. We are hoping to send you a copy as well as the infants.

Love from.
Joanne and Chloe.

The parallels with the learning experiences of Karen are obvious, and the children describe a whole variety of presenting situations generated by the project.

In the school attention is paid to word structures, word families and phonics to ensure that spelling is systematically dealt with throughout the school in ways parents can understand and pupils accept responsibility for. All classrooms, starting with reception, have their own dictionaries and thesauri, and children are taught how to use these resources from the outset and how to refer back to them. Whenever possible, work is marked in the presence of the child so as to encourage negotiation and challenge. Might there be a more appropriate word in this context? Why not refer to a thesaurus to find out? Dictionaries are in constant use to check and extend use of vocabulary within the context of the work being undertaken. Older pupils have access to increased numbers of dictionaries and thesauri so as to match availability with increasing demands as pupils mature in their use of them. Different types of dictionaries are available, ranging from classroom editions to fuller, more elaborate versions.

The acquisition of grammar is, again, systematically approached, but is likewise linked to pupils' own writing, taking consideration of the different types required for different audiences. More formal grammar-type exercises are always approached in the context of a pupil's own writing, rather than as meaningless exercises in a vacuum. Children's higher order reading skills are carefully developed through the use of skimming and sequencing techniques as well as through use of indexes, dictionaries and the thesaurus, as appropriate. Much of this work requires interaction, and care is taken to ensure as favourable as possible teacher/pupil ratios at these times. The use of the main idea and searching for supporting details in a text becomes immediately translatable in terms of using and understanding the school environment. When children are entrusted with the responsibility of taking adults around the school, this understanding of the whole in relation to the parts is of the utmost significance. Year 6 juniors visit an authority residential centre in Cumbria each year, and two of the three booklets prepared for the work to be undertaken there contain glossaries, to encourage development of a critical vocabulary appropriate to their work in that environment.

Teachers and Children Sharing: Language as Felt Experience

Written work is shared at formative stages, with the emphasis on presenting benefiting what is ultimately produced. When the children write, so do some of their teachers. When teacher and artist in residence both participate in this process, the richness is all the greater. One artist's work involved delicate layering processes, revealing facets of her personality and life experiences, past, present and future. The artist, Anne-Marie Quinn, wrote,

> Between the two rooms
> a cord
> woven, constructed
> of ourselves.
> A rich weaving
> it can be grasped fiercely, pulled taut
> handled if necessary.
> A straightforward connection through touch
> Then light dances over delicate strands
> movements textures shift
> like reeds in a gentle current
> opening their threads to receive and sift
> in the play of light its surface textures,
> fragile
> as barely there as old silk
> but there nonetheless
> We finger its structure quietly,
> smiling.

Anne-Marie's writing indicates links which have been carefully cultivated between the Murphy Room and the classroom — indeed between studio, classroom and Drumcroon. Within the intimate gallery atmosphere extraordinary descriptions revealing deep poetic insights were produced by the children, too, as Richard, aged 11, illustrates:

Scattered here and there clothes hanging out of drawers,
Flowers cascade out of the drawer.
I go to look.
Inside there is a mystic world covered in flowers.
I shut that drawer and open the next.
Inside are all the happy moments of my past,
On a roller coaster,
In an aeroplane,
Birthdays,
Christmas,
Getting my first swimming medal.
They all started to flow out.
I try to catch them, but my fingers pass through.
They are intangible thoughts just out of reach.
I close that drawer,
and I look at the top drawer.
I notice that it is all boarded up, locked away, best forgotten.
As I take away the boards the drawer bursts open,
allowing the discarded unhappiness to escape.
I try to force the drawer back in,
backing away from the escaping sadness.
It has all flown out to haunt me for eternity.
I push the drawer slowly once more.
Just like Pandora's box,
Only hope is left.

The reference to Pandora's box is interesting in that one group had been to Drumcroon to the Rose Garrard exhibition. In her work, Garrard deals with female stereotyping, both now and in historical terms, using Pandora as one of the key figures from mythology so treated. In connection with a 'Held, Connected, Restored' theme, references to Pandora consequently found their way into the school, epitomized in a display opposite Richard's classroom. A wooden chest had a lock on it and the wording, 'Remember Pandora, don't open the box!' Richard had not been to the Garrard exhibition, but was able to make an important lateral connection through the school's strategies for sharing.

A further value of these approaches is made manifest in that a small number of pupils would use the Murphy Room on their own. Leon, in such a situation, quietly watched Anne-Marie at work, writing the following there and then, with no teacher present. The ground has already been thoroughly prepared, so that pupils can work independently for sustained periods of time.

Everything is set.
I like the colours she uses and the way she mixes them.
She uses words in her pictures.

On a poster is a line I particularly like.
  'I promise to hold you in my mind
  as a cupped hand protects a flame.'
A thought for the future.
Words to return to in a longer life.
Words I like the feel of.

There is music, it is very peaceful.
You want to listen to it over and over again.
You can concentrate to the music, there is no singing.
I like it without the singing, you can use it for background.
Her movements are easy,
Some sharp, some slow.
A working expression, a whole body concentrating.
Undisturbed but at the same time available.
Every movement is considered.
Working with slow skilful hand movements.
Never rushing, covering areas with detail.
Thinking, stopping, looking, choosing wisely,
tearing little bits and sticking them.
Mixing water with glue,
Using chalk, pencil and tissue paper.
planning in her book,
Storing poems like her mother did,
Storing letters in fragments,
Old photographs,
Holding them in her book, holding them in her mind,
As the cupped hand protects the flame.

Here, indeed, is evocative realization of the Plowden proposition that children 'write most easily and imaginatively about their homes, their hobbies and interests, about things seen and done in science, mathematics, geography and on school visits'.[15]

Sometimes initial drafting and considered piece come together on one sheet of paper; Joanne wrote the following, using the content, form, process and mood model to aid her thinking.

Delicate pictures. Anne-Marie loving and caring for her child Bella. Delicacy shown by the sorts of colours — pink, cream, light brown, beige, and a little purple — suggesting a beach silent and peaceful/soft shape and mood. Skin colours of a baby. The shape is always curved and sympathetic to the rest of the picture. She looks as if she is in a world of her own imagination. She cuts out everyone and everything except for the music and the picture created in her mind. She is engrossed in her work.

Joanne then wrote:

> Concentration in her face as she works. If I disturb Anne-Marie I feel as though I have affected the picture in some way. If she turns to look at me to see what I want, she stops the flow of her working style.
>
> Music helps Anne-Marie to find ideas. She also uses parts of photographs of her and Bella. Pictures about her life. I think that Bella is the main part of Anne-Marie's life. Photographs to help get the right shape, colour and image for a body. Anne-Marie concentrates on one section of work for a long time, when she thinks it's right she steps back and looks. She tilts her head in different ways looking for improvements that can be made.
>
> The colours blend together to create the right sort of mood. A kind of sympathetic mood so gentle and fragile. The shape is always curved and sympathetic to the rest of the picture.

Basic Strategies for Developing the Creative Use of Language

What child and teacher do is shared — the child sometimes reading his or her work to the group; the teacher sometimes doing so on their behalf. Drafting and redrafting are practised throughout the school, with children walking around and looking at each other's work. In this respect, an important formative experience was that of a group working in the urban environment during a practical workshop related to the Gerd Winner exhibition at Drumcroon. In this situation, it was natural for children to move around and see what each other was doing. At the time, though, all the children perceived this as copying. This aspect of sharing, to do with audiencing, is now implicit in *all* school practice, not just that to do with the arts. Pupils accept the concept of redrafting in the light of responses made known to them through the act of presenting.

The practice of teachers reading to children happens throughout the school — sometimes a book will be read over a period of weeks, at others a poem might be read. On occasions, video is used to record writing and reading aloud, and pupils develop the practice of taping their reading of their writing or a text, and replaying this with the text in front of them. The word processor is used as an aid to drafting from the infant stage upwards, and the computer is used in an incidental manner to aid spelling.

Time is allowed for second to fourth year juniors to read in silence. During this one hour session, pupils have a choice as to what they read. A further hour is also set aside for use of the school library, well stocked with a wide choice of books. By Year 6 stage, though, this set hour is scrapped; pupils are now expected to know how to use the library as needs dictate. The library is always staffed and accessible to pupils at lunchtimes. In the light of the National Curriculum and the tremendous pressures on time it has created, this time has to be held onto out of conviction. Cross-curriculum networking provides a main justification — science benefits as much as do arts activities, for example. The nature of intake necessitates that the principle is maintained; there are many who would never use a library or read contemplatively otherwise.

Book week is important in this respect. It is timed to coincide with parents' evening. Children go to a bookshop in Manchester, some fifteen miles away. It is the first time some children have visited the city, and they choose books — straight off the shelves — to bring into the school. They choose with the whole nursery to top junior spectrum in mind and range across fiction and non-fiction. Books are loaned for a week, allowing time for children to handle them and browse. All choose the book they would buy if they had the money. They review the book, taking account of format and structure, use of language, characterization, weighting in terms of heroine and hero, genre, and to whom it would appeal and why. They reflect on the terms with which they engaged with the book and which they would use to recommend it to others. This is a general school practice, but during book week parents see which books their children have chosen and why, with the option of purchasing or ordering them for home. Many take up the option. This means that school, parents and children work together to ensure that reading for pleasure develops both at home and in the school.

These clear and systematically used strategies ensure that development takes place throughout the school, with the inevitable proviso, of course, that some Year 6 pupils develop a self-image which can impede such concepts such as that of reading for pleasure in one's own time, whereas few Year 4 children have these distractions to contend with — learning of this nature cannot develop in an uninterrupted upward curve for all children all the time!

The Aesthetic Field: Language and Its Uses within Arts Contexts

The school has made use of writers in school (Adrian Mitchell, for example) and children are exposed to a wide variety of literature and encouraged to produce their own work in relation to this. Various contexts and a variety of models are used. 'Rhythms and cycles' was the theme chosen for the 1989 Christmas service, one of the few situations which required children to assiduously learn a text and commit it to memory with a view to speaking in unison. This service coincided with the dismantling of the Berlin Wall. Negative images of the wall were projected, with the children dancing in front of them. The children had very clear concepts about recycling through school display policy, etc., through all their preparations, and the notion of rebirth as symbolized by the unification of a country which had been divided, the television images indelibly fresh in their minds. Mark said, 'there had been lots of reports about the Berlin Wall on the news and it fitted with the theme of the whole Christmas Service . . . it destroyed the rhythms of friendship and relationships and it split families.' It has, of course, become a remarkable symbol of people-power in modern times, as Hayley understood, 'the people had ended the curse'. Gary wrote:

> We decided that we'd do the Berlin Wall because it shows how a wall can affect the rhythm of life and how conflict can separate a whole city of people. If people try to get over it they get pushed back and in the end the wall is broken and people make a new start and be friends. We thought we would do it because it shows the people being friends, then conflict happening between them, then a wall splitting them apart. After the years people have thought about it and think they could be friends and they could travel into the other half of the city, so the wall gets knocked down.

The children created and performed the music to the dance themselves, some observing that the ideas could be better expressed in dance than in words. The class produced a joint statement as an explanation of what they were doing;

> Time has its own rhythm, measured by the ticking of a clock. This can be interrupted, the clock may stop, but time is continuous. 12 o'clock a beginning and an end, day and night, never stopping.
> We represent cycles as circles, smooth flowing shapes. All things that are cycles return at sometime, they just circle round. The circle represents the whole of something that isn't divided, it is a friendly shape — uninterrupted — a symbol of peace.
> A rhythm is in a poem, in music and in the sound of a river repeating itself over and over again, the rhythm of its life, the rhythm of its growing.
> Cycles are continuous patterns. Preserving natural cycles is very important. They are at risk from humans, from our industry and our greed.
> Cycles can be represented by circles spinning round with different things happening. Celebrations fly out and happen, this is repeated on and on for years. As long as the circle is spinning the celebrations will go on and on.

Within this context, the pupils understood what was being said in T.S. Eliot's *Four Quartets*. They loved the passage, willingly committing it to memory. Their own writing was undoubtedly shaped, in part, by their understanding of the Eliot piece. Emma observed that, 'Our choral speaking was about going round and starting again from the end, that is like a cycle.' The Eliot passage used went as follows:

Round and round the circle
Completing the charm
So the knot be unknotted
The cross be uncrossed
The crooked be made straight
And the curse be ended.

Time present and time past
Are both perhaps present in the future.
And time future contained in the past.

What we call the beginning is often the end
And to make an end is to make a beginning
The end is where we start from.

We shall not cease from exploration
And the end of all our exploring
Will be to arrive where we started
And to know the place for the first time.[16]

Louise, aged 11, produced a decorated piece of writing and its second section contains a passage in which the debt to Eliot can be discerned — the concepts are her own, but clearly heightened and clarified through the association.

When you are thinking
the things you think about
are often in your head like a rhythm.
You can imagine that it is raining pots of gold in your garden,
and you were the richest person in the world.
The past is full of good and bad.
The good future is ahead of your past
like pictures in your mind.
The future is crystal clear as the past is
leading you to your future.
The things that you think about
are often in your head
like a rhythm
trying to arrive where they started.

Ursula Le Guin is an author who can prove difficult for a number of young children, the books being quite abstract in their form and presentation. However, some children are extremely responsive to works like *A Wizard of Earthsea*.[17] One pupil writes about *The Farthest Shore*[18] by the same author,

The main characters are Sparrowhawk the Archmage of Roke whose
real name is Ged and Arren the prince of Enland whose real name is

Lebannen. Arren is a person that is sensible but can be foolish as well. In the book it speaks mostly about him and his feelings.

Sparrowhawk and Arren have to find a source of evil that is causing wizards to lose their spells and forget their names. A name is a secret to yourself and other people that you trust and love. You have a used name and a true name. The true name you keep as a secret and the used name everybody knows.

I think the Farthest Shore is a good book but I liked the Wizard of Earthsea better because the Wizard of Earthsea was more about Ged and how he was hunted by the shadow and how he sought to hunt the shadow to name it.

Writing about *The Wizard of Earthsea*, Alex, aged 11, concluded,

I enjoyed the book of The Wizard of Earthsea because it was a well described, fantasy, adventure book, when I got the book I liked the picture and thought I was going to like it and I did. I am into fantasy books and this book was like one. Ged lives in Earthsea, a fantasy world but a world which is flat. At the beginning of the book you will find a map of the archipelago of Earthsea.

Shortly after reading this book, Alex produced a powerful passage which is descriptive but also picks up on the abstract qualities and strange imagery he had discovered in Le Guin. Rather than copying anything directly from the book, though, Alex reused the substance as basis for an examination of the self, producing an evocative and haunting piece in the process. He vividly illustrates the statement in *English in the National Curriculum* which reads, 'An active involvement with literature enables pupils to share the experience of others. They will encounter and come to understand a wide range of feelings and relationships by entering vicariously the world of others, and in consequence they are likely to understand more of themselves'.[19] This is not all, though; he has visited the Lucy Jones exhibition at Drumcroon, seeing there her self-portraits in which she depicts her disability, one half of her body being paralyzed by cerebral palsy. She spoke to the children about her good side and her 'dark' side, and Alex has made the essential cross-reference, relating this to the concept of having two names because we all have two sides to our personalities. Alex wrote,

A misty world, peaceful but too peaceful,
A mysterious unexplained balance between good and evil.
You can walk in swamps and not get stuck,
You can breathe fresh air but feel sick.
Black dead trees, that when touched, crumble,
then sprout into green shrubs when reaching the ground.
Everywhere you tread you grow grass
so streams can flow.

You see yourself in that green landscape,
Where everything is bright and cheerful,
While your spirit is in darkness.
Your spirit is lost.
You cannot find your real self.
Looks can betray you,
You have to dig deeper to see a true being of a person.
Even when you win a fight, you lose, because you have to fight.

You have to fight for a good cause,
Because if you fight for fame you get hated.
If you fight for other people's freedom, you win,
even if you lose the fight.

Ursula Le Guin would doubtless have approved of the nature and content of Alex's storytelling achievements, for she;

> . . . resents a mindset in which male and female, science and art, rationality and magic are held apart. Stories, she believes, can bring them together, and it is 'when children start to tell stories that they begin to be people'. Ursula Le Guin, too, would like to be remembered as a teller of stories, not as a genre writer: 'I don't want to stay in the ghetto. I want the freedom of the city'.[20]

An extraordinary illustration of a pupil effectively using the form of a writer occurred in relation to fourth year pupils writing about a set of entangled roots that were being incorporated into their school sculpture trail. Mark had recently read a book which inspired him to assume a form of writing which was totally distinct from that of the rest of the group.

> At the beginning of eternity there was a tree. In the tree was a nest with two eggs. One black, one white. The tree looked after the eggs as if they were its own. The tree made them warm in the cold season, and kept them cool in the warm days of the hot season. It protected the eggs from flying stars.
>
> One day in the warm season the black egg started to crack, and out of the egg crawled a baby. The baby stayed in the nest until it grew to be a beautiful young woman. When she climbed out of the tree she walked round the bottom of the tree, and from the roots there came beautiful flowers which protected the tree from any danger.
>
> The woman became the Goddess of warmth.
>
> A month later in the cold season the white egg cracked open, and a wolf cub crawled out. It took a matter of weeks for the cub to grow into a strong and gentle wolf. The wolf walked round the bottom of the tree, and up from the roots there came a strong wooden fence, to keep danger from the flowers.

The wolf went off and became a strong winter warrior.

On the sixth day of the warm season the woman, who had been named Summer came back to the tree. She was ill. She crawled back up the tree into the nest. She ate one of the blossoms of the tree and died at the end of the summer.

The winter warrior returned, dying. He didn't have enough strength to climb the tree, so he died in the flowers below.

An interesting example of work in one curriculum area leading to unusual explorations in others is illustrated by the use of Schools Loan art works in relation to a science-based project on the theme of flight. The display was mounted adjacent to the second year junior class which was studying the topic. One of the pieces featured was a coloured etching by Michael Oelman from a sequence telling the story of the flight of Icarus. This naturally led to the study of the classical myth. Stuart, a second year junior, communicates his obvious knowledge and understanding of the story in his close scrutiny of the etching, a work which held a fascination for many of the children.

When I looked at the picture the first thing I saw was Icarus flying through the sky. Then I saw the V shape it reminded me about how birds fly in the sky. The picture looks real because of the colours, the sky looks as if the sun is setting with an orange yellow glow. There are white little birds in the yellowy orange sky as well as Icarus with his huge feathered wings. It looks as if the candle wax is melting and the feathers coming off, and he's falling into the Mediterranean Sea below. The little house looks like the palace of King Minos with the labyrinth beneath it and the minotaur is in the labyrinth. There is a trap door and the people have to pull it up. I think it will need about five people to lift it up because it's so heavy. It might be the entrance that Theseus used when he went to kill the minotaur. The grass on the other side might be another island or a field and some hills.

The use which Marshall made of Beethoven's *Pastoral Symphony*, and its greater significance to her work, has already been noted. The Plowden Report[21] comments on the unsatisfactory state of music then, suggesting that it 'will have to be tackled systematically and resolutely', a process which still has a long way to go. It notes that ' "musical appreciation" has lately fallen a little into disrepute, partly because what used to be done under that name was often ineffective and partly because, rightly in our opinion, the best way of learning to appreciate music is to make it.' However, it goes on to emphasize that 'there is a place for listening to good music', and any teacher can ensure that children are regularly exposed to such music, given the availability of recorded sound today. 'Young children's listening powers are usually exhausted fairly quickly and the choice of music, the occasion for listening and the duration of the performance all call for great judgement on the part of the teacher. There can be a link here with other branches of the curriculum'. Examples of such usage will already have been noted, and in the context of related arts experiences listening powers can be dramatically extended, to the point where children can become engrossed in the *1812 Overture* from start to finish, wanting to then hear it all over again.

The context involved an examination of the theme of Conflict. This stimulated the use of the *1812 Overture*, with Year 5 children's own making taking the form of visual representation through art work of the forms and imagery suggested by the piece. This was followed by an interpretation and evaluation of the experience in written form. Initially, 'they were not told anything about the piece of music, no one already knew it, they could listen to it as many times as they wanted to — which they did, over and over'.[22] The children made use of content, form, process and mood as a basis, illustrating their 'ability to extend a common vocabulary across art forms'. One child wrote,

> *1812 Overture* — As the music came to my ears it flowed swiftly, first was the light tone, for this I used felt tips and ink. I saw as my vision, a peaceful little house. I saw a pattern with green swift lines and blue lines rather like the sea. It swayed smoothly like the wind, and then came the heaviness. For this I used pastel, paint and dark pencils. The lightness and heaviness were there pushing and shoving, the heaviness roaring strongly — the power was tremendous. The lightness was twinkling like stars with all its might. In the middle I drew a haunted house. I blew with straws, with blue and green ink over the top of it, and there were shadows in the windows. I drew sharp quick zig zags around it with rain tumbling down thick and black, with fierce looking ink at the side. I drew a cat and a mouse, the cat was darting past the hallways and rooms, the mouse scurrying past as fast as her little legs would carry her; for this I used dark pencils with bits of felt peeping in, with the heaviness rolling against it. Paint and pastels over the top gave it a real heavy look, slithering in and out of each other like a snake.

Another pupil wrote the following;

> In our picture of the 1812 overture we used different shades of grey we mixed colours with paint and also did different patterns using pastels and scratching with scissors on top. We did powerful drawings and calm drawings. The pictures were the ones we saw in our heads whilst listening to the music. The patterns and colours were the different tunes we picked out in the music. I did a Grand National because at one part of the music I seemed to hear horses galloping and people cheering. In the music we saw the calm sea right at the beginning, the rough sea came almost immediately after. We put chalk

lines on top of the sea, and rubbed it in. The colours we used for the rough sea were blue and black mixed together. The chalk on top gave it quite a ghostly effect. The rough sea was mostly the main effect because all the way through, apart from the time it went calm, the music seemed to represent a rough sea, and a little boat being tossed about on it. The black streaks coming down were supposed to be lightning. We didn't do them yellow because they wouldn't look right against such a dense black sea.

A further pupil, in a relatively short passage, gets very close to the actual content which inspired the *1812 Overture*,

In our minds we thought of war and battles. We thought of a pattern for the music. It was very hard to think of patterns. At first it was a lot of scribble and then we did the painting. We drew some ships and tanks in our minds and then we thought of the colours for the ships, tanks, aeroplanes and war field. What made us think of war was the powerful music then the soft music made us think of peace again.

— not that correctly recognizing what the content is meant to be is necessarily the point of the exercise! As the 'nightingale and the cuckoo sang their little trills, and the theme wound its way in again' in the *Pastoral Symphony*, one of Marshall's children declared, 'That tune's a swan'.[23]

'I'm going to put a swan in.' I was dubious — swans were becoming a bit of a cliche with us, I felt. I said, 'I don't think Beethoven wrote a swan into it, Bev.' She looked up at me with eyebrows raised nearly to her hairline. 'How *do* you know?' she said. There was no answer to that, so she got her way. Her swan was the most glorious swan ever. . . .

Janet Mills in *Music in the Primary School* uses this extract to make the point that 'we should not let the supposed meaning of the music obscure the music itself. . . . Limiting our thoughts about a piece of music to some known stimulus can limit the listening itself.' On the other hand, Penderecki's *Threnody to the Victims of Hiroshima* 'takes on a whole new level of terror once one becomes aware of the subject matter'.[24] It is therefore of interest that some pupils got close to the underlying content of the *1812*, but equally it provoked an intense level of listening which allowed the imagination to soar.

The Conflict theme focused the children on their own urban environment; the time was that of the Toxteth riots, and the children were confronted with daily media imagery from both newspapers and television. In contrast to that poetical evocation of the Cumbrian landscape already recorded, ugliness now came to the fore:

I switched on the television. The news was on. Riots with mobs and police. Mobs have sticks and stones. Police have guns, shields and plastic bullets. Madness in town. People sent crazy with the noise at night. People crying because their sons or daughters are injured, even dead. I have a feeling of sadness in my body. I hope it doesn't go worse than it is now.

Black and white newspaper big black headlines. Riots and the disturbing madness of the mob. Violence is everywhere. Pushing and shoving. Big black pictures of terror and violence. Just these little words giving me these powerful pictures in my mind. Stabbing and killing, a cry of pain. Oh no, she's dead! Does anyone care? Does anyone have any feeling? Who is guilty?

The children readily identify with the situation, for they, too, live in an urban environment. To conclude this examination of their use of language in creative contexts, a collective piece of writing by fourth year juniors communicates an extraordinary amount of information about the environment in which their school is situated and in which its pupils conduct their lives — a very different world to that of the Cumbrian landscape which so affected Jeff!

A place where there is vandalism and litter
People bustle
cars going too fast along the roads
old people having a chat at the corner
The litter problem could be solved
By a few more bins
but even that might not work.
Some people just can't be bothered
Vandalism on walls
Drain pipes and traffic signs
If Tyldesley had a place
where the teenagers could go
to mess around
Maybe they wouldn't get so bored
No more scribble and doodle
all over walls
It doesn't do anything for them
The Market Place
that is supposed to be done up
It looks like we've gone back in time
old fashioned lamps
black seats
black tree frames
everything needs livening up
bright paint
instead of dull black all the time.

All the shops
they could do with a new lick of paint
shops that are empty
shops that will change over night
From one thing to another
everywhere busy
workman's drills droning on
the clack clack as they hack at the earth.
The one way system
cars that take no notice of Tyldesley
just drive right through it
searching for a parking place
Yellow lines
the dreaded traffic warden pacing up and down
Stray dogs wandering around
It's a nice place to be
but what confusion!

There are current pressures, with moves already afoot, to start penalizing pupils for their spelling mistakes as part of the drive to raise standards. When children give expression to potent ideas such as are inspired by arts engagements they put themselves at risk. They are giving expression to complex and subtle ideas and have to search for the most appropriate word or turn of phrase. They are consciously engaged in extending their use of vocabulary. It is better that they do this in a situation of mutual trust and support than that they rely on a restricted range of words, however mundane, out of fear of making a mistake. We all of us use only a small proportion of the range of vocabulary of which we are conscious. Education should constantly seek to enable children to utilize their range of words to the maximum. Artistic contexts are those best suited to increasing that percentage, especially when approached within the matrix of making, presenting, responding and evaluating. This extended vocabulary then also has the potential to inform and enrich learning in every other area of the curriculum.

Such an extended vocabulary, albeit with the occasional spelling mistake, provides a far better basis for adult life than the use of a safe but restricted one governed by fear. What this chapter forcibly illustrates, though, is that for this to be achieved, a school must have a rigorous set of teaching strategies in place. The fallacy that gave child-centred approaches such a bad name was that all children were naturally creative, and for this to happen, all the teacher had to do was to create a pleasant ambience. Crucial to the strategies illustrated is that of children understanding something of the vast range of possibilities they can draw upon through awareness of the writings of all manner of adult writers, particularly — but by no means exclusively, at this stage of education — those writing for childhood audiences.

References

1   The Plowden Report (1967) *Children and their Primary Schools*, Vol. 1, London, HMSO, p. 19, paras 54–55.
2   Marshall, S. (1966) *An Experiment in Education*, Cambridge, Cambridge University Press, p. 127.
3   *Ibid.*, pp. 172–3.
4   *Ibid.*, p. 186; all the examples of Marshall's children's writing which follow are taken from Chapter 5 of her book, pp. 183–214.
5   *Ibid.*, p. 201.
6   Plowden (1967) p. 220, para. 605.
7   Marshall (1966) p. 164.
8   *Ibid.*, pp. 136–7.
9   *Ibid.*, p. 131.
10 *Ibid.*, p. 171.
11 *The Bullock Report* (1975) London, HMSO, p. 167.
12 Cooke, A. (1987) *Writing: An Art Form for All Children*, unpublished, pp. 84–86.
13 *English in the National Curriculum* (1989) London, HMSO, p. E6.
14 This extract and all other Tyldesley County Primary written examples used in this chapter have been provided by the school.
15 Plowden (1967) p. 220, para. 605.
16 Eliot, T.S. (1963) *Four Quartets*, London, Faber and Faber, pp. 13, 58–59; also *Oxford Dictionary of Quotations* (1985) London, Guild Publishing, p. 202.
17 LeGuin, U. (1968) *A Wizard of Earthsea*, London, Heinemann.
18 LeGuin, U. (1973) *The Farthest Shore*, Harmondsworth, Puffin Books.
19 *English in the National Curriculum* (1989) p. D21.
20 Bigsby, C. (1990) 'North of the cocaine line', *The Independent on Sunday*, 30 August.
21 Plowden (1967) p. 252, para. 689 and p. 254, para. 692.
22 *The Arts in the Primary School: Some of the Arts All of the Time* (1990) Metropolitan Wigan, p. 13.
23 Marshall (1966) pp. 189–90.
24 Mills, J. (1991) *Music in the Primary School*, Cambridge Cambridge University Press, p. 84.

Chapter 7

The Art of Science and the Science of Art: Learning in and through the Arts

To me it seems that all sciences are vain and full of errors that are not born of Experience, mother of all certainty, and are not tested by Experience; that is to say, that do not at their origin, middle, or end, pass through any of the five senses. For if we are doubtful about the certainty of things that pass through the senses how much more should we question the many things against which these senses rebel . . . although nature begins with the cause and ends with the experience, we must follow the opposite course, namely, begin with the experience, and by means of it investigate the cause.

Leonardo da Vinci[1]

In schools where there is work of quality, teachers are always sensitive to the nature of this relationship between the child and the world and to the need to create an environment which feeds curiosity: '. . . an environment where rocks and shells, creatures and bones, grasses and earth are considered together with the vast range of man-made things which surround and fascinate the child. . . .'

The Arts in Schools[2]

The Aesthetic in Nature and the Artistic: Two Essential Areas of Experience

Properly taught, both the arts and the sciences engage children in the full use of their senses. Until recently, the sciences suffered the same neglect at the initial training level that the arts are currently experiencing. The National Curriculum has so changed the status of science in the primary curriculum that, in many schools, virtually everything that children now do is science-led, with some science requirements addressed in purely subject specific ways — but all too often involving little or no use of the senses. In many schools, a whole year's projects and topics are definitively listed in advance on staffroom notice boards, ensuring an inflexibility in learning — inert and sterile, just as Clegg feared, with cursory, superficial approaches to topic work, the arts frequently featuring as little more than servicing agencies for a science-driven curriculum. In consequence, a polarity between science and the arts is developing, to the ultimate detriment of each. Neither fully flourishes in its own right, nor does it inform the other. The consequent neglect of sensory experience, fundamental to both the arts and sciences, is damaging to all children's education.

David Best insists on the distinction between the aesthetic and the artistic; the aesthetic response to nature is distinctly different to that to a work of art, where the response is governed, at least in part, by the artist's *intention of purpose*. This distinction is of particular relevance to primary teachers, who can otherwise believe that they are dealing with all the areas of experience, including the 'aesthetic and creative' when, in fact, they are only dealing with one aspect of aesthetic experience — that relating to natural phenomena — while completely ignoring the whole area of artistic experience. With the pre-eminent position afforded to science by the National Curriculum, and the consequent diminishing of the place of the arts in many teachers' eyes, this is a critical issue at the present time. Given the sheer volume of science requirements allied to its 'core' status, some schools have adopted the attitude that the curriculum must now be science-led, further impairing the balance between the aesthetic in nature and in art. In any coherent curriculum, both should be experienced in equal measure; work in one area is no substitute for that in the other, but this whole field of activity is currently causing untold confusion.

Best criticizes the Gulbenkian Report *The Arts in Schools* for conflating 'the two concepts throughout'. He is concerned to point out the 'greatest educational danger',

> . . . which is that, if the same experience were given by our relation to these natural objects as by our relation to the arts, then we should not need the arts to give the experience. 'Aesthetic education' could be achieved by taking children on nature walks, and encouraging them to be observant in various ways.[3]

The confusion in *The Arts in Schools* to which Best alludes is particularly apparent in the chapter on primary provision. Attention is drawn to an earlier section in the report on the 'aesthetic and creative mode' which states that this 'embraces more than the arts'. The report then continues:

> Looking through a microscope at an insect's wing; examining shells and fossils, plants and the local environment can be rich sources of aesthetic experience. The arts are the characteristic ways in which we record and reflect upon these experiences. Aesthetic experience, like creativity, should be fostered throughout the curriculum, as well as the arts.[4]

It is obviously highly desirable that childen, from the earliest of ages, become sensitive to the wonders of nature in such ways. Indeed, this book places considerable emphasis on the significance of heightened environmental awareness, with it obviously valued as a desirable experience in its own right. However, the key role which artistic response plays in this process is also fully stressed; for the child to most effectively 'record and reflect upon these experiences', a third vital element in the equation is the related study and response to works by artists of all kinds. This study, vital in its own right, also significantly heightens environmental awareness.

Aesthetic Issues and the National Curriculum

This is a particularly crucial issue at the present time. By legislation, the secretaries of state have altered the initial concept of a broad and balanced curriculum for all pupils by making art and music optional at key stage 4. This action is justified on the grounds that pupils can get aesthetic experiences *elsewhere* in the curriculum — but where? Given the construction of the National Curriculum, art and music provided the only *guarantees* of aesthetic experience of the crucial artistic type. It is more to do with chance than entitlement whether or not pupils do gain any adequate aesthetic experience — of whichever type — elsewhere in the curriculum.

The confusion and conflation to which Best draws attention is particularly acute in the National Curriculum *Physical Education for Ages 5 to 16* document. It propounds the notion that the aesthetic comprises anything and everything, from the optional dance component through to anything which, however loosely, might involve the open air and nature:

> Aesthetic experience is concerned with heightened awareness of perceived qualities — qualities of line, form, design, and dynamics. The range of qualities to be found in skilful activities is extensive. For example, outdoor education can play a special role in fostering the value of sensory experience as a basis for appreciation of sensory qualities like light, temperature and texture, and for the aesthetic appreciation of the environment; games and athletic activities can help pupils to learn to appreciate the finer points of form, display and contest; gymnastics and dance skills and movement can illustrate the dynamic qualities which make them so exciting or satisfying.[5]

Everything conceivable is thrown in here — the conflation is complete. There is, for example, the implication that, simply by being outdoors, aesthetic experience takes place — most certainly not the case, even with regard to aesthetic responses purely in relation to nature. The reader's attention is drawn to Chapter 12 of Best's book in this Library, *The Rationality of Feeling*, where he makes specific reference to sporting activities: 'Yet in the case of purposive sports, which constitute the great majority, it is clearly merely a contingent matter whether there is even *any* concern for the *aesthetic* manner of achievement: aesthetic qualities are not *necessary* to successful performance of purposive sports.'[6] It is important that this confusion about the aesthetic and the artistic, or of two distinct categories of aesthetic experience, is cleared up once and for all, for children's opportunities for genuine experiences embracing both aspects can be seriously diminished through confusions concerning conflation compounded by the expediencies of secretaries of state.

We have said, 'by intention', echoing many writers on this subject, but Best also queries this use of words, suggesting that, 'it is intrinsic to an art form that there should be the possibility of the expression of a conception of life issues'.[7] This definition is in accord with that of Abbs, as described in Chapter 1. He refers to Kant, for whom 'aesthetic response entailed an act of sensuous contemplation in which meanings were disclosed', of a perceptual rather than a conceptual nature, but 'nonetheless, ordered, moving and significant.'[8] Through the aesthetic, 'we symbolically discover and extend our nature within nature', a far more profound process than that defined by the PE Working Group, and one which certainly embraces life issues.

In similar vein, Rod Taylor made a plea to the Art Working Group, as set out in *The Visual Arts in Education* that they took greater account of *Content*, following publication of the *Art Interim Report*, in which it barely featured. It is therefore particularly disappointing to see another partial definition of the aesthetic in their final report, *Art for Ages 5 to 14*: 'The capacity to make aesthetic decisions is of central importance in art, craft and design. Here, aesthetic is taken to indicate the principles of taste in art: the study of beauty and, to a lesser extent, of its opposite, the ugly.'[9] This provides only part of the account, with this partial definition focusing only on those aspects traditionally associated with a refined and tasteful elitism. It is most unhelpful. Taste in art is a shifting, rather than fixed, entity and is prone to the fluctuating whims of fashion, as opposed to being founded upon deeper, more significant values. Through the Library on Aesthetic Education, Abbs has sought to emphasize and restore the original meaning of the word *aesthetic* — 'things perceptible by the senses, as opposed to things thinkable or immaterial', states the *Oxford Dictionary*. It was through a misapplication in Germany in 1830, relating it to 'criticism of taste', that the word took on connotations of taste and beauty. It is important that the original broader definition influences and shapes educational thinking in these mechanistic times.

Attitudes as to what is deemed beautiful or ugly in one era frequently change dramatically in another. Taylor, in making his plea, drew attention to the *Observer* photograph, released at the time art educators were still absorbing the Working Group's *Art Interim Report*, of the charred Iraqi soldier dead in his burnt out jeep on the retreat from Kuwait. However 'tastefully' composed, this 'ugly' image addressed the most powerful and profound life issues; the photographer was dealing with artistic considerations of great import, addressing content through the most uncomfortable material of the utmost relevance.[10]

These issues are brought sharply into focus in the relationship of the arts to science in the primary school. It is here that the aesthetic in nature and the artistic can mutually benefit and enrich each other — or their forced separation lead to the relative impoverishment of each! With science taking up around twenty per cent of curriculum time, some schools are constructing science-led projects which unashamedly marginalize the arts, with them then becoming servicing agencies which afford little or no opportunities for children to experience the aesthetic *as it appertains to the artistic.*

Through these confusions to which Best draws attention, many schools can delude themselves that they are adequately dealing with the aesthetic because they *do* encourage the use of microscopes, magnifying lens, etc. — maybe even taking their children on nature walks! Secretaries of state can likewise pretend that they are remaining true to the promise of a broad and balanced education when, in reality, the curriculum is being seriously distorted by denial of proper access to the arts and the artistic. The temptation to capitalize on these misunderstandings caused by conflation is highlighted in the PE document, but is compounded by the inadequacy of the Art Working Group's view of what constitutes the aesthetic.

Positive Interactions between the Arts and Science

Given the, hopefully, temporary distortions to the curriculum created by the phased introduction of the National Curriculum, the arts — mainly coming at the tail end, as they do — have suffered, particularly as teachers have tried to take account of each successive demand placed upon them. From the outset, the National Curriculum was conceived in terms which elevated some disciplines and devalued others. In establishing this new hierarchy, science has become the dominating force in the curriculum, often distorting it to an undesirable extent and to the detriment of other curriculum areas: it is now many years since Read wrote, 'In the end I do not distinguish science and art, except as methods, and I believe that the opposition created between them in the past has been due to a limited view of both activities. Art is the representation, science the explanation — of the same reality'.[11] His words, 'in the past' were written almost *fifty years ago*; they are more pertinent than ever today.

Extending the Science 'My Body' Project through Arts Experiences

In this vein, though, one national initiative which has periodically brought science and the arts together in ways beneficial to both has been the science and health education 'My Body' project. Treated narrowly, 'My Body' can fail to develop much beyond the naming of the parts of the body, children even chanting these in unison as the teacher points to each part in turn on a diagram made by drawing around a child lying on the floor. Once adequately allied to artistic experience, however, this project can come alive through unusual combinations of factual information, scientific scrutiny and felt experience.

One deputy headteacher, conscious of the severe limitations in children simply learning about where particular organs are located, the naming of the parts of the body and the healthy caring for one's teeth, took steps to bring an artist who dealt with the figure into the school so that subtle understandings of a more personal and feeling nature could be addressed. Small groups of children went into the studio of the artist, Melanie Young. The deputy made arrangements to ensure that all the teachers involved 'be released from their classes, [and] can spend some time with Melanie while she is working with the children, particularly in the initial stages, so they can see what kind of approach she has'. This was essential for them to capitalize on what the children experienced there, and also constituted an invaluable form of school-based in-service. She also talked a lot with the artist,

> . . . about what the children were doing in their own aspects of the project and then individually with the class teacher. They were able to pinpoint areas which they would particularly have liked to have developed artistically but didn't quite know how. She's looked at children themselves and their bodies in terms of what they've gone through in the classroom and expressed it through faces, movement, physical appearance of the body.
>
> She's put all these strands together and communicated right through what everybody has been doing. It's a way of expressing to one another what's gone on in a different age band. She's really put across the idea of the well-being of the child, and what it really is that makes us feel well, and happy, and a whole being as a proper person. Their whole delight with their body — with their person if you like — is just coming right out at you.[12]

Insights into Self through Art

An extraordinary example of these mutual interactions between arts and sciences through 'My Body' occurred at our school when Anne-Marie Quinn undertook her first residency, working with a second year junior class. The residency also tied up beautifully with the Amanda Faulkner exhibition at Drumcroon, creating an unusual triangular relationship which led to the most profound realization of 'My Body' concepts, as Glennis Andrews testified:

> A working Partnership: School —— Artist —— Gallery
> Through this partnership a richness was possible that otherwise could have been elusive.

1 A section of 'The Arts in the Primary School' 1993 exhibition of the school's work in the Manchester Metropolitan University PGCE Birley Gallery. It shows the varying scale of work which has arisen out of its partnership with Drumcroon and performance groups, and its use of the environment, urban and rural, including representations of the school building.

2 The main downstairs corridor at the commencement of a new school year.

3 Part of the same corridor showing the school's musical instruments on open display, accessible to all pupils, and an exhibition of textiles and ceramics in support of an African dance residency.

4 and 5   Two displays on the same section of corridor, each following visits to Turnpike Gallery exhibitions, one to 'Ikats' and the other to 'Tune Up'. A Lamp Bookshop display of stories from different cultures is used to contextualise 'Ikats'; see chapter 7 regarding technology work stimulated by 'Tune Up'.

8 Children chose to make interlocking jigsaw shapes as a solution to how best to present their work arising from the Ludus Dance 'Crying Out Loud' residency. (See page ?)

6 A different view of the same corridor showing infant work generated by a visit to Drumcroon's Anthony Lysicia exhibition. On the left are watercolour paintings made out of doors during the visit. Beneath sketches of themselves are plaster panels which directly utilise data drawn from the sketches.

9 Weaving became a well-established school tradition. Every class contributed to the 'Four Seasons' weavings developed in relation to 'Colour, Structure, Texture', a combined science/art Murphy Room exhibition which utilised Wigan Schools Loan Collection art works.

7 An upstairs landing linking mathematical concepts, weaving and 2-D and 3-D structures.

11 Y3 and Y6 pupils working co-operatively in the Y6 classroom in preparation for a Ludus dance residency on the theme of communication.

10 A child using a sketchbook, involved in intense scrutiny and concentration. A section of corridor display, rather than the classroom, provides him with the necessary stimulus.

13   An area of the Y6 classroom showing a wide range of informative art reference material and objects carefully displayed to contextualise and in support of pupils' classroom work.

12   Two children showing a visitor round their school, explaining how the mood of a Y6 classroom environment has been shaped by schools loan, their own work and natural materials all being brought together.

14 A dance residency by the Ghanaian teacher and performer Edith Proctor. The large textiles piece was produced by Y3 pupils in preparation for the residency; it incorporates Ghanaian symbols made known to them in advance by Edith.

15 Anne-Marie Quinn at work in the Murphy Room. The residency spanned two exhibitions, 'Hold, Protect, Restore'phasing into 'Passing Through'. (See chapters 5 and 6 for Vicki's writing about Anne-Marie at work, her use of Content, Form, Process and Mood in relation to the breast feeding pastel paintings on display and other resulting language work.)

16 A Y4 pupil studying an Amanda Faulkner painting in school from the standpoints of Content, Form, Process and Mood. It was made available by the artist at the time of her Drumcroon exhibition and was used in relation to 'My Body' project work. (See chapter 7.)

17   The Murphy Room on the upstairs corridor is clearly signposted for the benefit of pupils and visitors alike.

18   Children in discussion with visitors in the Murphy Room during the inaugral exhibition featuring pupils' work generated by Ian Murphy's residency of the previous year.

19 The design on a puppet booth causes a rainbow to be thrown across the children's model of stages in the life of a river from its source to the sea. This model featured in the presentation to parents about the work they had undertaken in the Duddon Valley. (See chapter 7.)

20 Y6 self-portraits developed from Drumcroon workshop charcoal studies made during their visit to the Lucy Jones exhibition. Lucy was in residence and drew alongside the children. (See chapter 6 for Alex's language work developed from this stimulus.)

21 School-based art INSET with teachers working alongside Duncan Ratcliffe, the school's Enterprise artist at the time. These sessions arose through the reception teacher attending a course at a neighbouring school run by the artist Susan Ross, a member of the Artists in Wigan Schools Scheme at the time.

22 A drawing of the Wigan Pier made in situ by a Y6 pupil while based at Drumcroon during its 'Gerd Winner' exhibition. The project grew out of the school's strong environmental studies tradition and marked the beginning of its close partnership links with the Centre. This study provides vivid evidence of heightened environmental awareness; see chapter 2 for a written example from the same project.

23 Working to a design brief, and in relation to Drumcroon's 'Art of Design' and the Murphy Room 'Hold, Protect, Restore' exhibitions, children made containers to hold a poem, story or book of their choice, each vessel being designed to be in harmony with its contents.

24 Christine Merton talking to children about her work during the construction of her 'Passing Through' sculpture, the waiting mothers in the background likewise finding plenty to talk about.

25 'Passing Through' nearing completion, a cloud of steam rising as tar is poured over the logs, binding them together, by a father, one of an extensive group of parents and friends of the school who assisted the artist throughout the project.

Many of the steps taken were tentative, the results precious. . . .
Surely the 'My Body' science project must somewhere be about
making self-connections, be about exploring, drawing out and making connections with hidden, inner selves, physically and mentally.
Drumcroon, with the Amanda Faulkner Exhibition, offered a wonderful extension to this. Children and adults sharing a viewing and
reading of the work. All of us making our own self-connections.

The exhibition and the work undertaken with the 'My Body'
project provided a context for the testing and challenging of attitudes
and social values that should not be avoided.[13]

Ex votos were a recurrent motif in Faulkner's work and became particularly
important to the children. The artist's use of them derived from the time she
had spent in South America where it was customary to see *ex voto* offerings
on church altars. Made out of wax, these took the form of the diseased limbs
or organs of the friends and relatives being prayed for. They increasingly
fascinated the artist;

> I love the images of hundreds of carvings of bits of bodies on an altar
> . . . I removed it from the religious sphere, or rather re-examined it
> from my own perspective. I made it part of my own language by
> fragmenting the bodies in my work as a manifestaton of damage. The
> woman in the piece is putting herself back together, metaphorically
> speaking, regaining her integrity.[14]

Immediately on their return to school, the children made drawings of
themselves. In many of Anne-Marie's recent works, written phrases can be
discerned, some clearly legible, others fragmentary and mysterious with key
words in focus and others collaged over in whole or in part. Elements of
Faulkner's work rapidly merged with those of Quinn. The children readily
incorporated words into their drawings. Extracted from these, many can stand
alone, almost as poetry. Claire's, for example, gives expression to the most
intimate feelings about her own body:

> delicate thoughts flowing through my skin and blood
> trying to reach a place where they can settle.
> Things I hate on my body.
> relationships
> touching
> hands holding their relationship together
> legs appearing next to my body.
> I hate wearing slippers.
> Lost thoughts.
> Hard and strong, but delicate.
> My stomach is warm and gentle.

Things I like on my body.
Peeling back old to new skin.
Warmth of skin.
I hate the scar on my left arm.
Swirling scarves.
I feel great on the picture of my body.
I love the bit of blue in my eye.
Clothes touching.
I love the wind rushing over my body.
Skin holding me together.
Sun shines through my skin.[15]

As their work developed, the children began to use a range of materials and processes which they combined in quite complex and subtle ways, handmade paper being a crucial central element throughout. Through these means, Claire was able to develop further the initial concepts to which she had given expression, as the artist explains:

Words and ideas that were clarified yesterday and externalised, have now appeared in the paper book. Claire has followed the threads with a lot of her written ideas — linking to different parts of her body. That feels very satisfying — to actually make the connections like that, and draw it all together in her way, back and front, enjoying both her heavily worked tissue and paper 'front', as well as the almost accidental beauty of the back — the lovely qualities in the paper itself joined by raffia and thread, now with words. A joy![16]

The development in Claire's thinking from the first thoughts set down on her drawing are clearly recorded, and reveal how she chose to make use of symbolic ideas derived from the Drumcroon visit well into the project:

The best part of my body is my hands because I can feel my skin and hold things I like. When I broke my arm I felt sad because I had a scar on my arm and the skin had gone. If I imagine the inside of me it is like my bones are gathering round the organs of my body. My skin is a mask to cover up the inside of me.

I think of my stomach as a maze where my thoughts get lost. My stomach is gentle and squashy, but when my stomach rumbles I feel that something frightful has got lost in my stomach and is grumbling. I love the feel of clothing like scarves, warm things that hide old skin. When I feel nervous my stomach goes all tense and tells me my feelings. I imagine the inside of me as dark passages leading everywhere.

We went to Drumcroon to see Amanda Faulkner's exhibition and we saw her drawings. She had about 5 ears and 3 arms floating about the picture. Then when we looked at it closely it had things she liked. I could tell through her pictures whether she was sad or happy. When we got back we did our drawing with charcoal. When I was drawing it I did 2 people on it and me. I did 3 ears, and one arm was in the right place but I put the other touching another. We wrote words and sentences like relationships, and my ears are listening to the rest of my body.

I felt brilliant after doing the work with Anne-Marie. I did two people on it because I like having friends and I wanted to show friendship, I did 3 ears because I was showing my ears listening for messages and my stomach rumbling. I put 2 hands touching because I like the feel of touching hands.

The *ex voto* aspects of Faulkner's work, allied to the layering processes and techniques characterizing that of Anne-Marie, led to developments in the project extending far beyond its customary range and scope. The children's developing sensitivity towards their bodies was further dramatically heightened by a whole new range of associations they were now able to make in relation to the layering methods used in the shared making of a handmade paper book. David recorded the following extraordinary passage about this activity:

We were going to make a book out of paper. We made ourselves. We made the paper out of pulp. When the paper was dry it felt like it was part of me. I felt the paper was keeping me alive. . . . I felt my body was really important. We discussed how we felt about it. . . . The book was of me and I felt I was exploring every part of my body. When we were doing the work with Anne-Marie I felt like I was finding passages inside my body and finding treasures.

I liked wrapping the thread round a piece of fragile thread and it was like skin wrapping round flesh. Because I was writing sentences about the body I was finding a friend in my body. My friend was showing me hiding places. I felt like I was finding a friend in my book. My skin gave me instructions to do art with Anne-Marie.

In similar vein, Thomas wrote:

When I was making my paper and putting pastel on tissue paper I felt I was putting myself together and when I was putting my piece of paper in my book I felt as if I was putting the inside of me in my skin and it felt I was being made. . . . My picture is about the softness and beauty of our skin, and the warmth of my skin. The words in my picture make me feel safe about my skin. I drew clothes on my picture because it is about warmth and safeness of our skin.

As the project unfolded, teacher and artist had to respond with particular sensitivity. The pupils were handling issues of great sensitivity concerning themselves and their own intimate feelings. Were these dimensions too private to share, or in the sharing would the project move further forward? Anne-Marie recorded:

> So now it comes to sharing this with the rest of the class, which I think is a vital part of the process — to share and pass on this enjoyment, this celebration of themselves which has been a very delicate, personal probing and peeling back. But it has to be done carefully — not to be intrusive — both 'parties' have to understand its importance.

Intimate Experiences Shared

Anne-Marie had worked closely with a target group within the class, but the whole class became involved in these deeper layers of significance brought about by the sharing process, a fundamental dimension of all the school's work. In evaluating the project, the school identified a number of key factors which guaranteed the richness and depth of the experience. The children engaged with original art works, in both the school and gallery contexts. They already had experience of making handmade paper — it had been a regularly used technique since its introduction into the school by the artist Elizabeth Stuart Smith, some eight years previously. Consequently, the children were able to use it naturally as a means of expressing and communicating ideas, as opposed to having to find out about a process from scratch. Year 5 pupils became intrigued in the uses of paper, with younger children subsequently assisting older ones to further their practical knowledge of these basic processes and materials. They also had previous experience of using writing creatively, so were used to the idea of translating ideas into different forms. Work in dance supported the project, though not to the same intensive levels as in visual arts. The artist knew the school and the children the artist, and the school's respect and care for the children's work certainly had a part to play in the preparedness of the children to reveal themselves so intimately through their work and their responses to it. Finally, there was a supportive overall school policy.

Also of the utmost importance was the fact that the class teacher was the science coordinator for the school, and was completely in sympathy with the broader dimensions of the project — by no means always the case! She believes that when science is addressed in isolation at this level, it can become very clinical and cold:

> Art puts that different side where there is feeling to it. Feeling is the strength of it in that respect, because it just puts that emotion into it. 'My Body' illustrated this . . . we'd talked about the brain as an organ, and the heart, and so on, and then the skin. But the visual arts

put that aspect of the feeling into it. Because of your brain and you, you have to survive in a sort of scientific way, and if your heart fails, all right — you die. But what I am saying is, you are a person and all these organs fit together to make you — but there is more to it than that! There is a sense of character about you, and what makes people sensitive. I think that has to go with it; I don't like to make them remote from each other.[17]

Some schools have kept their nerve in a period of dramatic imposed change. In these, the relevance of arts experiences is still valued and the benefits to areas like science is becoming increasingly clear. Understanding of a purely factual and theoretical nature then grows into deeply felt experience through practical activities which engage the senses in positive ways. The science coordinator is so adamant on this point that there is no question of the arts being diminished because, whatever the pressures, 'we've got the arts running alongside'. When science and arts subjects successfully come together, the work becomes more enjoyable 'and it is very positive'. She feels that the phased introduction of the National Curriculum has not proved detrimental in any way to the arts disciplines in her own school, because of a clear shared philosophy: 'As for the arts, I do not feel — and I am sure the whole school does not feel — that there has been any great feeling of pressure that, "Oh! We have still got to run that, because . . . it is actually part of it".'

Creativity in the Arts and Sciences

The secondary-based controversies which rage around the separate disciplines frequently bemuse primary practitioners who have an obligation to 'deliver' every single attainment target and programme of study across the whole range of core and foundation subjects as they appertain to the age and level of their children. One such controversy rages around whether an acceptance of the notion of a generic community of the arts means combined arts teaching or not, and arguments that learning to paint a picture in no way help when it comes to composing a piece of music. To the outsider, such arguments can seem obtuse and bizarre and there are those who feel that an insistence on these kinds of arguments has weakened the arts case to such a degree that a secretary of state felt confident enough to diminish further the place of the arts by making art and music optional at key stage 4 in the sure knowledge that deep-rooted divisions among arts educators would ensure fragmented and ineffective opposition.

These arguments have raised further issues about the nature of the arts in relation to the sciences. Best argues that advocates of generic arts operate with 'caricatures of the sciences, mathematics, etc. which, contrary to still-common oversimple assumptions . . . involve, or *should* involve; imagination, intuition, interpretation, creativity *as much as the arts*.'[18] The use of the italics is interesting, for countless young people at the latter stages of full-time education still emphasize that learning in the arts involves them at deep and personally expressive levels at a profound remove from their experiences in other curriculum areas. Whatever the undoubted imaginative and intuitive potential of the sciences and mathematics, this is not being realized for many, many individuals. It is likely to be a long time before this situation is rectified, given current developments and the emphasis on paper and pencil tests as the favoured basis for gauging ability in the core areas of the curriculum. The notion of the arts informing work in the sciences and related curriculum areas is therefore still of vital importance, and it can be realized at least in those primary schools which have an appropriate philosophy matched by strategies.

Limitations in National Curriculum Technology

Since its introduction as a foundation subject, there has been concern about the nature and future of technology. At the secondary level, it comprised the fusion of five previously distinct subjects, but with the role art might play left in abeyance pending the recommendations of the Art Working Group. In the meantime, technology has developed with art's key role ignored, or with it subsumed within technology to the point where it cannot adequately address its requirements as a foundation subject in its own right. Technology at the primary level is more open and less gender hampered, for at the secondary level the two dominant disciplines of home economics and craft, design and technology came into technology with lamentable records of gender-biased approaches. Imaginatively implemented in the primary sector, even in its present form, technology can afford considerable scope for children to explore the nature and properties of materials and their uses, and it would be unfortunate if proposed revisions rendered the subject more narrow in scope, as well as the curriculum as a whole. The revisions as planned would appear to diminish regrettably the scope for design activities of a practical nature.

Addressing Technology through a Gallery Experience

The introduction of technology as a foundation subject led many primary teachers to enquire as to what this 'new' subject was. However, its introduction has helped many teachers to see relationships between different disciplines, brought together through practical activities requiring application of design principles. The school's Year 2 teacher sees art, science and technology as all linked through the understanding of what materials will and will not do. 'What paint will do, what cellotape will do, what pastel will do — all the materials that you use, it might even be just using the scissors properly. Creative art seems the best way of using the materials without the child being inhibited'. She cites the Turnpike Gallery *Tune Up* exhibition as being particularly fruitful in terms of developing technological understanding and awareness:

> Although it was an 'art' exhibition, it was wide open for anybody to take a technological slant on it. You could do cogs and gears and what made things move. Observational drawing from that exhibition led to a greater insight into why the machines worked. It linked the parts, and because most of the exhibits moved the children could see that actually happening. While they were drawing it over a period of time, perhaps an hour, which is a very long time for infants to be drawing and to be concentrating, they could get the mechanism and see the actual mechanics of the exhibits.[19]

The scale of the exhibits was also important. They 'were huge', and the gallery staff performed a vital function, arising out of their in-depth knowledge of the exhibits. 'They had somebody pointing out what was happening and they moved — that was the important thing — they were exciting. They had had gallery visits before, but this was something very different'.

> Their vocabulary was widened and they actually used the words cogs and gears, and we were able to use words like lever and machines. We got a toy as a result with the cogs, and they were able to deduce a lot that perhaps the game wasn't aiming for — it was just a simple little game with cogs. The initial idea was to make a roundabout, but some of the children were beginning to work out that little cogs went much faster than big cogs and that they would get horizontal movement from a vertical cog — they couldn't translate that into their own work, that was too hard because of the limitations of the materials rather than their understanding. . . . It enlarged their vocabulary, both scientific and technological.

The stimulus provided by *Tune Up* stimulated the children to envisage a whole range of possibilities, some of which were subsequently developed in the classroom.

The authority technology coordinator was impressed by the understanding these infant pupils showed. They clearly understood fundamental principles of mechanics and gear ratios through the direct experience of the art gallery. 'They could have gone to the Science and Industry Exhibition in Manchester and seen the same principles at work, without maybe understanding'.[20] The Turnpike exhibits had no purpose other than as Heath Robinson-type constructions. The group fully understood why a half cog was so important, though. Their own large-scale drawings made 'the gallery experience concrete for them'. They added additional bits of paper to their drawings to indicate various parts of machinery with counter movements, or what stood forward in space etc. Inevitably, a considerable amount of 'prodding and questioning' took place to ensure that they fully thought through the mechanisms they were designing. From a technological standpoint, the Turnpike visit made real what so often remain purely theoretical problems: 'How many times does this cog have to turn to move that?'

The teacher also brought construction kits into school. The pupils learned to control movement, they were able to link cause and effect, and began to utilize gear ratios to meet their requirements at an instinctive level. Another important feature of the exhibition, in contrast to much of the technology which still takes place, was that it was gender-free. Both girls and boys responded with equal excitement and interest, while in the classroom subsequently the 'discoveries' of one child were shared with others, once made. Of particular fascination to the children were the 'exploded' cars in *Tune Up*. These were displayed vertically on the walls and generated a great deal of discussion about the relationships between their two-dimensional appearance and the three-dimensional shapes normally associated with these forms and objects. Such insights were further affirmed as the children sought to convey the third dimension in their paintings.

Technology as a New Discipline

Technology is a 'new' subject and primary teachers can approach it confidently in that light. In the secondary sector the picture is more complex and fraught because already existing departments, particularly that of craft, design and technology, laid claim to technology from the outset, invariably perpetuating outmoded practices without seriously addressing the envisaged developments. There is therefore a very real danger that the emphasis on skills-based and uncreative approaches traditionally bedevilling this curriculum area will unduly constrain the broader scope now possible in technology. No such constraints need affect technology practice in the primary school.

Non-Statutory Guidance states that 'Design and technology is an activity which spans the curriculum, drawing on and linking a range of subjects'. It describes 'a way of working in which pupils investigate a need or respond to an opportunity to make or modify something'.[21] It emphasizes the need for pupils to use enterprise and work as members of a team, and to meet deadlines while reconciling such conflicting requirements as 'quality, speed and cost'. 'As their experience grows they will understand that technological development rarely ends, since the evaluation of a product offers new possibilities for improvement'. The Working Group's statement that: 'The various processes involved, such as imaging, modelling, planning, making and appraising are not undertaken in sequential isolation, but interact and feed each other continuously', provides an invaluable link with the aesthetic field of making, presenting, responding and evaluating in the arts.

Technology is fundamentally concerned with design and, indeed, the Working Group had seriously considered calling the whole discipline, rather than one aspect, 'Design and Technology'. NCC felt that this could cause unnecessary confusion. However, technology is conceived as a practical subject, with children learning through doing much of the time, so design is fundamental to, and inseparable from it. It is therefore worth noting the Design Council's description of design used in its *Design and Primary Education* publication, which placed great emphasis on what it called 'design-related activities':

> Design is the way in which we try to shape our environment, both in its whole and in its parts. Anybody setting out to design anything — an object, a room, a garden, a process or an event — will be trying to mould the materials, space, time, and other resources which are available to meet a need which she or he has identified.[22]

With regard to designing, the document continues:

> It requires us to listen to others' suggestions as to how a problem might be tackled, and to others' ideas about how any solution fulfils the function envisaged. Problems relating to design do not simply lead to a 'right' solution predetermined by the teacher or some other authority, but require the exercise of discrimination.

Bearing these aspects of design and technology in mind, it is worth looking at a relatively unusual primary project in that it involved the pupils in the use of basic film techniques and processes. These were employed in relation to the first Design and Technology attainment target: 'Identifying needs and opportunities for activities by investigating a range of contexts', but addressing all four attainment targets in the process of what was undertaken.

Affording Insight into Basic Film and Television Processes

The technology coordinator, in addition to responding to the *Tune Up* visit, was likewise impressed by the technology involved in the Year 6 pupil presentation to adults of their Duddon Valley week early in the school year. She attended the presentation, as did parents and governors. Use was made of all the art forms, but considerable technological expertise was developed in their use of film and media processes and techniques required to make a tape/slide sequence. Pupils often have access to the school video recorder, individual children often being given the responsibility to document a particular event, but tape/slide can prove ideal for primary classroom use. Groups of children made direct use of it during the course of the actual lesson. They learned to control materials in relation to time, choosing and sorting images to match most effectively the messages they wished to convey. It was a real situation, for what they were doing in class was in preparation for a public event. There was an onus on them to communicate their Lakeland experiences as clearly, concisely and as graphically as possible.

Film and Television is the most ignored art form in every sector of education; 'a grand irony', suggests Abbs, as 'film is not only the one unique art form developed in our own century but also the most unequivocally popular'.[23] Secondary sector resourcing problems are, as always, inevitably more acute at the primary level. Nevertheless, through the use of tape/slide techniques, any school can provide its children with opportunities to sequence images, involving their use in real time. Not only can pupils gain insight into the fascinating world of film and television — they are developing essential technological skills.

It has been emphasized that the children live in a somewhat bleak urban environment, and a strategy they are regularly taught to adopt is that of compare and contrast. They consciously make comparisons between their school surroundings and those they encounter in the remote quiet of the rural Duddon Valley. There is invariably an area of the school environment devoted to the juxtaposing of these aspects of their work with that of artists and writers who have likewise addressed one or the other. One Murphy Room exhibition on the theme of the Changing Landscape brought both aspects together, with the delicate plaster works of Sue Peterson providing a distinctive bridging link between urban and rural during her residency.

While in the Duddon Valley, every child has the opportunity to record his or her sensations photographically, as well as through a wide range of other means. This continuous engagement with related imagery inevitably informs their responses and selection of composition and images. Some of the children's imagery effectively captured transitory and elusive aspects of the rural environment. Though they were many miles and months removed when they presented their responses to others, their writing effectively conveyed their experiences: 'Mist, cloudy skies, blowing in the wind. Clouds swirling in the mist. Orange skies, glowing like fire'; 'Shattered rocks surrounded by mist. Ghostly looking skies. Mountains hidden by the scary mist. . . . Sheer drops. The black silhouettes of mountains towering above'; 'Whispering trees chanting in the wind. The towering landscape flooded with nature and colour'.

They had to work to a deadline, with the performance date planned sufficiently in advance to enable the maximum number of adults to attend. A timetable was devised to ensure the most effective utilization of available time. This allowed for an important initial open-ended experimental phase for the pupils to establish an overall 'feel' and flavour. In turn, this ensured greater richness and coherence of form and order once they had to focus on the final shape and sequencing. Important judgments had to be made: which set of images most effectively conveyed a point, and which had to be rejected to make the most telling sequence? The time allotted to specific aspects of the Duddon experience helped the children understand how they can control and manipulate circumstances to their advantage, and the use of voice-over techniques involved the recapping of experiences and their organization in different ways.

The Technology Working Group referred to imaging, and these children were involved in 'mind-mapping', moving sequences around and ordering and reordering these as appropriate. Skills of presentation were being developed, with them recounting a journey that was both physical and mental. The audience was mixed and varied, and the children effectively conveyed what they had done while in the Lakes, and how they had done it. It was a vital experience, both memorable and enjoyable, but certainly not a holiday. The sum total of what was communicated was more than any individual child could have conveyed to family and friends.

There were a number of presentations, the pupils sharing each others' experiences, for the audience also comprised peer group members with others in the class sharing what they had not necessarily seen or done themselves. Simple, but nevertheless extremely important skills were highlighted — putting the slide in the right way round and up, knowing what the correct sequence was for future use, manipulating sound and images so that the children could control and order them, using a light box to organize and sequence thoughts and ideas, redoing to better synchronize sounds with images, etc.

The children were learning about basic film techniques essential to understanding how images and sounds can be organized to communicate ideas and concepts. In doing this, they were harnessing technological processes to meet their needs. These enabled them to communicate with a wide range of people, both peers and adult audience. Parents were given a rich picture of the depth of learning and the insights their children gained during one week in the Duddon Valley and further substantiated in the classroom. Parental confidence in education can easily be eroded in the present climate of blanket media and unending ministerial criticism of education. Here they shared in their children's achievements through the slide/sound presentation and the related displays filling the classroom, with the sequencing idea carried into their written work. Individual pupils' ideas and phrases were extracted and drawn together into one corporate passage, resequenced to give it coherence and meaning, with the children working in partnership. Through such empowerment they could express and communicate vivid word pictures:

Leaves drop as slowly as the night drops.
The air gets filled with the sound of the water's rhythm smoothly
    flowing down with the current.
The magic feeling of the tune of the flowing water of the river.
Ghostly whispering sounds at the birth of the river.
The earth is soft and slippery, springy surfaces, soft and free.
You can feel lonely but be surrounded by many people.
Heavenly white mists drifting slowly unites the ground and covers
    the land.
Mountains seem to be the sides of a hole with everyone and every-
    thing at the bottom.
It's a wonderful view, a place to be treasured.

Restless trees swaying and bending in gusts of wind.
Valleys embroidered with ferns and flowers.
The wind is woven through the moorland grasses.
Shadows of the sun finding places to hide and rest.
The dark green hills protect their patches of murky yellow.
A grey mean landscape just above the fells with the ghostly looking
    fort on Hardknott.
Jagged rocks looking like graves.
All you can hear is the ceaseless river flowing.

Besides gaining invaluable insights into their children's Duddon Valley experiences through this use of slide/sound techniques, parents could also place the performance into a larger whole, understanding something of the depth and breadth of learning a special week had generated.

Utilizing Multi-Disciplinary Arts Stimulus

The school has made use of Drumcroon since the Centre opened in 1980 to the point where many pupils perceive Drumcroon as almost an annexe of their school:

> We go to Drumcroon because it follows with our image. . . . We do displays from Drumcroon, we have them up because we like the artists; Wigan is an artistic place. We have been down to Wigan to visit with our school. There is a link between Drumcroon and our school — it is that they have pictures on the wall. It is important to have Drumcroon because we can understand about art and feelings a lot more. We have workshops and the way people pass on information about the pictures makes me understand more about the life of a picture and how the artist feels about the paintings.

Drumcroon exhibitions frequently extend beyond the showing of just paintings, however, some involving other arts disciplines with the visual arts in dynamic and fruitful ways. When Horse and Bamboo took over the Centre for a whole term, the result was a marvellous coming together of all the art forms in ways emphasizing how the school curriculum embraces more than is prescribed by National Curriculum core and foundation subjects. It underlined Herbert Read's view that the arts disciplines, in total, 'form a unity which is the unity of the harmoniously developing personality'; a unity with profound implications for the personal and social education of all children.

Horse and Bamboo is a community group who bring together 'the skills of painters, potters, actors, performers, sculptors, musicians, printers, weavers, dancers, embroiderers and others to make a work which no person could make singlehandedly'. Their second Drumcroon residency, *Body Image*, was of a whole term's duration. It had many unusual features, the first being that the main gallery took on unusual characteristics. This was no conventional gallery exhibition! Secondly and most unusually, teachers were banned from entering it until the 'Postview' at the end of the term, on the last evening of the 'exhibition'. The catalogue stated:

> We wanted to utilise the power of play to encourage the imagination as fully as possible. The exhibition became a labyrinth, with a personal cassette machine guiding each child through its passageways. Thus participants would all be taken by different routes, each one with its own stories and soundtrack attached. Teachers would be strictly banned (!) from taking part in the exploration of the labyrinth. In part their role would be to draw together the individual experiences of the children in discussion sessions, and help guide the children in the task of imposing some kind of order onto the resulting material. The teachers would also have the support of staff from the Wigan Education Drama Centre and Drumcroon in their efforts to create a performance with the children.[24]

The project turned on its head the notion and usual practice of the teacher being in control, making the important decisions. Even though every attempt might be made to involve children in the decision-making involved in a project or theme, they usually know that most of the initial planning and thinking has already been done.

Twenty schools, covering the full 5 to 18-year age span and including the special needs sector, were involved throughout the term, a representative teacher from each attending an evening meeting with the company and Drumcroon and drama support staff. Schools then made an initial visit, every child going through the labyrinth. Two further visits followed, the first to watch a performance by Horse and Bamboo, the second for the children to perform to the assembled members of the company. There was a six week period between the initial visit and the children's performance.

The children found the role reversals stimulating and exciting; it was they, not the teacher, who were the most informed. One pupil commented that she could tell lies to the teacher without her knowing — not that she wanted to tell lies about what she had experienced, of course! 'Our teacher was confused. She must have found it almost impossible. She felt very frustrated. She felt left out and very jealous. I think she felt very excited waiting for us to tell her what it was all about. . . .' The teacher acknowledged that most of these comments were accurate; the school philosophy is that children should work in an environment that is somehow sympathetic to the project in hand, 'but how did I accommodate this when I didn't know what the source material was?'

Yes, I was confused and frustrated as I sat and listened, trying to make sense of 20 versions of a visit to Drumcroon's main Gallery.

Everyone over-excited, interrupting one another and unable to keep still, a state of affairs that continued for a whole day. A term's work loomed ahead and here was the source material, the inspiration, a verbal and physical tangle of third year juniors. Yes, there was a hint of jealousy. I wanted to see what they had seen. Yes, I did feel excited, because there was an educational risk — the tables turned — I was very confused as to what exactly my role was — where do we go from here? The control and responsibility for their work had been handed over to the children, and they had a stimulus around which they could explore all the areas of the Arts — music, visual arts, crafts, dance, drama and literature.

In the event, the children used their new-found position of power responsibly and the teacher, 'received warm encouragement from the children when they felt our classroom display was reflecting the feel of the labyrinth'. The classroom was near to a spare one — destined to become the Murphy Room in due course — and the carpeted television room was next door, meaning that work could develop freed from the constraints of availability of the school hall. The children were used to being trusted to go off to work something out in a small group as necessity dictated, knowing that there was the expectation that they would return and present their work to the rest of the class.

They would watch and respond, whether or not the piece was fully resolved. Girls and boys worked naturally together in close knit groups, generously helping and supporting each other. They were used to expressing their opinions, and had worked through early stages of experimenting with musical instruments, perhaps in response to an abstract concept or to fit a pattern of movement. Both timetable and timescale allowed for different patterns of group activity, discussion and quite extended periods of concentrated work. 'Their only burden was my ignorance of the material and experiences of the labyrinth'.

The Drumcroon catalogue, normally in every school before the beginning of each exhibition, was made available at the Postview on this occasion. It revealed that the sources for 'Body Image' revolved around five areas of imagery and story, all loosely connected by the central theme of metamorphosis. They were as follows:

i) *The Mask Shop*: Here the children meet a mask maker. They are shown different types of mask, and given some advice on maskmaking. They are told a story about the mysterious transformations afforded to those who wear masks!

ii) *The Shrine*: A cave through which various types of icons can be glimpsed. We try to show how formal devices can create images of secular, or religious, power.

iii) *The Tomb*: A source of stories of resurrection and the 'other world', but also an attempt to deal with the mystery of this one.

iv) *Creation Myths*: A rich source of stories, as well as an excuse to deal with tales, often written for children, which play on the magical transformation of inanimate objects such as toys. 'The Little Tin Soldier', 'Pinocchio', 'The Gingerbread Man', for example.

v) *The Workshop*: For each group of children we provide a workshop in puppetry and mask-making, aimed primarily at widening the definition of the meaning of 'puppet'. In the labyrinth the children also come across a workshop. Here they are invited to make their own contribution to a room full of puppets, totems, dolls, fetishes, and scarecrows!

The mask-making and puppet workshop took place in the Drumcroon basement, following the experience of having gone through the labyrinth. Children had the opportunity to test out their own shadow puppets, having seen the beautiful silhouettes created by Balinese ones. They created bird and animal heads which could be worn, inspired by the sheer size and scale of larger versions worn by Horse and Bamboo members, which they had tried out by themselves.

In the resulting classroom discussion, a common theme which emerged from the children's descriptions of their various experiences was 'Creation'. They found books about creation in the school library and were fascinated by the different interpretations of the Biblical creation story. The teacher recalls:

> We used Greek myths, books in which animals act as humans, and ones in which humans were changed in some way. Books about famous artists were displayed, Rodin, Rouault, Giacometti, Lowry, Leonardo, Michelangelo, the Tomb of Tutankhamen. The idea of gods, idols and worshipping received attention, and an Indian girl spoke about her Moslem faith.

The project rapidly became a model of how much responsibility for their own learning children can take on, when afforded the trust. Their written statements provide invaluable clues to do with their own decisions and reactions to the processes of making and presenting, of great import to teachers worried about allowing such scope and trust. They were conscious of the responsibility involved in being 'in control' of their work, and of how important and transferable the processes they were using were. They also emphasized the need for mutual cooperation:

> After we had seen the labyrinth we thought it was about creation, so we based our play on creation. But you get frustrated when you can't decide which idea to use . . .
> We got a large piece of paper to plan it out on, which was a good idea, because you could cross things out and put different ideas in . . .
> First of all we started off with one big sheet of paper, we all put down our ideas, some of ours were disagreed with and some were

put on the sheet. But if anyone thought of a better idea then the other one got scrubbed out. After that the process got more and more interesting, because we got more and more ideas . . .

The build up on our plans was incredible, because we started off with an empty white sheet of paper, and in a few days we had so much information that we had filled two big sheets of paper. It was like some kind of topic, because their performance, their exhibition, and our performance were all to do with creation.

When we kept discussing it over and over again we kept changing things and crossing them out. This process took a long time but it was worth it in the end . . .

The group's second visit to Drumcroon was to see Horse and Bamboo perform *The Amazing Journey of Cabeza de Vaca*. By this time there was already the beginning of an exciting classroom environment, a resource area of books and photographs, an extensive range of materials 'and a PLAN'. Horse and Bamboo's performance demonstrated a wide range of puppetry techniques, and after watching it the pupils decided that certain further refinements were required:

After we went watching Horse and Bamboo's performance we got better ideas for the play and got a second plan to add better parts in. On the second plan we chose all the characters, but not for definite, so we could change people . . .

We decided to have a male creator and a female creator, because we couldn't decide whether a creator was male or female . . . like a god.

When we did our second plan we started to make things and kept on going to different places to help each other. When we finished with all our things we did it at Drumcroon.

The Horse and Bamboo performance caused the children to reappraise what they were doing in the classroom, with a second plan growing out of the initial one through a very important redrafting process. Further practical aspects had to be sorted out next, and to aid these a mother came in for a day and a half each week. Decisions about scale and size were all taken by the children themselves, and they employed a whole range of techniques and processes in preparing for their performance. They were conscious of working within a timescale, all their puppets, masks and costumes obviously having to be finished in readiness for the performance. The children worked together throughout — nothing was the property of just one person.

The music was also composed cooperatively, with three children deciding to be the orchestra. Sounds and patterns were tried out in conjunction with a group who were practising dance. In the end, the music was composed by the three in response to what was happening in the performance. In one child's words, it 'took a long time to make, but once the musicians had got the idea of it, they kept adding things as they went along'. To arrive at an eventual performance in which all component elements could come together in harmony, many dilemmas had to be resolved. Finally the big day arrived:

> I felt nervous when we set off for Horse and Bamboo, because I did not want to show our play to them. . . . As I first went in I felt shy and tense, and I sat there for ages. I sat there for so long that I went shy again. . . . When Gary put my mask on I felt very confident and knew what I had to do. . . . When we were all in the circle I was relieved because I knew the performance was nearly over, but I couldn't lose control of the play.

All the children, having to do their own performance, commented on how nervous and tense they were on this final visit. One child had been very upset and could not cope with going through the labyrinth alone on the first visit, yet felt able to write after the performance, six weeks later: 'Underneath all the tension and anxiety I was quite enjoying it and I thought it turned out very well. Although I was scared I was confident'.

Reflecting on the event, the children were clear about what they had achieved, and conscious that their performance had been well received. 'They had all applauded so much that I knew we had done very well, I felt radiant and very pleased', yet there were still some hurdles to be cleared: 'I was worried when they asked questions because we might not have been able to answer all of them'. There were also important insights arising out of the performance: 'I like how when you're a puppet or moving a puppet, you can take over control of it . . . this is strange because you can put a little puppet on a big person, and a big puppet on a little person'.

All the work was displayed in Drumcroon but on its return to school the children's was shown combined with the Horse and Bamboo puppets, willingly loaned by the group. The Drumcroon performance was repeated in the school hall for the benefit of the rest of the school. Other classes wrote to the third years about their performance, and it was decided that because there were many interpretations of dance, drama and puppetry, the class would write to every teacher and class in the school, offering two things in particular: they would work with small groups, and talk about their performance, and they would take guided tours around the corridor displays, explaining their own work, that of Horse and Bamboo and the puppets. 'We wrote some letters to all the classes in the school to say we would show them around the corridors because all they saw was everything being taken down, then these puppets being put up, and they walked round and messed with them'. The letters of Christian and Laura are representative:

> I would like to invite your class a few at a time to come with me so that I can show them the display of the Horse and Bamboo Performance. If you could give me a time when you are free to let them look

at the display, I would be happy to show and explain it. Also I would like to meet them in groups just to talk to them about our performance which we did in the hall and ask them if they liked it or if they didn't and what were their favourite bits.

Christian Eaton.

I hoped you liked our play and would you like us to talk about it and tell you what it was about? Also would you like us to show you around the display with the characters on it that Horse and Bamboo used for their performance and the things we used for ours. I would also like to know if you would like to try and make your own puppets for the display and whether it would be convenient or not. Thank you very much for your letters, you had some good guesses on it but most of them weren't right. I'll tell you one thing I wasn't carrying a bird cage and Gary wasn't carrying an orange tree.

From Laura Willis and class 6.

In addition to offering to take other children around their exhibits and discussing the hall performance, Laura adds a third element by inviting other children to make their own puppets and add them to the display, making it an organic entity within the school rather than a fixed one. Two classes responded to this suggestion, making puppets of their own. The one created by Year 3 was very tall and thin, and sufficiently close in quality for the parallel with Giacometti's sculptures to be drawn. This led to the first years coming upstairs to the Year 5 classroom for the Giacometti book, spending a whole session talking about his sculpture in relation to their own work.

These activities extending back into the school, beyond the lifespan of the Drumcroon event, meant that children were practically involved for one whole term and well into the next. Their work embraced all the arts and the project was a model in terms of cooperative learning and creation. The stimulus and expectation at the outset were both high, and the children rose to the occasion through their equally high levels of achievement — with important seeds planted for the future: 'I think we can use the drama again and the confidence we got from performing to other people'.

During the performance they communicated through mime, dance and music, and they created visual effects in relation to these art forms. They confidently discussed what they were doing, and were happy to share, refer to literature, explain how things were created verbally and through visual representations. Their work was recorded on video, and subsequently used in other contexts, while their artwork and three-dimensional constructions became an invaluable school resource — too important to die with Horse and Bamboo finishing at Drumcroon!

I think they took too much time and effort and care to be just deserted and thrown away in a corner and forgotten about; Yes, and I think we did well seeing we're not experienced and we only had about two and a half/three weeks or something like that — I liked the way we worked it out, doing different things, making things, and discussing it. I really enjoyed doing it.

The four phases of making, presenting, responding and evaluating were fundamental to the project throughout. Over a period of many weeks they took a variety of forms, some of which were extremely successful in extending the benefits of an initial stimulus experienced by one group into the wider school community. Far more children ultimately benefited than just those who went on the Drumcroon visits, though undoubtedly some of those will remember the experience well into adulthood. Skilful teaching and commitment ensured that the experience was built upon in many ways so that, in turn, it became a model of good arts practice within the school, but with the three Drumcroon visits unforgettable high points.

On most out-of-school visits, children usually encounter one or two art forms brought sharply into focus, but just occasionally all the arts can combine through ventures of this kind, adding up to one glorious whole. Not only that, but the experience was then shared with younger children who had been unable to experience the Horse and Bamboo labyrinth — creating a wider school involvement. The arts provide the ideal focus for the whole school to come together, perhaps on an annual basis, through participation in projects involving every class and pupil in the school.

References

1   Richter, I.A. (Ed.) (1977) *Notebooks of Leonardo da Vinci*, Oxford, Oxford University Press, p. 5.
2   The Gulbenkian Report, *The Arts in Schools: Principles, Practice and Provision* (1982) London, Calouste Gulbenkian Foundation, p. 53.
3   Best, D. (1990) *Arts in Schools: A Critical Time*, Birmingham Institute of Art and Design, an NSEAD Occasional Publication, p. 3.
4   *The Arts in Schools* (1982) p. 52.
5   *Physical Education for Ages 5 to 16* (1991) London, HMSO.
6   Best, D. (1992) *The Rationality of Feeling*, London, Falmer Press, p. 172.
7   *Ibid.*, p. 173.
8   Abbs, P. (1989) *A is for Aesthetic: Essays on Creative and Aesthetic Education*, London, Falmer Press, p. 172.
9   *Art for Ages 5 to 14* (1991) London, HMSO, p. 55.
10 For further information and plate of this image, see Taylor, R. (1992) *Visual Arts in Education*, London, The Falmer Press, p. 34.
11 Read, H. (1943) *Education through Art*, London, Faber and Faber, p. 11.
12 *The Arts in the Primary School: Some of the Arts all of the Time*, (1990) Metropolitan Wigan Arts in School Publication, p. 45.
13 Taylor, R. (1991) *Artists in Wigan Schools*, London, Calouste Gulbenkian Foundation, p. 19 (appraisal of residency and gallery visit by Glennis Andrews).

14 *Amanda Faulkner Catalogue* (1989) Wigan, The Drumcroon Education Art Centre.
15 Taylor (1991) p. 29.
16 *Ibid.*, p. 29. Subsequent artists and pupil writings are taken from school's documentation of this residency.
17 From a recorded interview between Rod Taylor and the school's science coordinator, Viv Burrows, now deputy headteacher at the school, 1991.
18 Best, D. (1992) 'Generic Arts: An Expedient Myth', Corsham, *Journal of Art and Design Education*, **11**, 1, p. 34. Best argues that Abbs, in particular, but 'like many arts educators', is guilty of this caricature approach; for Abbs' response see *Journal of Art and Design Education* **11**, 3.
19 From a recorded interview between Glennis Andrews and school's Year 2 teacher, Liz Surman, 1991.
20 From an interview with Carolyn Yates by Rod Taylor and Glennis Andrews, 1991.
21 *Non-Statutory Guidance, Technology* (1990) York, National Curriculum Council, p. A1.
22 *Design and Primary Education* (1987) London, The Design Council, ref. 3.3.
23 Watson, R. (1990) *Film and Television in Education: An Aesthetic Approach to the Moving Image*, London, Falmer Press, p. ix.
24 *Horse and Bamboo Catalogue* (1985) Wigan, The Drumcroon Education Art Centre.

Chapter 8

All of the Arts Some of the Time: Communal Celebration and Cultural Festival

Indeed, separate timetabling can place artificial boundaries around activities which, with young children especially, should be seen as an integrated part of day-to-day experience. The most important thing is for teachers themselves to recognise and respond to the opportunities for creative and expressive work which continually arise in the primary school.

. . . there are many opportunities for joint schemes of work involving music, dance, drama, visual arts and the rest — both as part of the daily curriculum and also for specific projects and events. This kind of co-operation can enrich the cultural life of the school in general.

The Arts in Schools[1]

Working Together Cooperatively

The concept of 'some of the arts all of the time' has already been addressed; within the primary school context, a counterpart, 'all of the arts some of the time' is equally worth embracing for some stage in every school year. It epitomizes the principle of periodically bringing all the arts together in a celebratory manner for the benefit of both school and wider community. If we determine that this might also be for *all* pupils, the benefits multiply tenfold. In the process, an invaluable opportunity is afforded to enrich learning and the curriculum and for staff to engage in a vital form of school-based in-service with a potential to develop specific skills and insights of immediate practical relevance. The arts also suffer in some schools because of constraints of space; even in the most disadvantaged, though, it is possible to compensate by shifting the focus sharply onto the arts for this set period of time, their needs then determining how space is used to maximum advantage to provide children with rich artistic experiences.

In emphasizing the differences between primary and secondary practice, the Gulbenkian Report suggests that there are 'very few organisational problems in developing the arts in primary schools. Their success or otherwise leans heavily on the attitudes and resourcefulness of the class and the headteacher'.[2] The above quotation also makes it apparent that these attitudes are equally as applicable to activities which lie outside the confines of the standard school day, though the Report clearly emphasizes the need to establish the arts 'as part of the daily habit of education'. From what has been outlined so far, however, whatever resourcefulness class and headteacher manifest, still more can be achieved when a *whole staff* work together cooperatively, treating the arts as an integral and essential part of a whole-school policy in which they feature as the cultural right of all children. To facilitate this every school should have an arts coordinator who, in addition to establishing standards and values through his or her own classroom practice, also accepts a responsibility in terms of curriculum development in, and organization of, the arts for the whole school.

Organizational problems besetting the primary school have increased considerably since *The Arts in Schools* was written in 1982 — most significantly through the National Curriculum requirements of particular subjects generating strategies more akin to those of more formal secondary school-type timetabling and approaches. It would be equally wrong to discount the influence of those who systematically seek to undermine the primary practitioner with accusations of declining standards, the need to return to 'real' teaching, etc. aimed at imposing ever more formal methods of teaching and organization, allied to paper and pencil testing, with all its limitations: 'Memory should not be called knowledge'.[3] It is all too common to see these and related influences mitigating the creative and imaginative approaches so fundamental to a balanced education and learning in and through the arts. Too often,

> we ask them to expose themselves to a stimulus we provide, whether it is an object or an idea, and moreover we ask for a *total* response, not merely an objective statement or the perfect repetition of an exercise, but for imaginative participation in a situation. Once this is admitted, it becomes apparent that the 'subject' we choose must be worthy of their absorption; we must have confidence that the situation into which we plunge them is capable of bearing them up and carrying them to a new synthesis, a new point of rest.[4]

Living Powers concludes with a manifesto requiring 'that each school develop a coherent aesthetic policy', and 'That each school has at least one yearly arts festival in which a representative selection of aesthetic work is formally and informally presented to the community'.[5] In the primary school, both requirements can intertwine in significant ways, the annual event growing out of a coherent course, with staff and pupils working together on activities which aid mutual trust and development of a shared philosophy. These can then manifest themselves throughout the school year, with the pupils experiencing the arts on an in-depth basis throughout every phase of primary education. This annual event in which all ages participate on equal terms has the potential to extend children's artistic horizons by revealing new aspects, providing scope for the kinds of surprise which can give rise to the illuminating experience. By thus bringing together all aspects of school arts policy, a focus is also provided for negotiation with the secondary sector, essential to facilitating the closer ties necessary for the achievement of a more seamless arts education; too many pupils still experience a disconnection in their arts education in the transfer from one phase to the next.

Reappraising the Christmas Service and Nativity Play

In many schools, Christmas is the time when a coming together of the arts traditionally takes place, through the focus of a carol service or nativity play. Performances can be stereotypical in format and content, though, with little variation from one year to the next, offering little scope for pupils to interact as active participants because of their clichéd nature. Children often recite predictable lines composed for them by adults. Equally, these events are essentially extra-curricular, unrelated to other learning taking place throughout the year. The curriculum, normally sacrosanct, is now abandoned — possibly for several weeks. Countless rehearsals and the memorizing of lines and stage directions take over. Invariably the privileged few obtain the prize parts, the majority having little or no worthwhile involvement. The overriding requirement that an essentially adult audience is impressed leads to a contrivance which has little or nothing to do with the children themselves or their educational needs:

> One Christmas we did 'The Twelve Days of Christmas'. . . . We got 'Seven swans a swimming' and they virtually told us what to do. . . . They drew the swan shape for us and we had to stick the bits of rolled up tissue on — it took us hours doing them, and we had to stick all these stupid bits of paper on the shape of the swan. They even drew the beak in for us and everything. . . . I suppose the teachers did as much as they could to make it look respectable. I suppose they felt that when we were left to do them on our own they looked a mess.[6]

Examples are legion of teacher-controlled activities of this type, affording little or no scope for pupil creativity of a dynamic, imaginative and interactive nature. Sometimes children do rebel — apocryphal stories abound, such as the child acting the inn-keeper saying, 'Yes, come on in, there *is* plenty of room in the inn'. Given current approaches to parent power and the Parent's Charter these pressures are increasing, the limitations and shortcomings of many adults' own educations becoming criteria for imposition on their offspring too; the desire to replicate one's own education, as opposed to children receiving more in the light of changing needs and circumstances, can be strong and pervasive. Parents have a vital role to play and should obviously be actively involved in their children's education, but ideally through a closer partnership with the school and based on an understanding of its aims.

The above contrivances need not remain the norm. The principles and types of provision and practice outlined in this book provide a philosophical and practical basis for performance events of a genuinely educational type to become a focus for a whole school involvement of a creative, imaginative nature. Long-term preparation and follow-up rooted in the mainstream curriculum characterize them, the actual presenting providing the central hub in an extended programme of learning set within a larger framework. Such projects provide a basis for all staff to become involved in school-based arts INSET capable of informing their work throughout the school year.

Our case-study school is situated in an area where the Afro-Caribbean and Asian community comprises less than 1 per cent of the population, with the Christmas service still very much part of the local tradition. What is actually presented is, in fact, at a far remove from the conventional evening of this type. The school consciously retains the word 'service' and selects a range of carols the audience can immediately recognize and sing, providing something to hold on to while the pupils address issues of import to their lives in society today. The International Evening is the equivalent in communities with a different ethnic mix, the main principles being eminently transferable. International Evenings drawing upon fundamental aspects of curriculum content likewise avoid the pitfall of tokenism and can further nourish and enrich the mainstream curriculum. In this modified form, therefore, both the Christmas service and the International Evening can address current national and world issues commensurate with the needs and concerns of all their pupils.

Transitions, Timescales and Some Essential Stepping Stones

Worthwhile curriculum development takes place over considerable timescales — the success or otherwise of a national curriculum can only be gauged over many years! In this light, it is worth examining how the school's Christmas services, in keeping with the above criteria, evolved. In the process, many of the principles already outlined in this text are inevitably reiterated. Prior to Wigan's involvement in the National Arts in Schools Project in 1986, the annual service incorporated presentations from each junior class, but in the form of separate performances not drawing upon curricular work. Presentations were specific to the event, without a common link other than that of the forms used — work in music, drama, art, etc. Corridor decoration was determined by the season, and was quickly put up and taken down again, making it expensive both in terms of time and materials.

The form of the service was that of community carols interspersed with the retelling of the Christmas story, all done in a candlelit setting. It contained various musical presentations — singing and large recorder ensembles, and was coordinated by the school's music specialist. When she left there was a dilemma about what to do. Nobody was capable of orchestrating a performance of that type. This led to a shift towards other types of performance.

The thematic form dates from 1987. The intention was to focus on something that could be reflected through the whole school, informing the curriculum and growing out of it, extending in relevance beyond the Christmas season. Themes were negotiated, the shared decision involving all junior staff. Staff ran their own form of INSET in order to generate and share ideas prior to involving the children. The themes addressed each Christmas to date are:

1987 — Harmony and Discord
1988 — The Earth and Our Responsibility to It
1989 — Rhythms and Cycles
1990 — Links
1991 — Journeys/Passing Through

All four junior classes worked on these themes. The infants present their own nativity play, with each class also working around a theme, but with both juniors and infants contributing to the overall school environment — everybody is thus aware of the environment and its significance.

Preparation, Planning and Practice

Planning for the Christmas service starts just before the autumn half-term, the common theme arising out of the initial staff discussion. It provides a basis for the event itself, incorporating ideas and issues already developed in the respective classrooms, extending curricular work as a whole and feeding into future planning. The theme has to accommodate a broad range of values and interests, worthy of the children's absorption and able to carry them to 'a new synthesis, a new point of rest'. Staff discussion is rigorous and references are brought together for consideration, prior to use. These are selected to range over time and place, taking account of national and international perspectives. Such issues-based approaches can prove controversial:

> We do take world issues. I remember when we took the issue of Third World Poverty, at the time of the Ethiopian trouble. A number of the parents said, 'Do you really think they understand this?' They probably think, 'When I was that age I knew nothing of this', and perhaps some of them want to be kind, in a way. Perhaps nowadays people just see it on the news and think, 'Oh, it's that again!' So for them to actually understand, yes, children can actually be brought into issues and can understand. It could be just as basic as looking at similarities and differences: 'Well, how are they different to us? What

do they have that we do not have? What do we have that they do not have?' You might just take it at that level.[7]

Staff have to be clear about the scope and importance of the work prior to sharing it through discussion with their children. It is necessary for each to retain an openness to ideas if they are to involve their children fully in the subsequent negotiations necessary to determine the class's contribution and form of presentation.

> We start working on that Christmas service at about October, after the half-term when we come back. So basically we have got about five or six weeks. But it is absolutely intense work. The junior staff decide on the theme, and then we work for quite a while deciding which aspects to deal with. Each teacher tends to choose their own but, having said that, the children within the classes then tend to go through an exploration of whatever strands you have taken out of that theme. Sometimes, of course, you go back to the children and say, 'This is our main theme. What aspects should we look at?' They work very much in the planning of it and deciding what is to go on, and the formation. So they see it from an absolute nothing to the final drama or piece of dance, or whatever.

Through the range and nature of the experiences provided over many years, children are enabled to make informed choices regarding the communication of ideas, utilizing a wide range of arts practices. From Year 3 onwards, using shared themes, they systematically build on practical experiences founded upon making and presenting, allied to ample scope for response to and evaluation of their own work, that of their peers and of established arts practitioners.

The way in which chosen themes are translated and interpreted rests with each individual member of staff, but regular meetings ensure all staff are aware of overall structure and planning. At a later stage, agreement is sought as to how the evening might fit together as a whole, taking account of the varying form and content of the presentations. Considerable thought goes into how aspects of the theme might most effectively be communicated, taking account of the arts scope already available within the school — dance, drama, music, singing, puppetry, visual arts, choral speaking, individual statements, slide projections, sound effects, etc.

> One value is that the whole junior department work so intensely for those five or six weeks, but it is perhaps the only opportunity in the whole year we actually get to work as a whole department. Also, mine see what Year 6 are doing and what Year 3 are doing, and how it links. They see what is going on and they know what is going on in the meantime, and when they see how it all comes together, it's amazing, because they say, 'Oh, yes! That goes with this, and they've

done this because. . . .' It is lovely the way they see how their part, which may be a quarter of the whole, fits in and why it fits in. . . . It is actually a process of thought and a process of working.

The actual presentations, supported by displays within the school environment as a whole, take place on a raised stage in the main school hall, using staging units borrowed from a local secondary school or other local institution. The units are adaptable, allowing for different arrangements and placings within the school hall, providing a fresh impetus and different scope each year. The size of the audience makes it necessary that the subtleties of dance and gesture are made as visible as possible — an important consideration in terms of building individual confidence. Each class presentation is interspersed with a traditional approach to lusty carol singing, with all the audience participating. The Year 4 teacher admits that inevitably,

> We always get people who say, 'What has this to do with Christmas?' It is running the tradition with this other strand. We actually keep that basic tradition of the carols and the Christmas readings, but we try to put it — with the readings more so — into some sort of relevance for what we are about . . . I think there is a total trust in what we do and what we are about, and there has got to be that.

The only circumstance in which there might be hostile challenges would be if neither school nor curriculum were stable: 'Parents know what we are about'.

Pit Prop Theatre Links and Issues-Based Approaches

Each Christmas service has a broad enough theme for each class to take a distinctive aspect, and it is generous enough for major contemporary issues to be addressed. For many years, the school has enjoyed an extremely close working relationship with Pit Prop Theatre, who work in Wigan schools on a regular annual basis. Their work is issue-based, and *Blood Lines* was to have an important bearing on the content of the 1989 Rhythms and Cycles service. *Blood Lines* vividly illustrated the power of the arts to provoke and challenge accepted attitudes, dealing with issues of race and colour. Concept areas covered included justice, nationality, freedom, racism, difference, discrimination, power, exploitation, violence, truth and falsity. It was a comparative study, spanning the thirty years from 1959 to 1989 — from post-war austerity to the credit boom, National Training to Employment Training, and colonialism to colonial independence, covering issues of immigration, discrimination, deportation, and racist abuse.

It was designed for top juniors and Pit Prop performed it to Y6 pupils during the autumn term of 1989. It, and the extensive support material, afforded many opportunities to explore ways in which we use language to convey particular meanings, selected key words being *neutral, positive* and *negative*. How and why do we give certain words loaded meanings? The teachers' pack included the following passage,

> Although coloured immigrants have been present in Britain for cen-
> turies, it is only since the early 1950s when Commonwealth immi-
> grants flowed into this country from India, Pakistan, and the West
> Indies, that the colour question has become a problem.

Why not 'black people' instead of 'coloured immigrants' and 'were urged to come' instead of 'flowed into'. Is 'the colour question' the same as racism, and 'a problem' for whom?

In support of the drama, the children were also introduced to such litera-ture as the books *The Fat Black Woman's Poems*[8] . . . by Grace Nichols and *I Know Why the Caged Bird Sings*[9] by Maya Angelou. Questionnaires ensured that facts as opposed to myths were addressed — the actual percentage of black people in relation to population as a whole (4 per 1000), for instance. The teachers' pack included the statement:

> The characters in the play are real for the children and they represent
> a black presence in the class which could be crucial in follow-up in a
> white or predominantly white group, to enable work to come from
> concrete black experience rather than suppositions (abstractions) which
> could be mistaken.
>
> Their importance is also in helping children clarify their thoughts.
> They will have identified with different characters, agreed and dis-
> agreed with them, and in thinking and talking about them will ex-
> press their positions on various issues, which they would be
> hard-pressed to touch on in a theoretical, abstract way.

The pupils' responses to *Blood Lines* are well documented, and illustrate how powerfully they were affected by the piece — and how they were indeed able to 'clarify their thoughts' effectively concerning issues of importance to all of us in a modern multicutural society.

> Sad is a lonely and confused feeling, the only way to get rid of sad-
> ness is by laughing and joking. Tina was sad when she first came to
> England, and all the people rushing past her and not stopping to help
> her. I feel that Joe was sad because of all the people calling him. I
> thought that Joe's mum was very sad when Joe died.
>
> I felt confused because one minute Michael is Joe's friend and then
> he's not. I think this is because Michael doesn't want to be called
> because he plays with a black boy. The feeling of sadness was on me

when Joe died, and when Michael had shot Joe. Michael was the only friend Joe could rely on at the time, but that gave Mike an advantage to use Joe. Earlier Joe was the only friend that Mike had, but he could have got rid of Joe when he got some more friends. The sadness comes when you have lost a friend or when you see someone being cruel to someone or something. The feeling of sadness can hit you and make you hurt. Also it can be turned into courage and give you advantage in fights.

Contrary to widely held views during the Child Art era, even relatively young children are able to draw upon the full breadth of their artistic experiences in relevant contexts, demonstrating the significance of the relationship between vertical and horizontal axes; *Blood Lines* was destined to surface again in the 1989 Rhythms and Cycles Christmas Service.

During the same term Y5 were working with Horse and Bamboo on a performance of the Book of Hours, using rod and shadow puppets, utilizing their own music to evoke the mood of the month of February as shown in Le Duc de Berry's *Très Riches Heures*. Planning for the Christmas service at the end of the term made use of this performance developed over the whole term. A central focus was to be the large puppet booth representing the February plate of the book. So as to make use of this and significant work developed in other classes' work, the theme of Rhythms and Cycles was chosen. Y5 had a fresh angle from which to explore their work, move it on and further develop it.

Year 6 were given a complete explanation of why Rhythms and Cycles was chosen as a theme, but chose to override their teacher's explanation completely when making their evaluation of the service. As far as they were concerned, the theme had grown directly out of their work on *Blood Lines*. In looking at the life and happenings of the late 1950s and comparing them with the present, they saw a rhythm in regarding similarities and differences echoing through the years. They had examined relationships interrupted by prejudice, lives altered by discrimination suffered by individuals and groups — our very existence was a cycle and our lives had their own rhythms. This led to an examination of happenings that could alter or prevent a rhythm or cycle having its rightful pattern. In this way, personal experiences probed in the drama piece, the subsequent examination of these and a probing of their own lives and attitudes had become more powerful than the choice of a theme determined by another class's examination of it in nature and the seasons. Their view was further influenced by groups within the class discussing the rhythms and cycles of fashion, again leading back to comparisons they had made between 1950s and 1980s styles.

This Christmas service all started on rhythms and cycles because of the Pit Prop play, we got rhythms from prejudice, how death interrupted the rhythm of life, the cycles were the cycle of life.

> We decided to do a piece of movement about the Berlin Wall because walls don't have to be built by bricks, they can be built by prejudice. We watched a play by Pit Prop and the story showed prejudice and discrimination.

> We decided to do the Berlin Wall because it shows how the wall can affect the rhythm of life and how conflict can separate a whole city of people. . . . We thought we would do it because it shows the people being friends, then conflict happening between them, then a wall splitting them apart. After the years people have thought about it and think if they could be friends and they could travel into the other half of the city, so the wall gets knocked down.

Their hold on this rich vein of stimuli led to important explorations of various art forms and the potential of each to facilitate the most satisfactory marrying of form and content:

> Dance and music explained it clearly because we showed how the conflict started and then the music showed the conflict.

> I chose to be in the movement because it was interesting and it is better than speech. . . . The music fitted with the movement because you could tell what the next feeling was.

> I think dance is better than speech because I can understand it better, because of the way people move and the expression that people gave on their faces and all the gestures on the movement. I would rather use my own interpretations in movement.

> When we put the music together we had to get some instruments together then we watched the movement then tried to put music to it. When we had the main idea we would go and see if we could make some music then we'd come back and try and put the music to the movement, if it didn't work we would stay in the class and make music to the movement. Then when we had got the main idea of all of it we would go and practise, and in the end we would keep on practising until we got it perfect.

Both axes of creativity interacted dynamically with each other, enabling the children to make the kinds of lateral connections so essential in a rapidly changing world. Once pupils become active participants in determining content and its formal means of realization, we move worlds away from the predictable Christmas service which remains constant from one year to the next. The arts provide an extraordinary vehicle for explorations of this nature when children are provided with access to the whole aesthetic field. Equally, the major life-issues being addressed demand generous timescales; deep-rooted prejudice and attitudes cannot be dealt with in a single forty minute Personal and Social Education (PSE) lesson!

A School Puppet Tradition

An invaluable art form within the primary school with extraordinary potential to bring all the arts together in purposeful ways is puppetry. It can involve children in a wide range of visual arts practices demanding constructional skills using two and three dimensions and textiles processes, lead to imaginative developments in dance and drama within musical contexts, and the writing of stories, plays and texts. Children can easily envisage the whole by creating environments on a scale they can practically control and realize. Puppet making enables children to meet many National Curriculum technology requirements in realistic ways. Children normally reluctant to perform in public often lose their inhibitions in identifying with the characters they are bringing alive through puppets of various types and scales.

The puppetry used in the Horse and Bamboo 'Months' work was given a further influence in the school by developing what was begun in 1988. Through participation in a Drama Centre puppetry project the school, with the support of the Drama Service, staged a series of workshops. Year 4 pupils then created a historically based performance based on their environmental work, utilizing their investigations of the road on which their school is built. Part of the Hogarth Collection of puppets was being exhibited in the school at the time, providing rich and relevant references on which to draw. This project was then displayed at the Turnpike Gallery in a Primary Science and Technology Fair during June 1988.

The following year, as part of the Wigan Performing Arts Festival, Nenagh Watson and Rachael Field presented a new puppet performance in the school called 'Discarded Memories'. Some of the art and written work is still in the school, and is used and reused to this day — Anne-Marie Quinn reclaimed some of the writing as part of her Murphy Room environment, and other creative mapping pieces became natural parts of the Passing Through displays relating, in turn, to the 1991 service around that theme. Another special feature of puppetry is the way children readily pass on to others the use of puppetry, thus developing and sustaining the tradition. Uses of puppetry in 1992 have clear resonances which extend back to 1988 and earlier.

It is interesting to note that the large puppet booth used in the Horse and Bamboo work and in the Rhythms and Cycles Christmas service was used again the year after for the Links theme — an appropriate passing on and link! Likewise, some of the work in that service was communicated most effectively by bringing together shadow puppetry, dance and music. In the Murphy Room, Quinn also made further use of a weaving originally constructed outside as part of an Earthworks project:

It's a weaving, a network of a web. . . . We did the web as part of the sculpture trail, at first as a try-out to see if anybody messed it up. Then we decided to keep the web as the main one. . . . The web was constructed by forming networks from the tree to the [school] sign. We used wool and string as materials to make the web. We used these materials because they are best to do a weaving with. . . . The web looks very fragile but when you keep weaving the wool in and out and making networks it makes it very strong and hard to get through. . . . We thought we could weave around the tree as well and make the tree locked in the weaving like a fly caught in a web.

Earthworks and the Origins of 'Passing Through'

The origins of the 1991 Passing Through service can be traced back to the summer term of 1990. Earthworks was an authority-wide initiative over a half-term period, planned in tandem with the related Drumcroon and Turnpike Gallery exhibitions. One secondary school converted an art room into a rainforest, creating a labyrinth which left the visitor unaware that it was in a conventionally shaped rectangular room. There were bird forms and sounds and, on completion of the project, Greenpeace took away all the materials for recycling. What often remain as vague concerns became extremely real to the pupils through a project which involved them in directly interactive ways.

The *Sticks and Stones* exhibition in the Murphy Room (see Chapter 3) was conceived as part of Earthworks. The title related directly to *Blood Lines* — a sheet with that title, focusing on the derogatory use of names, contributed to the support material. It now provided a focus for both exhibition and school sculpture trail. Each class considered how it might fit into their environmental work, and whether it was worth 'putting something extra' into their planning. The school's overall planning emphasized that 'Sticks and Stones needs to be a Cross Arts and Cross Curricular Project, with the possibility of being inspirational for our approach to environmental work';

The idea of PASSING THROUGH   Passage, transient, transit, memories, Naming places, Crossing barriers — real and imaginary. 'Rites of Passage' one stage to another. Maps.

'A walk is just one more layer, a mark, laid upon the thousands of other layers of human and geographical history on the surface of the land. Maps help to show this'.

The importance of JOURNEYING   How and why we journey. Aboriginal journeying. Shrines. Cairns. Ancient stone circles.

ALSO Standing stones, Prehistory/Mystery. Relationships between the person and nature. Weathering. Shape. Symbolism. Japanese gardens. Skeletons — Museum Loan.

The project would involve a tree count in the district, 'with possible links between schools to collect the information. We will also be planting new trees in a nursery tree area'. The desire to 'plan different routes' to a neighbouring primary school was to lead to a deep interest and insight into the work of Richard Long.

It is interesting to relate this project to the National Curriculum Art requirement that, by the end of key stage 3, 'pupils should be able to ... identify the conventions used by artists and assess critically their effect', leading to the programme of study that they 'explore diverse ways that artists working in different cultures produce images, symbols and objects, recognizing the main codes and conventions used to convey meaning'. As illustration, the accompanying non-statutory example is provided: 'Pupils could discuss and compare the various ways in which artists have represented journeys; e.g. Chinese scroll paintings, Aboriginal dream maps, Turner's notebooks and Richard Long's walks'.[10] The school has yet to do justice to Chinese scroll paintings; all the other examples are well known to its pupils. Many now readily identify with Richard Long and his work, for his activities relate to their own. On their visit to the nearby primary school, 'we counted how many steps it took us and how many trees we passed on the way there. . . . Altogether it took 3,751 steps and altogether we saw 195 trees'. It is also commonplace for children to collect materials associated with a particular point in the environment to be subsequently utilized in school-based work. *Sticks and Stones* demonstrated that primary pupils are able to make sense of Long, Turner and Aboriginal walkabouts if these are presented within properly thought out contexts.

Some understanding as to what constitutes sculpture was essential to the project, and each year group attempted to define what they thought sculpture was:

Y2 — Like a skeleton; Something in your head that's round like the world.

Y3 — Posh people have them in their houses; Like a pot; Something made of clay/wood.

Y4 — Something which is hand made, and has a shape and not flat against a wall; A piece of art from the mind or imagination, carved or moulded into a shape or form from different kinds of material.

Y5 — Clay and all kinds of bits and pieces put together and made into an art work; Something that is three-dimensional. I think that structures are sculptures like if you do a model.

Y6 — A piece of art that is three-dimensional and put on display; A chiselled shape made out of stone; Something that is not flat.

The sculpture trail would comprise Internal and External Trails, with existing material providing a basis: a plaster relief in the school entrance, made by pupils following their Duddon Valley visit working with Enterprise Artist Duncan Ratcliffe, who was based in the school for a while, the pig sculptures commissioned from Ted Roocroft, weavings and plaster figures. Each class could feature something for inclusion in the trail. The Year 2 teacher, for example, suggested an assortment of stones on a table to be moved around and 'patterns made with them or just enjoyed for themselves', while another class 'are building a totem pole'. The External Trail would be created during the half-term of the exhibition and 'will fit directly with *Sticks and Stones* . . . using the areas around the trees and the Wildlife garden. "I like the idea that art can be made anywhere, perhaps be seen by a few people, or not even be recognized as art" '. Year 4 pupils worked with Year 6 to create a guide around the sculpture trail in the form of a map with riddles and stopping points. All the information and the form was worked out on a large format, covering six tables, making it accessible to a number of pupils at a time, before reducing it to its final A3 scale.

Picking up on the Japanese garden idea, Year 5 helped construct a piece in the centre of the Murphy Room, complete with fountain. They called it 'Kokoro-Mochi', and the school's exhibition catalogue described it as follows,

> 'Kokoro-Mochi' is a sculpture which uses stone, wood, water and vegetation. The initial stimulus arose from talking about how buildings and landscape 'aged' (the weathering processes that acted upon them). We discussed how we could show this weathering process in the form of a sculpture. . . . The idea of the water 'dripping' onto rock and or/wood emerged strongly. It was felt these materials linked in best with the 'Earthworks' title.
>
> Emotionally, the sculpture has had a strong impact on all of us. It is seen as soothing, peaceful, a calm piece of work particularly in the restful atmosphere of the Murphy Room . . .
>
> We hope visitors to our sculpture approach the work in a quiet and reflective way. To look, to listen and enjoy, and to feel enriched in some way.

Two Year 4 Gallery Visits

In May 1990, as Year 4 pupils, the 'present' Year 6 had visited both the exhibitions associated with Earthworks, 'Changes', the Andy Goldsworthy exhibition at Drumcroon, and 'Time and Place' at the Turnpike Gallery. They were particularly responsive to Goldsworthy's work, having visited Changes first:

> There was the large sculpture in the Main Gallery of the circle and of the twigs. They found that fascinating, because when we walked in

it just hit them. I can always remember them just sitting there, and whoever was talking to them they just could not take their eyes off this. The thing they could not understand was how he had got this perfect circle in the middle, because they had some experience of working with materials, but they could not understand how he had got such perfection — for to them it was sheer perfection![11]

They saw a video while at Drumcroon, including film of the artist at work in the Antarctic:

The children were absolutely enthralled with it . . . we'd talked about people working in this way, and to see something like that makes it real, and to see the real person there in the snow, they thought that was wonderful — and the snow sculptures he made and the ice ones!

Back at school, they played a significant role in the construction of the External Trail:

We worked, really, through science and technology, and it was environmental. We decided we would like to make a Sculpture Trail. We decided we would not put it in the school, but actually out of school as near as we could put it to our natural environment. They worked in groups. Each group decided for themselves, first of all, what materials they wanted to use, and then what form their sculpture should take, and then where they would like to site it. They decided where they would like to put it and why they would like to put it there. So it was real technology-like planning and designing.

They all

actually did work in different materials. One group with twigs, another with slate. Another group worked with stone, another one wanted to work with reeds and leaves and different plant material, really, as a weaving. They decided they wanted to do something to make the hall steps at the back of the school where the railings are, a lot more attractive. So that was where they decided to work.

In the process, they discovered a great deal about the nature and properties of materials — 'they were really hitting problems!' A group making a twig ring discovered that only certain types of branches would bend, but cuttings from the headteacher pruning her willow tree came to their aid. Some of it looped out as it grew, but no way would they resort to using cotton or string: 'It had to be natural'. So involved in this concept did they become that they accused Y6 pupils of cheating by using string and the like. It had to be explained that they 'hadn't been to Andy Goldsworthy, and they weren't following the same line of thought as we were'. Accepting that two distinct lines of thought can legitimately be simultaneously followed was an important learning experience, especially as they felt so strongly about the values implicit in their practice.

The Construction and Siting of the 'Passing Through' Sculpture

The central focus of the Turnpike exhibition was a large installation piece constructed by Christine Merton — 'The main feature of Christine Merton's work — an installation based on the traditions of past industry in the local area and the use of a Turnpike as a stopping point on a journey'. The artist used materials representative of the dying local industries. North West Arts, the regional arts association, provided funding to locate the piece permanently in the local environment, a country park seeming the obvious location. However, the warden, supported by a vociferous councillor, took exception to the abstract nature of the work and vehemently opposed its siting there. Would such opposition kill the project?

An obvious solution was to site it in a school's grounds — an obvious aim being that of producing more informed and aware adults in the future. The school had recently acquired an additional area of land for use as a wildlife area — an obvious location and one where it would be used and cared for. Christine Merton took up residency at the school for a week to work on and supervise construction of the sculpture. The Turnpike Gallery Officer at the time of the exhibition had clung tenaciously to her desire to locate the sculpture, though it would have been easier to give up through sheer frustration. She naturally took great interest as the sculpture took shape in its new home during that week.

> Prior to the residency children at the school had been jointly responsible for many of the elements involved in the planning and development of the outdoor site, with its landscaped and wildlife areas. Teaching staff and the school's artist-in-residence (Anne-Marie Quinn) had also been working with children investigating the theme 'Passing Through', the title of Christine's sculpture, and the title of a previous project she had devised relating to the piece which she used when the work was first installed in the Turnpike Gallery.
>
> This preparatory work with the children was invaluable in giving them a greater insight and understanding into what would be involved during the week and the inherent meaning of the sculpture. At the end of each working day when special time was set aside it enabled them to discuss with confidence the work that Christine was doing with them, and made links between their own work in relationship to hers. Groups of children came to the site on a regular basis

throughout the day, recording progress through note taking, drawing, sketching and observing. They were able to handle the materials
and tools she was using and watch an artist solving problems in a
practical way through the manipulation of materials.[12]

One child, 'was responsible for videoing the day's work at regular intervals',
while 'some were working with the artist-in-residence collecting materials
from the wildlife area to incorporate in paper-making'. She noted that, arising
out of such rich stimuli, the cross-curricular implications of the work were
also considerable.

> . . . its potential to range across the curriculum was taken advantage
> of by the staff. Mathematical concepts (measuring, sorting, classify-
> ing, making plans) were being reinforced, science and technology
> (through direct handling and observation of materials and their pro-
> perties) were being explored, new social skills were being learned,
> language was being extended and developed, the geography and his-
> tory of the locality were studied within the context of the theme and
> when the sculpture was completed its presence and the atmosphere it
> created within the space where it was sited led to the deputy at the
> school seeing its new potential for stimulus in music and dance. All
> of this generated from, and based upon the sculpture and its theme of
> 'Passing Through'.

This breadth of cross-curricular learning, thoroughly considered and envisaged in the planning on the project from its earliest stages, is of particular note
at a time when many teachers are bemoaning the lack of scope for creative and
imaginative teaching because of the dictates of the National Curriculum. This
was not lost on the many parents who took a great interest in the project as
it unfolded, two in particular becoming an inseparable part of it,

> Two fathers were daily helpers on the site, working from nine in the
> morning until well after the end of the school day. The week began
> tentatively, with them feeling unsure of their role and the use they
> could be to an artist, but as the week progressed I watched a working
> partnership develop between helpers and artist so that by Thursday
> they were confidently offering advice on how to solve constructional
> problems, taking initiatives relating to the pouring of the hot asphalt
> and were able to discuss with Christine each aspect of the sculpture's
> development. I know she found this help and support invaluable.

One father 'stayed on', building a pathway from school to sculpture, taking
care to use 'materials that are sympathetic to the sculpture and its site'. Interestingly, the site had been an iron foundry where many parents and grand-
parents had worked. The school acquired a corner of the site as a green play
and wildlife area, the rest becoming a small residential development. The

foundry was being demolished at the time of Earthworks, and one of the sculptures in the Internal Trail was built with materials reclaimed from the site, the roof slates providing natural surfaces upon which to write about the foundry. The sculpture became a Tree of Life, embodying the notion of the new rising from the ashes; 'we have done a tree that is made from metal from the foundry site next door'. Alan's writing makes apparent the complex significance of both the piece and the foundry site!

THE TREE

A tree is a symbol of life, decorated by all sorts of metals, mainly rusty because they were scattered all over the waste land from where the foundry was. The discarded foundry has been brought back to life as a tree, but not a natural living creation, dead but alive.

We have put it in the centre of a spiral, symbolising reclaiming and peace and harmony to trees. Telling people what is happening to trees around the world, trying to save them. It puts me in an angry mood but also sad. This is because of what is happening to the rain-forests, and also because of the foundry being demolished. But I'm glad, because the foundry will not become a discarded memory, the tree will represent Grundy's Foundry passing through time in a rhythm or cycle of life. The brick spiral like a vortex sucking the threatened life of trees in, throwing itself to the centre, transmitting messages. Telling people what they are doing to the world.

As the sculpture took shape outside, the Murphy Room was also being transformed in keeping with the Passing Through theme, three key elements — networks and patterns coming together, stations, and journeying — providing points of focus within the room and establishing links with other areas throughout the school. Anne-Marie Quinn achieved an imperceptible transition of ideas from the 'Held, Protected, Restored' mother and child theme of the summer term to 'Passing Through' in the autumn. The combination of displayed writing and art works provided many points of reference, some immediately tangible, others subtly complex and intangible, making the space contemplative and inviting. During the summer term half of her residence, every class came to her in the Murphy Room, whereas during the autumn term things were being taken out into the school from there; Anne-Marie herself was now working out in other areas of the school.

School-Based INSET for 'Passing Through': Deepening Perspectives on Music

The focus of an arts-based annual event is in itself a basis for invaluable school-based INSET through the pooling and sharing of enthusiasms and expertise. Even the most enlightened school needs to look outside itself as a prerequisite for future growth, however. Local authority INSET provision has until recently provided the first and most natural agency. The relationships between art, the arts and technology in the National Curriculum provided a major strand in a residential Wigan Art and Design conference in March 1990. Another focus was the authority-wide Earthworks project, the related Drumcroon and Turnpike exhibitions, and related land art and environmental issues. Glennis Andrews was a course member. Feeding this information back into school triggered some of the thinking which shaped Passing Through.

As a Wigan Arts in Schools Coordinator, she had been instrumental in developing the concept 'some of the arts all of the time'. The school having lost its music specialist, she decided to accept a responsibility for music — though specialist she was not! The range of musical instruments in the school was extended and an attempt made to take greater cognizance of music throughout the school. A wide range of school-based INSET encompassing a multiplicity of art forms took place in the preparations for Passing Through. Many primary teachers find music the most difficult art form with which to engage; it is seen as the art form demanding most specialist expertise. These insecurities have intensified with foundation music requiring specific subject time, particularly as 'the music curriculum should include the three activities of performing, composing and appraising', with attention paid to 'the history of music', 'our diverse cultural heritage' and 'appreciation of a variety of other musical traditions'.[13] How might the primary teacher take account of these requirements in ways which provide full access to the aesthetic field? Initial training limitations in the arts have already been highlighted, with art and music now optional at key stage 4 restricting training further. Collaboration between the school and an authority music advisory teacher was to prove particularly significant. She was sympathetic to the school philosophy based on her Arts in Schools involvement, having 'guested' as a pianist at previous school Christmas services arising out of INSET work on the Christmas themes. Close links with the authority Music Service have developed over a number of years.

Her INSET was designed to address the school's perceptions that creative music making needed to be more vigorously developed. It had suffered neglect in some classes, with an over-reliance on taped music. However, the Music Service had also worked on a long term INSET basis with the infant department, an infant teacher regularly attending the Sound Base creative music course. The resulting work helped foster an already important feature of school practice, that of older children working alongside younger ones. For example, Y6 and Y2 worked together, sharing music making and also working with Anne-Marie Quinn to create corridor installations, one on the bottom corridor, one on the top. Both were related to each other, the Murphy Room and to the 'Passing Through' sculpture outside. Cairns, made by every class from reception to Y6, were made of found materials and also provided stopping points — moments along the way.

Merton's sculpture had a central opening or passageway, symbolic of a gate or turnpike, and it was fascinating, especially at the construction stage, to observe how the symbolism of this affected children. Some braced themselves before running through from one side to the other. The music INSET was therefore 'based on the theme of people who could have passed through the "gate" and what their feelings/emotions/demeanour were/was as they made their journey. It is a journey of life and the "gate" is the catalyst'. Life's journey requires that each of us pass through various imposed structures, all of which can help us grow and develop as people — whether the passing be from sorrow to joy, or from joy to sorrow. What might be a dangerous passing for some could be of the daily robotic type for others. In what variety of contexts might people have passed through Leigh's Turnpike in the past?[14]

All the arts provide rich references to journeys, both literal and metaphorical. Music abounds in them — Marshall's use of one from town to country in Beethoven's *Pastoral Symphony* has already been noted in Chapter 5. Three particular musical compositions were introduced to stimulate related critical and active listening in relation to 'Passing Through': i) Mussorgsky's *Pictures at an Exhibition*, with specific reference to the 'Great Gate of Kiev' and the promenade which occurs after each sound picture, utilizing the rondo form A, B, A, C, A, D . . . ii) Julian Lloyd Webber's *Variations 1–4*, building on a theme, that is, a) gate, b) gate plus people, c) gate plus more people, etc. iii) Chris Rea's 'Tell me there's a heaven' and 'Road to Hell', parts 1 and 2, creating sound effects and layering of sounds — rain; windscreen wipers; radio; news bulletin — simple heavy brass — speaking/singing voice telling of a journey to riches which ends in Hell.

One session, focusing on the 'Great Gate of Kiev', was structured to encompass the full spectrum of listening, performing, composing and appraising activities.

> Listen to Mussorgsky's music 'The Great Gate of Kiev' from *Pictures at an Exhibition*. As the children are listening encourage them to discover clues in the music which suggest what kind of gate this might be. (The children might like to draw a picture of the gate they are hearing).

The practical activities initially used vocal, body and found sounds, and tuned and untuned percussion. Is the school's 'Passing Through' similar in any ways to the 'Great Gate of Kiev'? How has it been built? What is it made of? How are the pieces of wood arranged? Why do you think our sculpture is built in this way? What might be the artist's reasons in choosing those materials? Bearing all this in mind, we are going to create a sound picture of our 'Passing Through' gate, just as Mussorgsky did of the 'Great Gate of Kiev'.

Using woodblocks, drums, maracas, sticks, castanets, tambours and available found sounds, the children created 'sound chains' with an emphasis on sequencing, duration and dynamics, including use of crescendos and diminuendos. They were introduced to timbre in relation to producing imitations or echoes involving each in copying the sound patterns made by the first, discussing how and why sounds changed or were exactly replicated. They made group compositions, working on a presentation of chain or imitative sounds. Groups performed to each other, appraising and redrafting as part of the process. They recorded their work on tape and used this as the basis for movement and dance, one group playing while the other moved or with them combining playing and moving. A further activity involved them in layering sounds, representing their gate by layering them in keeping with the structure of 'Passing Through', giving consideration to beat, rhythmic patterns and motifs — a steady, strong hammer beat on the tambours and drums, a lighter 'tapping' rhythm on woodblocks and castanets, plus clicking fingers, a further light pattern motif and a circular swishing pattern imitating the faces of the block — with ample scope provided for the children to invent and develop countless patterns of their devising, linking with a whole tradition of work in the school in the visual arts and dance illustrating the transferable dimensions in what was being done.

The introduction of xylophones stimulated more developments of these ideas, with consideration now consciously given to harmony — as the logs in the gate fit together and relate — and, by giving a few children a limited selection of notes, to pitch. Pitch patterns were then layered over rhythmic ones. Children took it in turns to conduct the gate, thinking about how they might best make the sound go higher and lower as the shape of the gate ascends and descends. Care was taken to ensure that they could distinguish between loud and quiet (dynamics) and high and low (pitch). A vocal impression of the gate was also composed and performed, both in unison and as a round, again introducing layering and harmony. Song and percussion were brought together by a variety of means, in a variety of forms, binary and ternary, using introduction and coda, etc.

Next, the notion of passing through the gate was considered, and the different feelings this might arouse, as when going to work, to market, or when visiting. Secret or fearful travelling was considered, and the idea of sad and happy processions, such as for funerals and weddings. How do we move under the impulse of different emotions? How might different moods combine in one piece? Many forms and sequences were explored. The 'gate' and 'passing through' ideas might be arranged in rondo form, as in the Mussorgsky — GATE work GATE market GATE sad event GATE fear GATE celebration. A ternary form might be used: Sad event — GATE — Happy event. The gate could be the constant factor throughout, fading quietly as each musical motif passes through, and so on. This brief summary illustrates the relevance of the music INSET, for it was deeply rooted in the school's curriculum and concerns.

Into the Future

The 1991 Passing Through service brought all the arts together in a rich and stimulating evening. Year 3 focused on transport, Y4 on the journey through life's stages, Y5 on water as a life-sustaining resource and on injustice and imbalance, and Y6 on exploration. The theme certainly did possess the necessary depth to be worthy of the children's absorption and was 'capable of bearing them up and carrying them to a new synthesis, a new point of rest'. It has been seen how the whole grew out of concerns addressed in-depth through mainstream curriculum involvements over considerable timescales. The implications inevitably lead into the future. They do not conclude with the service; it signifies a comma, not a full stop:

> The focus was journeys because of a term's work around passing through — a term's work transferred into the Christmas service. Before we identified the theme we wanted to focus on we had to take a fresh look at everything in relation to a word or idea. . . . The work was done in-depth before the Christmas service — we wanted to draw all the strands together into a coherent whole. . . . The sculpture is a tangible legacy — we have got to be able to look at it and build on what has already been done.[15]

The spring term Murphy Room exhibition therefore took as its theme, 'Changing Landscape'. This offered many possibilities to pick up on and develop strands explored or just touched upon during the Passing Through project. It made extensive use of the Wigan Schools Loan Collection, with one-half devoted to the urban landscape, the other to the rural. It was staged two terms before art and music became foundation subjects. It met many National Curriculum requirements as a cross-attainment target project, as is illustrated by looking at those for art.

It offers a broad theme relevant to each key stage (key stage 3 as well as 1 and 2) ranging across AT1 and AT2, with potential to address all end of key stage statements in investigating, making, knowledge and understanding. It warrants revisiting at each key stage, thus revealing new layers of significance and meaning. It is able to facilitate in-depth practice of a cross-curricular nature, providing links with National Curriculum requirements in every core and foundation subject. The individual teacher can use it, adapting it according to age, stages of development and the backgrounds of any group. Equally, it provides scope for whole-school planning and usage with regard for continuity and progression, presentation and response, utilizing children's work, that of their peers and of established artists and designers. It offers a broad theme applicable to all curriculum areas, a focused theme or modular course covering a number of curriculum areas, or simply an art-led topic capable of embracing a number of curricular areas from an art stimulus.

Account might be taken of the personal landscape, as well as the physical and geographical. General considerations might include relationships between people and the environment, the familiar and unfamiliar, the wild and the cultivated, the urban and the rural, and the interior and exterior. Key concepts could include cause and consequence, change and continuity, similarity and difference, and chronology. In the primary context the topic would, of necessity, address the cross-curricular themes of environmental education, economic and industrial understanding and citizenship.

The theme provides ample scope to meet the requirements of many curriculum areas, while remaining consistent with Marshall's 'symphonic method'. Programmes of study can be used from relevant key stages in science appertaining to the natural and physical sciences, including evolution, climatic effects and the recording of the weather, the development and use of machines, the impact of invention and discovery in both the past and present world. In mathematics, there is scope for the gathering and interpretation of data, and for ordering according to shape and size, etc. It facilitates work at every level across all English ATs in talking and listening, reading and writing, including the examination of vocabulary and communication of a range of ideas for a range of purposes. There is scope for exploration of how technology transmits and reflects the circumstances, needs and systems of particular times, cultures and communities with respect to available materials. In history, the link can be made with core and supplementary units enhancing the pertinence of knowledge, understanding, interpretation and use of sources. There are obvious links between relevant artists, composers and writers being studied at a subject-specific level and periods in history, and of enriched experience of human and environmental geography on both local and global scales. Information drawn from field work and secondary source material can be utilized and explored. Music provides further reflection of the theme through compositions and performances by people working at different times and in different cultures and circumstances, including that of the pupils themselves produced through an exploration of the nature and essence of the theme. Dance offers similar scope and, with PE, the active examination of physical forces.

Many primary teachers feel constrained. Their schools, in attempting to develop whole-school approaches with regard to the National Curriculum are actually producing rigid straitjackets in the form of predetermined topics. The contribution of each subject is ticked off without the necessary debate as to how scope for imaginative and creative responses might be developed. The coming year's work in many schools is inflexibly prescribed in diagrammatic form on staffroom walls months in advance. Louise, age 11, illustrates how readily aspects of the Passing Through theme can be revisited and further developed through Changing Landscape, *but in an organic way*. Her writing about the foundry tree possesses elements regarding both the personal and physical landscapes, and provides evidence of practical inventiveness in pursuit of the satisfactory resolution of an idea.

> There is a tree at the back of the school, remains of a foundry, passing through age, passing through time. Rusty metal, concrete and furnace remains. It gives me a sad feeling because an old foundry has been demolished, but a happy feeling because we have saved the remains of the foundry. The metal is dead, but in a way it is alive, we have brought the metal back to life as a tree.

We collected striped bricks from the site to make a spiral around the tree. We used the symbol of the spiral because it is taking the tree into the future or back in time to bring back memories, and future life for the tree. There are some slates that we collected and scratched onto about the foundry and about trees.

We had quite a few problems, there were bits of wire and metal leaves that were sharp and pointed, and people could hurt themselves on them, so we put sponge over the pointed parts of the sculpture, they were shaped like leaves. Part of the process was mixing the concrete and holding the metal for about 10 minutes until it was stable in the concrete. Some of the metal kept slipping. We fixed the old bits of metal with wire strips twisted together with pliers. They had to be twisted tightly so that the metal won't slip about.

We sited the tree outside on a spiral brick or path. The tree is a symbol of strength. We hope that ours will be a long lasting construction. Builders use the tree on their advertising because trees last a long time.

A passage written by Glennis Andrews encapsulates a central part of the school's philosphy — in the realization and fulfilment of one context, seeds are sown that point the way to future possibilities through new beginnings. Her writing grew out of discussions with Christine Merton during the week of the sculpture's siting. It became part of the school's response and display, featured in the Murphy Room. Infants working with Quinn wrote passages from it using their fingers and mud from around the sculpture. It provides a further example of the importance of adults writing in schools, and the impact this can have on children. It further emphasizes how Passing Through strands then provide a weft and warp for Changing Landscapes when the vertical and horizontal axes of creativity are valued and cultivated in interactive ways which affirm each other.

Passing Through on the small repeated steps
of time
we create a journey
in times past and times present
we have harnessed the materials to hand
thoughtprints into earthprints,
layered circles of life.
Hands and eyes in harmony
with the inner sense —
the feeling,
that will build the structures,
trace the lines
soften the edges,
take the viewer

to the periphery
where reality is richly stitched and braided
by intangibles.
It's for us to unravel the strands
and extend the intricate web
that we weave around the network of our lives
and to pass through
to the Threshold of our understanding.

Annual events of this kind, bringing the whole school community together in celebratory ways, are more important now than ever. Centrally
imposed legislation is making many schools more dour, yet when all the arts
come together on these occasions, learning can be discernibly enriched and
enhanced. Increased levels of motivation and involvement bring a renewed
sense of purpose into the classroom — a realization totally at variance with
persistent arguments about there being no time for such activities, however
desirable they might be. Rather than the arts being marginalized by National
Curriculum demands, events of this nature further demonstrate their centrality. The late Harry Ree argued for more, not less, emphasis being placed on
these types of activities, for they frequently have lifelong significance:

> If we look back on our schooldays, what were the moments when
> something really important and memorable happened? And where
> were you when it happened? In the classroom? Doubtful. More likely
> in a play, a concert or on a theatre visit. On an excursion, at camp
> alone with friends and a teacher you were getting to know. But these
> events are regarded as frills, as peripheral little stopping places on our
> long educational trip. But the experience of many people points to
> the fact that such moments are central to learning and, therefore,
> what we should begin to do is to turn the school inside out — put the
> peripheral experience into the middle, and put the classroom experi-
> ence on the fringe.[16]

References

1 The Gulbenkian Report, *The Arts in Schools: Principles, Practice and Provision* (1982)
   London, Calouste Gulbenkian Foundation, p. 52.
2 *Ibid.*, p. 56.
3 Robertson, M. (1982) *Rosegarden and Labyrinth,* Lewes, Gryphon Press, p. 104.
   Quotation from a letter from Keats to Reynolds (first published 1963, Routledge
   and Kegan Paul Ltd).
4 *Ibid.*, p. 105.
5 Abbs, P. (1987) *Living Powers*, London, Falmer Press, p. 209.
6 Taylor, R. (1986) *Educating for Art: Critical Response and Development*, Harlow,
   Longman, p. 109.

7 From a recorded interview with Viv Burrows by Rod Taylor, 1991.
8 Nichols, G. (1984) *The Fat Black Woman's Poems*, London, Virago Press.
9 Angelou, M. (1984) *I Know Why the Caged Bird Sings*, London, Virago Press.
10 *Art in the National Curriculum* (1992), London HMSO, p. 9.
11 Viv Burrows interview, Taylor (1991).
12 O'Brien, S. (1991) 'Passing Through' (unpublished paper).
13 *Music in the National Curriculum* (1992) York, National Curriculum Council, p. 11.
14 Hull, C. (1991) 'Whole Staff Inset at TCP "Passing Through"' (unpublished paper).
15 Viv Burrows interview, Taylor (1991).
16 Ree, H. (1981) 'Education and the Arts: Are Schools the Enemy?' in Ross, M. (Ed.) *The Aesthetic Imperative; Relevance and Responsibility in Arts Education*, Oxford, Pergamon Press, p. 98.

Postscript

The Aesthetic Library and
the National Curriculum

The aesthetic dimension of human life extends across a wide range of human activities; and we ought to regard it as an inalienable human potentiality, as fundamental as the capacity for language. If a society cannot provide a facilitating environment within which the aesthetic potential of all of its members can find appropriate expression, then that society has failed.

... within the curriculum there is — or rather there ought to be — an *aesthetic field*, which requires a coherent defence. These writers conceive of the *aesthetic field* as a family of related disciplines, all of which are rooted in aesthetic response, and aesthetic expression. This is an emphasis with which I concur.

Peter Fuller[1]

A Negative Environment, Positive Possibilities

Enhancement, Enrichment, Enlightenment — these are the essential qualities which the arts can bring to all children's education; they should be at the heart of any entitlement curriculum. In the face of a multiplicity of pressures, they are being relegated in favour of *Economy, Effectiveness* and *Efficiency* — more readily acceptable in today's mechanistic climate. The late Peter Fuller wrote the above in the Preface to *Living Powers*, the first volume in the Library on Aesthetic Education. He went on to argue that our society *is* failing — and he was writing in 1987, shortly before a national curriculum became a reality. Had he lived, he would have been outraged to see only two arts disciplines as foundation subjects within it, with even these optional at key stage 4. Many high schools with end of key stage 3 option patterns favourable to the arts are reviewing these in the light of this decision — some have detrimentally changed them already!

The arts invariably suffer in times of economic stringency; this has been the case since 1979. As early as 1982, the Gulbenkian Report, *The Arts in Schools* was warning about the extent of the damage:

> In February 1981 HMI reported on the effects of cuts in public spending on education. In several passages the report comments specifically on the adverse effects on existing provision for the arts. These come through staff redundancies, reductions in part-time and peripatetic teachers and through deterioration or through the simple lack of facilities and equipment.[2]

Attention is drawn 'to the damage being done through retirement, redundancy and redeployment of arts specialists both in schools and in the advisory service'. A decade later, this process continues unabated — accelerating, if anything — confirming the report's concern:

> Nationally the situation is bleak and becoming bleaker as one authority after another is forced into making cuts in its budgets for music, drama and the other arts . . . Spending in the arts has never been profligate. What has been achieved — and in the past 20 years especially there have been a great many of them — have resulted from hard work, good-will and self-help. The danger now is that spending cuts, which may make small savings when compared with the total education budget of any authority, will devastate the provision for arts in education.[3]

The Arts in Schools also alerted readers to the harm to the arts through calls for greater educational accountability:

> The problems here for the arts do not lie in the need for accountability but in the forms it is so often assumed to take. Performance in public examinations is still taken as the main index of the success of a school. Any pressures to raise standards of education tend therefore to be transmitted through the examination system.

At the time, of course, this was an essentially high school-orientated issue; in 1982, nobody foresaw the full scenario of published league tables and paper and pencil testing for 7 and 11 year olds, with whatever could not be so tested deemed to be of relative insignificance.

Nevertheless, in 1982 Leslie Perry was getting uncannily close to the shape of things to come in terms of a three-tier National Curriculum favouring core subjects, followed by what are now being termed 'extended core' foundation subjects, with the arts relegated to the lowest tier. He anticipated the actual sequencing of National Curriculum subjects in terms of their introduction and assumed status; with just one exception — the new 'subject' of technology, born of the mistaken belief that it would be the nation's saviour in the economic world of market forces:

> ... let us now turn to the knowledge-based curriculum as it works out in subject detail. We find a group of core subjects, whose cognitive loading is everywhere present in the teaching of them. They are hardly thought to need justificatory argument, since their justification is obvious. They include mathematics, English and science, and recent literature runs true to type in accepting their position. There appears to be a second line of secondary school subjects of significantly high cognitive content to rank with the first, but the first always add strong vocational grounds to the educational ones, and rank as bedrock subjects for all secondary education, hence deserving a core position. The second group however which contains history, French and geography are clearly an important part of cognitive training. Finally, there is a group of creative and practical subjects. The hold of these subjects on the curriculum has never been so tight as that of the first two groups: they are constantly called upon to justify their existence, and are widely judged to be doing a minor function and worthy of a lesser share of curriculum time. These are art, music, drama, for example, and inevitably there we find craft.[4]

Perry is referring to the secondary school, but ten years later the arguments are both pertinent and applicable to primary education — there is even talk of French being reintroduced, it having been taught in some primary schools in the late 1960s and early 1970s. He *does* mention craft, with it in the lower tier; technology, an 'extended core' foundation subject, demands craft skills, but these are most likely to develop through art approaches — and art, of course, is in the lower tier, along with the other arts.

With regard to the bottom creative and practical tier, Perry observes:

> Their educational and vocational value are both questioned, and in times of economic stringency the question whether such subjects are necessary, or necessary on such a scale, or in such a form, is raised as a recurring procedure. Hence the present occasion, and the uproar, disturbance and pressures at present around creative subjects.

All this is in accord with Alexander's observations about the differing impacts of the 1982 Cockroft Mathematics and Gulbenkian Arts Reports, even though, 'if anything, the case made for the arts as a central "core" element of the curriculum was the more powerfully made'.

That the life-enhancing value of the arts is essential to any worthwhile education designed to prepare young people for adult life in a rapidly changing world has already been emphasized; *The Arts in Schools* shares the belief that this education must have an aesthetic component:

> To be fully educated, as T.S. Eliot noted, is to have some sense of where everything fits. This is the ground on which our first argument is based: that one of these distinct categories of understanding and achievement — the aesthetic and creative — is exemplified by the arts: music, drama, literature, poetry, dance, sculpture and the graphic arts. Not to attempt at some stage, and in some form, to involve children in the arts is simply to fail to educate them as fully developed, intelligent and feeling human beings.[5]

It is, however, within a negative climate with a disdain for imagination and creativity, that the National Curriculum has been introduced. With it comes all the paraphernalia for testing, league tables — introduced to ensure school competes with school and authority with authority — and the rechannelling of funding to support only what is centrally deemed to be worth teaching. Within this climate, the Library on Aesthetic Education has also been conceived and methodically published. How, if at all, do the two relate? Might one give added meaning to the other?

That the National Curriculum did not take proper account of the place and role of the arts has already been stressed — the above short résumé provides some explanation as to why this was the case. Consequently, the arts have been introduced in a haphazard manner, sometimes subsumed within other disciplines and at other times, belatedly. However, the Library on Aesthetic Education provides a rationale for examining the form each arts discipline has assumed in the National Curriculum and whether that form is an acceptable or partial one. Further, this rationale provides a basis for the arts to be conceived and treated as a related whole, collectively capable of offering that essential enhancement, enrichment and enlightenment, rather than remain the disparate entities their methods of introduction otherwise indicate. Many primary teachers are unhappy with this situation, finding it increasingly difficult to retain in their teaching what they know are essential values and approaches, so exacting have the dictates from above become. The overview provided by the Library on Aesthetic Education provides a creative and constructive way through the National Curriculum, though, and criteria as to how teachers might reassert values and approaches with relevance beyond the dogmas and dictates of the moment.

It is testimony to the various National Curriculum arts working groups that a primary staff can, in fact, apply the principles of the Library on Aesthetic Education to various arts subjects, and then impose a coherence that should have been there at the outset. This can best be seen by setting out the various attainment targets for each arts discipline in diagrammatic form, determined by the aesthetic field sequence of making, presenting, responding and evaluating — the aesthetic field itself fully facilitating the dual requirements of the vertical and horizontal axes of true creativity:

	Vertical		**Horizontal**	
	Making	*Presenting*	*Responding*	*Evaluating*
Art	Investigating	Making	Knowledge	Understanding
Music	Performing	Composing	Listening	Appraising
*Dance**	Performing	Composing	Appreciating	
English	Writing	Speaking	Listening and	Reading

(* The three for dance were subsumed within one AT in the Physical Education Final Order.)

Different art forms naturally used terms traditionally associated with them, yet the unifying relationships are immediately apparent as soon as they are placed within the context of the aesthetic field.

The Special Case of Drama

Drama, of course, does not feature as a foundation subject. It is subsumed within English; *English Non-Statutory Guidance* sees drama as 'not simply a subject, but also a method . . . a learning tool'.[6] However, David Hornbrook's assertion in *Education in Drama*, in this library, that drama as a learning tool has been to the detriment of drama as an art form is affirmed in the recent Arts Council Drama Report *Drama in Schools: Arts Council Guidance on Drama Education*. In reasserting drama as an art form, Hornbrook proposes three appropriate attainment targets as follows:

Drama   Making   Performing   Responding

With the National Curriculum still subject to change, perhaps it is still not too late for drama to be acknowledged in its own right, but changes in drama practice are required. It has suffered more than most art forms through partial conceptions.

Hornbrook demonstrates, that like other art forms, 'it is possible to reconcile membership of the wider arts community with the idea of drama as an independent educative force'.[7] Abbs emphasizes the extent to which drama has allowed itself to become a medium for learning, but how in the process it has, in the main, lost sight of the aesthetic:

> Drama was converted into an effective tool for enquiry which could be extended across the curriculum but, cut off from the aesthetic field, it forfeited any sense of intrinsic identity. Devoid of art, devoid of the practices of theatre, devoid of artistic and critical terminology drama became a method of teaching *without a subject*.[8]

Michael Marland finds an 'excellent model' in the Arts Council report; 'it is in fact a model for any school curriculum'.[9] In an article on the report, 'An art in its own right', he cites Lord Palumbo who sees drama as 'an art form with its own discipline and methodology' — it can indeed be 'a teaching method', but 'is first and foremost an art in its own right'. The report emphasizes the need for 'critical reflection' from an early age, specifies that pupils should be taught to 'develop voice and movement skills' and a critical vocabulary if they are to 'respond discerningly as members of an audience' to professional productions in and out of school, as well as to their own work and that of their peers. Marland suggests that it reverses 'the almost anti-professional theatre stance of many drama-education pundits'. Any study of drama without direct reference to professional theatre is incomplete, and pupils should be taught 'to identify different styles of drama' and to 'understand drama from different cultures and times'.

The report belatedly does for drama what Critical Studies did for art and design education a full decade earlier. Whereas 'school art' as a term always carried the derogatory overtones of the critical outsider looking in, 'educational drama' was coined by drama practitioners *themselves* to forcibly divorce school drama from all other aspects. As a consequence, many primary teachers admit to finding drama and how to approach it something of a mystery. *Education in Drama* and now *Drama in Schools: Arts Council Guidance on Drama Education* assert that drama, too, can become dynamically interactive by taking account of the aesthetic field. Otherwise making, performing and responding remain locked in child drama approaches, and can only be dealt with in that order, making always having to come first — it always being *only* the children's making. It is interesting how frequently drama uses the stimulus of other art forms, yet so rarely its own! The Library on Aesthetic Education demonstrates how this deficiency might be rectified, drama becoming whole instead of partial by belatedly drawing upon its own history and contemporary practice, whether through texts or the theatre.

English and Media Studies in the National Curriculum

The Arts in Schools project used 'verbal arts' as a term to distinguish the artistic aspects of English. In arts terms, English poses particular problems, for its paper and pencil testing demands, and their nature, do not equate with it as an art form. Equally, the pupil writings interspersed throughout these pages demonstrate the extent to which pupils' use of language and its development is enhanced and enriched through artistic contexts which offer them something to say, through felt experiences. It is in the desire and quest to express and communicate what has been so strongly experienced that these children so effectively extend their range and comprehension of language. Nevertheless, the belief that 'the basics' are only being taught when such involvement is precluded persists, creating a strange ambivalence with regard to English teaching, with it often not even perceived as being an art form. However, English attainment targets can be placed fairly and squarely within the aesthetic field, as has been illustrated, so there is ample scope for the aware, creative teacher.

Film and television do not, of course, feature in their own right, though there are references to media studies in all the English material. *English Non-Statutory Guidance* states that, 'For all children, including those with special educational needs, audio and video tape, film and photography can be ways of enabling them to communicate and build their self esteem'.[10] It also places emphasis on the need for interpretation and comparison of non-verbal scripts, including television, radio and computer displays, stating that, 'the whole range of media material can be used'. This means, of course, that the English attainment targets can be seen as being equally applicable to media studies, but it should also be emphasized that media studies occupies a place within every art form; images, whether single or in sequences, can be primarily concerned with the visual, the dramatic, etc. Over a period of time, therefore, the primary teacher might take account of every arts attainment target in relation to media studies, according to the nature of activities and their direct relationship to each art form (for example, there might be times when the emphasis might be upon sound and at others on the visual).

Dance within Physical Education

The initial training implications of art and music being made optional at key stage 4 have already been highlighted. Dance's toehold in the curriculum has always been a slender one, and the decision that it, too, should be optional at key stage 4 is further compounded by the NCC decision 'that only games should be compulsory in each year' of key stage 3.[11] Its time allocation in initial training is already extremely limited and will inevitably remain so, while a large majority of those wishing to become primary practitioners will enter higher education with little or no experience of dance beyond their own primary school days. To further compound the problem, it is possible to read the seventeen programmes of study 'applicable across all four key stages' without thinking beyond physical education; there is nothing of the aesthetic here to assert the importance of dance as a major, if neglected art form in the school context.

These fears are not allayed on turning to the 'activity specific' programmes of study for key stages 1 and 2. These are of an essentially practical nature, with just the odd turn of phrase which, for those conversant with notions of the aesthetic field, can be turned to account, as when it is specified at key stage 2 that pupils, 'in response to a range of stimuli, express feelings, moods and ideas and create simple characters and narratives in movement'.[12] Without an awareness of aesthetic field implications, however, a teacher could conscientiously interpret what is specified without even realizing that a fundamental area of dance experience was being neglected.

Art, Music and the Aesthetic Field

In their final forms, art and music sit most clearly within the aesthetic field. The vertical axis relates directly to AT1 in each, the horizontal to AT2. Nevertheless, great controversy surrounded the NCC decision to reduce three attainment targets to two in art and music, with 'Knowledge' (it was originally applied to music as well as to art) widely interpreted as indicating an insistence that children are taught history — and specifically that of Western Europe — with an undue emphasis on facts divorced from response and practice. Though these critics' concerns are not fully allayed with publication of the Final Orders for both art forms, any teacher with a grasp of the significance of the aesthetic field, and able to utilize the structures and principles set out in these pages, will have little difficulty in meeting statutory requirements while remaining true to the values and principles of this Library.

With regard to the reduction of three ATs to two, perhaps it is more fruitful to think of art and music now possessing four each — nothing of substance recommended by either working group has been lost. The problem of mentally retaining the three for dance as proposed by the PE Working Group is much more precarious, for they now disappear altogether from the Consultation Report stage onwards!

One strongly expressed argument against the reduction to two ATs was that this artificially divided the curriculum on a fifty–fifty basis for both art and music — one half would be practical, the other an unrelated form of theory. To allay this fear, a two to one weighting was proposed, though how this might be applied in practice is not clear. Does the child with remarkable insight only warrant half of what the child with making skills can achieve? These problems are inherent in the Interim Reports for both art and music. The Working Groups, like their predecessors, each claimed a holistic view of their disciplines, splitting them into ATs for clarity, each one identifying a key area of a discipline. Each attainment target was then followed sequentially throughout each key stage, with the onus on the teacher to put them back together again to provide a holistic view — a little like repairing Humpty-Dumpty! Though non-statutory, the highly influential examples scattered throughout both the art and music documents contribute further to this fragmented picture.

The relevance of each attainment target to the whole would have been immediately apparent if the three attainment targets had been set out *across* the page instead of one always being led down it, key stage by key stage. The examples for understanding, making and investigating in art and composing, performing and appraising in music (as set out in the Working Group documents) could then have been formulated to interconnect. To illustrate this at Wigan INSET meetings, one key stage 1 'Understanding' example was specifically used: 'Pupils could consider how themes, such as 'Mother and Child', are represented in different kinds of art; e.g. icons, sculptures by Henry Moore, the paintings by Leonardo da Vinci and Mary Cassatt.' (NCC later added 'and in African tribal art'.)[13]

In what context might an infant teacher address this theme? Presumably a practical one, so why not make the connections explicit so as to facilitate 'holistic' work from the outset, as follows:

Understanding	*Making*	*Investigating*
The 'Mother and Child' in art: icons, Moore, da Vinci, Cassatt, African tribal art.	Children making studies from posed mother and child.	Children bringing in photos of themselves as babies, or of younger brother or sister, etc.
Studying original works in gallery or school: Quinn, Faulkner, Utamaro, etc.	Developments from studies taking account of the following:	Creating displays of baby clothes, shoes, pram, toys, etc. brought in by pupils and teachers.
Utilization of relevant catalogue, teachers' notes, artists' statements, material.	• A set of shapes and colours expressing feelings about mother and child theme	Children and teacher finding mother and child images in papers and magazines
Visit appropriate artists in other venues — schools, studios, etc.	• A set of shapes and colours which remind one of a woman holding a baby.	Exploration of the theme using the school or local library.
Responding to artists' work by sketching/ note-taking (using C,F,P,M as an aid).	• A set of shapes and colours which fill the required space pleasantly.	Compare images of child, with those of parents and grandparents as children.
Classroom Contextualization in support of theme	• Having reconciled all the above, translate into pigment applied to surface.	Pupils sketching at home in support of theme.
Language developed through engagement with theme.	Presentation and discussion arising out of work on theme.	Selecting relevant words to convey ideas about theme.

(• These represent Mood, Content, Form and Process, in that order, and provide a basis for identification of material to contextualize further the theme with material which can be drawn from a wide variety of sources, including all the arts.)[14]

All the themes addressed throughout this book readily fit within this frame-work. It makes explicit the relevance to planning and practice of the aesthetic field of making, presenting, responding and evaluating. For example, the use of the 'Great Gate of Kiev' in relation to Passing Through provides evidence of how children's musical practical engagements in relation to a theme can be affirmed through the practice of others — very important, given a tendency among musicians to argue that there is insufficient time for this form of wider treatment, music educators having rather belatedly accepted that children can, in fact, make 'Child Music' when provided with a range of appropriate instru-ments. As a consequence, a tendency to re-rehearse all the traditional Child Art arguments is still strong in this art form.

With this structure in mind, once NCC had added Knowledge as a fourth component, it was simple and natural to regard this as equivalent to a fourth attainment target, rather than bemoan the reduction of three ATs to two. One simply added a fourth column to the above diagram, and facilitated an im-portant debate about the interface between knowledge and understanding: Can one possess forms of knowledge yet not understand? Can one understand through feeling responses without any knowledge of facts and contexts? Is there scope for knowledge to be interpreted as a form of knowing to do with apprehension through the senses? A long overdue debate at the national level about the interface between knowledge and understanding, and their relation-ship with practice is urgently required. These issues appertain equally to music and art; it was the music lobby, though, which attracted most media attention in the futile argument about numbers of attainment targets, with art riding on its coat-tails as a very poor second.

In conclusion, therefore, the Library on Aesthetic Education does pro-vide a rationale enabling primary teachers to give coherence to the arts in the National Curriculum. Further, where inconsistencies do exist, the rationale empowers a school to rectify them as, for example, with regard to the partial nature of the dance requirements within physical education. In rectifying serious omissions, the practical aspects of dance assume greater significance when placed within the aesthetic field, because of the dynamic interactions now made possible. Ample evidence now exists to indicate that, within the context of this field, children's practice can then transcend the norms of school dance, art, music, drama — whatever, for art does grow out of art as well as out of strongly felt responses of a purely personal nature. Once a school recognizes and facilitates this, many, many children can constantly surprise us with their ability to give potent expression to ideas and concepts about im-portant life experiences and issues. In the process, they are being better pre-pared for adult life in that uncertain future. For this preparation to be adequate, it is their entitlement to be provided with an education founded upon a rec-ognition of the importance of enhancement, enrichment and enlightenment.

References

1   Abbs, P. (1987) London, The Falmer Press, Living Powers, p. xi.
2   The Gulbenkian Report, *The Arts in Schools*: Principles, Practice and Provision (1982) London, Calouste Gulbenkian Foundation, p. 6.
3   *Ibid.*, p. 7.
4   Perry, L. (1982) 'The Educational Value of Creativity', *Crafts Council Conference for Teachers*: 1982 Report, London, Crafts Council, p. 26.
5   *The Arts in Schools* (1982) pp. 19–20.
6   *English Non-Statutory Guidance* (1990) York, National Curriculum Council, p. D11.
7   David Hornbrook (1991) *Education in Drama: Casting the Dramatic Curriculum*, London, The Falmer Press, p. 156.
8   *Ibid.*, p. ix.
9   Marland, M. (1992) 'An art in its own right', *The Guardian Education Bulletin*, 28 March, p. 28.
10 *English Non-Statutory Guidance* (1990) p. D16.
11 *Physical Education Consultation Report* (1991) York, National Curriculum Council, Letter to Secretary of State at front of document, page unnumbered.
12 *Ibid.*, p. 25.
13 *Art in the National Curriculum (England)* (1992) London, HMSO, p. 5.
14 A variant of this diagram was first produced for Wigan National Curriculum INSET purposes for use with primary teachers. Feedback indicated that it did a great deal to make the *Art Interim* and *Art for Ages 5 to 14* documents far more accessible.

Index